CHRISTIAN
HIGH SCHOOL
RELIGION SERIES

Saved by Grace

A Study of Christian Doctrine

Student Book

By Garth D. Ludwig
   Roger Riggs
   Ronald J. Schlegel

CPH
SAINT LOUIS

Write to Library for the Blind, 1333 S. Kirkwood Road, St. Louis, MO 63122–7295, to obtain *Saved by Grace* (Student Book) in braille or sightsaving print for the visually impaired.

Unless otherwise stated, the Scripture quotations in this publication are from The Holy Bible: NEW INTERNATIONAL VERSION, © 1973, 1978, 1984 by the International Bible Society. Used by permission of Zondervan Bible Publishers.

Scripture quotations marked RSV are from the Revised Standard Version of the Bible, copyrighted 1946, 1952, © 1971, 1973 by the Division of Christian Education of the National Council of the Churches of Christ in the U.S.A., and used by permission.

3 4 5 6 7 8 9 10 11 12   07 06 05 04 03 02 01 00 99 98

Contents

To the Student

In the last session of this course you will read about an insight from God that changed Martin Luther's entire life. One day while studying **Romans 1:16–17,** Luther realized that his relationship with God did not depend upon what he did, but on what God had done. He could have peace with God, because Jesus had died for him, and his sins were forgiven.

That is grace.

God extends that same grace to you.

The pages of this course and the Scripture you will study during this course reveal more about God's grace. They reveal the sin of your natural condition; they reveal the satisfaction Jesus made for your sins; they reveal the way God caused Jesus' redemptive act to effect salvation for you personally; and they reveal the new life in Christ which God has given to you.

It is by grace you have been saved, through faith—and this not from yourselves, it is the gift of God–not by works, so that no one can boast. For we are God's workmanship, created in Christ Jesus to do good works, which God prepared in advance for us to do (Ephesians 2:8–10).

UNIT 1
Salvation Part 1

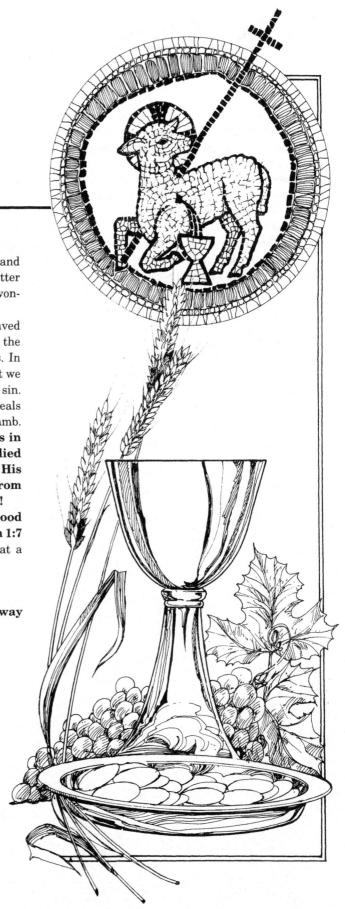

ROMANS 1:1—5:11

The big human problem is sin, sinful nature, and sinful activity. In the first eight chapters of his letter to the Romans, the apostle Paul reveals God's wonderful plan of salvation.

In **Romans 1:1—5:11** we discover how God saved us from what we *do;* in unit 1 we will look at the first aspect of salvation, the forgiveness of sins. In **5:12—8:39** we learn how God saved us from what we *are;* unit 2 will focus upon our deliverance from sin.

In this first unit, then, we will see how God deals with our sins through the precious blood of the Lamb.

"God demonstrates His own love for us in this: While we were still sinners, Christ died for us. Since we have now been justified by His blood, how much more shall we be saved from God's wrath through Him" (Romans 5:8—9)!

God is satisfied with His solution. **"The blood of Jesus . . . cleanses us from all sin" (1 John 1:7 RSV).** The first unit of Romans shows us what a marvelous cleansing it is!

Behold, the Lamb of God, who takes away the sin of the world! (John 1:29)

SESSION 1

Paul, the Man and His Message

ROMANS 1:1–7

Strange, isn't it, how we can say the same words and put completely opposite meanings into them? Say, "I belong to you." What would you mean if you were a black slave in early 19th-century America, and you said it to your owner? What would you mean if you were deeply in love for the first time, and you said it to your loved one? Same words. Very different meanings.

In the introduction to this masterful book of the New Testament, the apostle Paul tells his readers, "And you also are among those who are called to belong to Jesus Christ" **(verse 6)**. Even if you have never thought about it before (or perhaps especially if you have never thought about it before), write out a brief paragraph starting with these words: "I belong to Jesus Christ. What that means to me is . . . "

In your paragraph, honestly describe whether or not belonging to Christ seems restrictive or freeing, "under the thumb" or comforting. Also mention whether or not you feel a sense of belonging to Christ.

IN THE WORD

Verse 1: Paul, the Man

1. Carefully read **verse 1.** Paul describes himself as a servant of Jesus Christ and an apostle, one who is set apart for the Gospel. Check the introductions in Paul's other epistles. In how many of them does he identify himself as "servant"? as "apostle"? In your own words, write down why you believe he makes this identification.

2. Paul wrote this (and all his letters) in Greek. Interestingly, many English versions of the New Testament softened Paul's word. The Greek word means "slave" instead of "servant"—and not a high ranking slave either, but *doulos,* the lowest class slave (like a galley slave chained on a Roman ship!).

"Paul, a (galley-)slave of Jesus Christ," might be the way the first-century reader would hear this letter. Why in that class-conscious society would Paul's self-identity be shocking? What 20th-century word would convey the same kind of impact?

3. Paul's legal and social status in the Roman Empire was not as a slave at all! In fact, he was a Jewish Pharisee (highly respected among Jews) and a Roman citizen (a rare combination). As a Roman citizen, Paul (formerly known as Saul of Tarsus) had legal rights which most Jews did not have. What impact would this information have on Paul's first readers? Why do you suppose Paul began his letters this way?

4. Paul was also an apostle. Literally, that means "one sent out by Christ." An apostle was hand-picked by Christ Jesus to this holy office. An apostle spoke or wrote precisely what Christ Jesus wanted him to speak. We call the New Testament writings the Apostolic Word, or Scripture. Whose Word is it really (see also **Galatians 1:1, 11–12**)? Why does Paul make such a major point in his introduction about being an apostle?

Verses 2–5: The Message

Paul was very conscious of his Jewish readers, so throughout his letter to the Romans he used Old Testament references to support his teachings. In **verse 2** he said that the Gospel he preached was promised by God through His prophets. Paul was not just another crackpot with a crazy new idea for a cult. Rather, he was the ordained apostle and messenger of the Gospel of Christ.

Examine what Paul was saying about Jesus in these verses. Briefly list a description of Jesus from this section, as though you never heard about Jesus before.

1. What surprising things would you discover about

Jesus? How do you know Jesus is a real man? How do you know Jesus is really God?

2. What surprising thing did Jesus accomplish that no human ever before accomplished?

3. Paul's message-proclaiming task is calling people to belong to Jesus Christ. How do you know that you are one of Paul's audience (verse 6)?

4. The *we* in verse 5 is the so-called *royal we*, such as a monarch or government official might use. Paul is not speaking just as Paul, the man. He is speaking as an official of the kingdom of God. Therefore Paul speaks with authority. Why is it important that the message Paul proclaims is not seen as just Paul's personal opinion? What strong comfort do you receive from knowing that "you belong to Christ" is Christ's promise to you and not just a matter of human opinion?

Verses 6–7: Called to Belong; Called to Be Saints

Not only are you called to belong to Jesus Christ (verse 6), you are (at the same time) called to be saints (verse 7). Later in this course, we will go into much more detail as to how sinners can also be saints. For now, take a quick look at what Christ called you to be:

1. The word *saints* is a radical word! Literally, it means *holy ones.* How can Paul honestly use such a word to describe us?

2. Saints are people who have been taken out of the main stream and the ordinary, and set aside for God's purposes. Compare this with 1 Peter 2:9–10. From what have you been removed? To what have you been set aside? What was God's purpose behind calling you to belong to Him?

3. We are saints, not because we are good, but because God is good and is in love with us. That's why we have been called to belong. How does this Good News from Paul's message make you different from the world? Are you different from the world, even if you don't feel different? Explain your answer.

4. Paul's message is so great that it's unheard of outside of Christianity! Apparently that's why he makes use of his apostolic authority—so we know that this comes right from the mouth of God Himself! We belong to Jesus Christ because Jesus Christ called us to belong. Look closely at verse 7. What moved Jesus Christ to call us? How does that make you feel?

WRAPPING IT UP

Paul, a called apostle, writes to you, someone called to belong to Christ. Why does Paul sound excited about his message? Why does he make it sound exciting for us?

LOOKING AHEAD

Read Romans 1:8–17 for the next session. Expect God the Holy Spirit to work mightily in your life just as He did in Paul's.

Through Him and for His name's sake, we received grace and apostleship to call people from among all the Gentiles to the obedience that comes from faith. And you also are among those called to belong to Jesus Christ.

Romans 1:5–6

SESSION 2

Profile of a Saint

ROMANS 1:8–17

An old adage says, "A friend doubles your joy and halves your sorrow." How great we feel when someone shows genuine pleasure over a good thing that has happened to us! Likewise, how important it can be to have a sympathetic shoulder to cry on in bad times! But friends like these are hard to find. Most of us experience a twinge of envy when good things happen to others, even our friends. We may feel left out, wondering why this good thing couldn't come to us, too.

Take a few moments and think about your best friend. Think of the last time your friend received something terrific. Honestly evaluate your own feelings when you heard the news. Were you happy or envious? Was your rejoicing genuine, or could you have won an academy award for best actor?

As this section of Romans shows, a different and deeper kind of friendship can take place among Christians. Paul, who was once Saul of Tarsus, persecutor of the church, now demonstrates a strong, brotherly kind of love for God's people in Rome—people he had never met! He thanks God for their faith; he's anxious to visit them to bring them a spiritual gift. He can hardly wait.

What in the world caused this change in a man like Paul? What could he and the Roman Christians be sharing? What is it that not only rids our hearts of envy and feeling left out, but actually increases as we share it? Of course, it has something to do with Christ Jesus, but is it something that Christians today, including you, have?

IN THE WORD
Verses 8–10: Thankful

1. When something especially good happens to you, what do you do to express it? Suppose that you are

- a young man and just elected to be captain of the football team;
- a young woman and just elected president of the student council;
- a young writer, and just today a letter from the editor

of a national magazine arrived. He is buying your story, and it will be published soon; or

- an instrumental musician, and you were just appointed to first chair in the Metropolitan Youth Symphony Orchestra; this is the kind of news you live for. What do you do?

2. Paul felt that something great had happened for him. Although he had never been to Rome, the church there was growing and thriving. He rejoiced that God was mightily at work and the Spirit was calling countless people into faith in Jesus Christ. This is the kind of news Paul lived for. He was overjoyed. What did Paul do?

3. Reread **verses 8–10.** Write out a list of some of the things Paul did to express his thanks.

What does this tell you about the changed Paul? about the church in Rome? about Christ Jesus? What message does God have here for you and your local church?

Verses 11–15: Encouraging One Another

Paul longed to see the Roman Christians so that **"you and I may be mutually encouraged by each other's faith" (verse 12).** It may seem incredible to us that a mighty warrior of God like the apostle Paul needed encouragement from other Christians. But he did. Read the following portions of Paul's letters to other Christians, and comment:
2 Corinthians 7:5–7
Colossians 4:11
2 Timothy 4:9–11

1. From the above texts, point out where Paul feels he is

    a. afraid;

    b. deserted;

    c. downcast;

    d. harassed and tired; and

    e. needing help for ministry.

2. From the above texts, point out what other Christians did to make Paul feel stronger and uplifted. Explain why, if you were in Paul's situation, you would appreciate this kind of friendship and help.

3. In your notes, relate some incident when you

received comfort from a Christian friend. Have you ever had times when you wished a Christian friend were around, but wasn't? Explain. How can God give us encouragement even at times like these?

Verses 16–17: The Righteous Live by Faith in Christ

What's the Point?

It may seem extraordinary (and unusual!) that someone as "mighty" as Paul speaks so candidly and so strongly about his need and love for other Christians. Perhaps we do not speak that way. We may feel that not needing others is a sign of strength; that we should be able to handle all our own problems—including our spiritual problems—on our own.

1. But the point that Paul is showing us is that Christ Jesus not only *doesn't want* us to live the Christian life alone, He knows we *can't* live it alone. Why not?

Christ's people share something that nobody else in the whole world believes. Every force in the world puts pressure on us *not* to believe it. The one Jesus calls "the prince of this world" broadcasts powerful propaganda against us to make it seem foolish and too ridiculous to believe.

2. Have you ever been in the minority—on any question, issue, or opinion? If so, describe in a short paragraph what you felt like. Were you ever tempted to hide your true feelings? opinions? beliefs? Imagine finding one friend just at that time. How would that friend help you stick to your true feelings and beliefs?

3. The apostolic writer also spoke about encouraging one another. Read **Hebrews 10:24–25.**

a. What kind of "meeting" was he talking about? What would take place at those "meetings"? Christians have those very same kind of "meetings" today. Identify your "meeting" place.

b. The writer is urgent! Why? Because "the Day" is approaching. What is that Day? Why does knowing about that Day make our gathering with other Christians urgent?

The Gospel: God's Dynamite

Jesus Christ gave us His Gospel. For altogether sinful human people, it's powerful news. Would self-admitted sinners ever expect to hear that

- the all-holy, all-just God turns out to be our Father, and He's longing for us to come home to Him?

- His Son, Jesus, put Himself out on a limb to pay the cost for our sin?
- He loved us to death (His death, not ours)?
- Jesus rose again, beat death at its game, and now shares His victory over sin and death with us?
- all this is a gift! It's free!

That's powerful news that blows the doors of heaven wide open!

1. The Gospel is the "power of God." The word for power in the original Greek is *dunamis.* From that Greek word Alfred Nobel coined the term *dynamite* for his new invention.

a. How is the Gospel very much like dynamite, especially to those who think they are too far gone for God to love, care for, and save?

b. How is the Gospel very much like dynamite for you? Relate one incident when Christ Jesus' Good News (Gospel) sounded especially good to you.

2. Paul is "not ashamed of the Gospel" because it is God's power to save sinners.

a. In your own words, explain why a proud, independent person would be ashamed of the Gospel.

b. On the other hand, why is it absolutely Great News that salvation has been earned for us by Christ Jesus?

3. Salvation comes to us through faith. But faith is not a work we do either; we cannot crank ourselves up to believe. The Good News here is that faith also comes to us as a free gift from God the Holy Spirit.

Reread **verse 17.** It does not mean, "Only the good people live by faith." It means that sinful people who trust in Christ Jesus are considered by God to be righteous. This news changes our whole relationship to God! For instance, how can it change the way we pray? worship? serve? feel about ourselves?

LOOKING AHEAD

Read **Romans 1:18–23** before the next session. Why does God reveal His wrath to us? How does the wrath of God affect you?

I am not ashamed of the Gospel, because it is the power of God for the salvation of everyone who believes: first for the Jew, then for the Gentile. For in the gospel a righteousness from God is revealed, a righteousness that is by faith from first to last, just as it is written: "The righteous will live by faith."

Romans 1:16–17

SESSION 3

The Wrath of God

ROMANS 1:18–32

What makes you angry? Take a moment to think about your answers to this question. Then read the verses for today's session. If you look carefully, you may be surprised to find that many of the things that make you angry also upset the Lord.

How do you feel when you are ignored, when people around you act as though you didn't exist? How do you feel when you are telling the truth and no one will believe you? How do you feel when those you care about are mistreated by wicked and unjust people? Do these things ever make you feel angry?

We know that our emotions have been distorted by sin. Human anger differs from God's anger; God's anger is always just, always righteous, always holy. We can't really understand it. But thinking about our own anger and the things that provoke us can help us *begin* to understand God's anger (wrath) and why sinful human actions provoke it.

IN THE WORD

Verse 18: Reasons for God's Wrath

Two words from this verse summarize all the things that provoke the wrath of God. What are the two words, and how would you define them?

Verses 19–20: Ignorance Is No Excuse

1. Paul goes on to say that people who are guilty of these things are also guilty of suppressing the truth. What does he mean? Find an answer for that question in **verse 19.**

2. Paul then says that no one has an excuse for not knowing about God. By creating and caring for the universe, God has given ample proof of His existence.

David wrote, **"When I consider Your heavens, the work of Your fingers, the moon and the stars, which You have set in place, what is man that You are mindful of him?" (Psalm 8:3).** On warm, star-filled summer nights we have all had thoughts similar to David's. List a few other experiences that have brought the reality of God's existence home to you.

Verses 21–25: Examples of Godlessness and Wickedness

As you read **verses 21–25,** find as many examples of godlessness as you can. (You should be able to list at least five.) As you discover these examples of impiety, put them into your own words and consider what evidence you see of each in our society today.

In **Genesis 1:26** God said, **"Let us make man in Our image, in Our likeness, and let them rule over the fish of the sea and the birds of the air, over the livestock, over all the earth, and over all the creatures that move along the ground."** Compare these words with **Romans 1:23** and **25.** How have humans reversed God's divine order. What kinds of idols does our society substitute for God?

11

Verses 26–32: Consequences of Godlessness and Wickedness

1. What do you do when you get angry? Most of us, at times, need a physical outlet for our anger. We yell. We kick. We scream. We slam doors. These are natural responses to a powerful emotion.

People commonly, though mistakenly, believe that God reacts in the same way. When we think of the wrath of God, we are tempted to think of Him raining down fire and brimstone upon deserving sinners. Paul's triple use of the phrase **"God gave them over" (verses 24–28),** teaches us that God often expresses His wrath in a much more subtle—and much more terrifying—way than fire and brimstone.

God responds to a society that has rejected Him by leaving them alone. He allows them to act out their choices in perfect freedom. When God removes His restraining hand from a society, moral decay is inevitable. When spiritual values no longer matter, physical experiences become all important. This leads to **"sexual impurity for the degrading of their bodies with one another."** That which our culture calls the "sexual revolution," Paul calls the wrath of God.

Reread **verses 21–28.** As you do so, try to find the logical progression that leads a society from refusing to glorify and thank God to homosexuality—all in eight short verses.

2. Godlessness in a society leads to wickedness in the individual or, as Paul says, **"a depravity of mind."** His litany of evil in **verses 29–31** numbs the mind. Christians cannot just dismiss these more than 20 examples of moral depravity as characteristics of a sick society. We see too many of our own sins in this list. Does this mean that we, too, are under the wrath of God? How do we, the children of God, differ from those described in **verse 32?** Explain the comfort available to us, who acknowledge our sin and repent of it.

LOOKING AHEAD

Read **Romans 2:1–16** before the next session.

The wrath of God is being revealed from heaven against all the godlessness and wickedness of men who suppress the truth by their wickedness, since what may be known about God is plain to them, because God has made it plain to them.

Romans 1:18–19

SESSION 4

The Judgment of God

ROMANS 2:1–16

Suppose you see a friend do something you know to be wrong. If you say something to your friend, are you judging that person? If you fail to say something, are you responsible if your friend gets hurt? What's the difference between judging and calling sin, sin? Many Christians do not understand this distinction and, as a result, make mistakes in one of two directions.

Let's get a bit more personal. When someone points out a sin in our life, we may be greatly tempted to say, "Who are you to judge me? The Bible says, 'Judge not.' " This may effectively silence a critic, but it is not a Biblical attitude.

Judging—sentencing someone to hell or welcoming someone to heaven—is God's business. On the other hand, the Bible tells us that when we recognize sin in the lives of our brothers and sisters, we are to help them recognize it, too. And we are to build one another up in love. **"Brothers, if someone is caught in a sin, you who are spiritual should restore him gently. But watch yourself, or you also may be tempted" (Galatians 6:1).**

Thus, we err by becoming indignant when we are confronted with sin in our own lives. We Christians also err often by having an attitude of self-righteousness. When we see an evildoer in action, we love to get indignant. We take great pleasure in thinking about how good we are compared with how bad the sinner is. How easily we violate the spirit of **Galatians 6:1** when we build ourselves up by tearing down another. This is why Paul says, **"But watch yourself."**

If we are going to help others deal with sin in their lives, as the Bible instructs us to do, we must first be aware of it in our own lives. The Pharisee and the tax collector, the saint and the sinner, all must come to God on the same basis, forgiven by the blood of the Lamb.

IN THE WORD

Verses 1–3: Judgment Is God's Business

In **Romans 1** Paul thoroughly describes what happens to people who reject God and go their own way.

He then turns his attention to his Jewish readers. He realizes that they will be nodding their heads in vigorous agreement with his description of the corrupt Gentile society. Paul wishes to expose their hypocrisy without offending his readers, so he begins with a tactful phrase—"you who pass judgment." He clearly directs his attitude, however, at the Jewish people **(verses 9–10)**. Paul then skillfully begins to show how his readers condemn and despise the Gentiles while they stand equally guilty of breaking God's laws.

Verse 2 asserts that God bases His judgment on truth. This surely threatens any hypocrite whose religion is all on the outside. In another way, knowing that God's judgment is based on truth holds great comfort for repentant sinners. Can you think of some ways in which it is a comfort for you?

Verses 4–5: A Misunderstood Blessing

Paul ended **verse 3** with a question: **"Do you think you will escape God's judgment?"** Paul seems to expect some of his readers to say, "Yes, we think so. If we are as bad as you say, why isn't God punishing us?" What answer does Paul give? For what is God waiting? What does this have to say to you about your own life?

Verses 6–15: Judgment Is Impartial in God's Court

1. Many Jewish people believed that being right with God (justification) was not a matter of belief, but of birth. Anyone born a Hebrew was a child of God—and nothing, not even unbelief, could change that. In what ways do Christians today show they are sometimes guilty of the same faulty thinking?

2. True children of God resemble their Father. Their actions clearly show their right relationship with God. Paul has not forgotten that **"the just shall live by faith"**; but he is pointing out to people who mistakenly believe they are right with God that justification will produce **"fruit in keeping with repentance" (Luke 3:8)**. Right living (sanctification) is a natural outgrowth

of being right with God (justification). Why is sanctification important?

3. Reread **verses 12–15.** As you do, note that Paul refers to two different kinds of law—one for the Jew and another for the Gentile. These are sometimes called "natural law" and "revealed law." Use the text to explain what you understand these terms to mean.

Verse 16: Judged by Christ

When was the last time you thought about Judgment Day? It's very easy for us to repress thoughts about God's judgment. After all, it seems like such an unpleasant idea. Perhaps the finality of Judgment Day makes us uncomfortable.

Perhaps, too, we find it hard to picture Jesus as a judge. We see Him as a baby in the manger, as a loving teacher, as the crucified Savior—but not as Judge. Yet, Scripture clearly teaches that Christ will judge the living and the dead. Jesus Himself said, "**Moreover, the Father judges no one, but has entrusted all judgment to the Son" (John 5:22).**

Verse 16 teaches two things about Judgment Day:
The day of judgment *will* come.
Jesus will judge the secrets of our hearts.

Neither of these truths need to be threatening to us as God's children. In fact, a believer can find a world of comfort in them. Do you think you might explain this verse to a little child so that the child would hear the joy of the Gospel rather than the threat of the Law?

LOOKING AHEAD

Read **Romans 2:17–3:8** before the next session.

God's judgment against those who do such things is based on truth. . . . This will take place on the day when God will judge men's secrets through Jesus Christ, as my gospel declares.

Romans 2:2, 16

SESSION 5

The People of God

ROMANS 2:17–3:8

How do you feel when someone tells you that you need to be more responsible? If a parent or some other authority figure says this, it usually means that they do not feel they can trust you or depend upon you. At best, it means that they do not think you can act reliably without supervision.

Almost all of us feel resentful when someone suggests these things about us. Few people can accept this kind of criticism objectively. In the text you read for today, Paul accused the Jews of not fulfilling their responsibilities as the people of God. He lists all their privileges and then points out their failure to live up to the responsibilities these privileges brought with them. Paul knew that most of his readers would object to his condemnation. He anticipates their objections and then proceeds to show how dangerous it can be to accept the privileges and not the responsibilities that come along with being children of God.

It is a reality of life—with every privilege comes a corresponding responsibility. Think of the privileges you personally enjoy. Do you recognize the responsibilities that come with each privilege?

IN THE WORD

Verses 17–20: Privileges and Responsibilities

1. Look over these verses once again. What privileges and responsibilities does Paul list as belonging to God's Jewish people?

2. Paul begins this section with the phrase "if you call yourself a Jew . . . " If he were writing to us today he might say it this way—"if you call yourself a Christian . . . " What do you think might follow from this statement? What responsibilities and privileges do you think the apostle might mention?

3. In one sense, we Christians have the same responsibilities as God's Old Covenant people had. To us, as to them, God did not say, "Just do the best you can." What standard do you find in both **Leviticus 11:45** and **Matthew 5:48?**

4. Paul has already begun to make it abundantly clear that none of us lives up to the standard God has set for us. In **chapter 3** he will nail the argument down still tighter. If we persist in thinking that our Christian responsibilities are things God demands of us so that He will accept us, we will fall into one of two traps: despair or spiritual arrogance. Why is this so?

5. The core of the epistle to the Romans clearly spells out an alternative. We could look at many different passages. For now, read **3:21–24.** You have probably heard these words dozens, perhaps hundreds (or thousands!), of times in your life. Regardless of how often you have heard them, why are they such Good News to those of us who do not—and cannot—live up to our responsibilities as God's people?

6. Now read **Romans 9:25–26** and **1 Peter 2:9.** According to these passages, how does God view His children? What privileges has He given to us?

7. Someone has said that our "Christian responsibilities" are simply "our response to His ability." What do you think that means? Why is it such an important concept?

15

Verses 21—29: Warning! Danger!

Maybe you've observed people who have abused their privileges and have gotten away with it. Even though such people might think they have escaped the consequences of their actions, they really have not. Little children become brats. Young adults become selfish and rebellious. Adults become hypocritical and arrogant.

Some people are just "takers." You can probably think of a few who get everything they want and never give anything in return. How do you feel about them? They don't make very good friends, do they? Yet we face exactly this danger. If we take in all the blessings of God and refuse to share them, we become negative witnesses. We become an offense to people and an embarrassment to God. This is Paul's evaluation of the Jewish people to whom he is writing.

Paul gives three examples of character flaws typical of the Jewish nation at this point in their history. Can you find and put them into your own words?
1. **Verses 21—23**
2. **Verse 24**
3. **Verses 25—29**

Verses 1—8: Objections

In the verses you just read, Paul has made some very controversial statements. He has said that the rite of circumcision has no value unless the circumcised person also yields to the will of God.

Jews held circumcision in as high a regard as Christians today hold Baptism. Circumcision was the symbol of Jewishness, of being God's person. So when Paul says that a true Jew is one who has experienced a circumcision of the heart and not just of the body, he expects a vehement argument.

Paul knew that whenever people deal with such an emotionally charged topic, matters can easily get out of hand. Think of the issues of our day that cause this kind of reaction—civil rights, abortion, or prayer in public schools. When people try to discuss such matters, emotion often takes the place of reason, and the whole argument becomes an exercise in futility.

Paul expects his remarks about the value of circumcision to produce emotionally charged objections from his Jewish readers. Consequently, Paul creates an imaginary dialog between himself and a Hebrew objector.

1. Rewrite **Romans 3:1—8** in your own words. Look at the four questions being asked by Paul's imaginary debator. Try to show by your choice of words how each question becomes progressively more foolish.

2. Choose one of the questions you just paraphrased and give an example of how young people today sometimes use the same arguments.

LOOKING AHEAD

Read **Romans 3:9—20** before the next session.

This righteousness from God comes through faith in Jesus Christ to all who believe. There is no difference, for all have sinned and fall short of the glory of God, and are justified freely by His grace through the redemption that came by Christ Jesus.
Romans 3:22—24

SESSION 6

We Are All Guilty

ROMANS 3:9–20

The Latin word *persona* means "mask." In Greek and Roman drama, the actors wore masks designed to show different emotions. The masks were larger than life and could easily be discerned from the back row of the amphitheater. If an actor's role demanded a shift from tears to laughter, the mask was changed. The theater preserves this ancient practice in its logo—the tragic-comedy masks.

The English word *personality* comes from that Latin word (*persona*). Our personality is our mask. Aspects of our personalities project an image of ourselves that is not real. Little children are quite transparent. When they lie, it's obvious. When they try to be devious, they fool no one (except perhaps other children). As children mature, they become better and better at wearing the right mask for the right occasion.

Look at your own behavior. Do you act the same way with your parents as you do with your friends? Do you wear one mask on Saturday night and another on Sunday morning? In varying degrees we are all guilty of this sort of play acting. Shakespeare was right when he said "all the world's a stage."

What are we hiding? According to Paul, it's our corrupt character. Human beings wear masks to hide a nature that has been corrupted by sin. We have a genetic disorder, a terminal illness passed on from one generation to another, a disorder for which no human remedies have been found. No matter how well we control our behavior, it is only a cosmetic camouflage over a nature that has been spoiled by sin. Paul concludes his lengthy argument **(Romans 1:18–3:20)** with this thought: no one can become righteous in God's eyes by keeping the Law. We are all guilty.

IN THE WORD
Verses 9–18: All under Sin

1. In the last session, we looked at four questions or arguments directed at Paul's Jewish readers. Now Paul poses one last question. Considering the privileges and responsibilities of the Jews, the people of God, are they any better off than the Gentiles? Paul says, "No! All have failed to keep the Law. All are sinners. All must be justified in the same manner. Jews or Gentiles, we are all under sin" **(verse 9)**.

As you look back over the first part of Romans, find and read the section where Paul proved the guilt of the Gentiles.

2. Where has he shown the guilt of the Jews?

3. In the sections you just read, Paul used logic and human reasoning to prove that all people stand guilty before God. Now he turns to an even surer method of clinching his argument for his Jewish readers. He quotes from the Old Testament to prove his point **(verses 10–18)**.

Paul uses a method of debate he learned in rabbinical school. The Pharisees called it "stringing pearls," and it was very familiar to the Jews. They would take a number of selected verses from a variety of sacred writings and develop an argument from them. The power of the argument rested upon the unchanging truth of God's Word. The "pearls" were always carefully selected and presented in an orderly way.

Find and read the six sections of Scripture Paul chose for his proof texts.

    a. **Psalm 14:1–3 (Romans 3:10–12)**

    b. **Psalm 5:9 (Romans 3:13a)**

c. **Psalm 140:3 (Romans 3:13b)**
d. **Psalm 10:7 (Romans 3:14)**
e. **Isaiah 59:7–8 (Romans 3:15–17)**
f. **Psalm 36:1 (Romans 3:18)**

4. Did you notice how beautifully Paul strings his pearls? Portions of a verse, whole verses, multiple verses—he joins all together to form one cohesive and powerful conclusion: "We are all under sin."

Jot down what you hear Paul saying about human character in **Romans 3:10–12**, and about human conduct in **verses 13–18.**

Verses 19–20: All under the Law

Paul has had too much debating experience to let his readers wriggle off the hook now. He reminds them of an obvious fact: what the Law says was intended primarily for those to whom it was given (the Jews). Paul has produced proof from their own laws. He quotes Scriptures given expressly to God's people, Israel, that they together with the whole world stand guilty before the throne of God.

Paul moves his argument to its inexorable conclusion: "No one can get right with God by keeping the Law." This produces one final question: What good, then, is the Law? Paul answered this unspoken question this way—**"through the Law we become conscious of sin."** Theologians sometimes call this the "second use of the Law." God's law exposes the sin in our lives. The Law helps us recognize our sinful nature. What things would we not consider particularly wrong if the Law didn't identify them as sin?

LOOKING AHEAD

All together, this section of Romans sounds very cheerless. We must confess that we are all guilty under the Law. Is there any hope for us? Read **Romans 3:21–31** for next time. As you do, see what a remarkable remedy God provides for the problem of sin.

But now a righteousness from God, apart from law, has been made known, to which the Law and the Prophets testify. This righteousness from God comes through faith in Jesus Christ to all who believe.

Romans 3:21–22

SESSION 7

Pardoned

ROMANS 3:21–31

When I was a child growing up in Milwaukee, like children everywhere, I couldn't wait for school to end and summer vacation to begin. Unfortunately I spent more of my vacation time than I care to remember as a prisoner in my own home.

My parents weren't cruel. I wasn't grounded for antisocial behavior. My confinement was caused by a tiny virus, so small that it escaped detection for years. This tiny virus crippled and killed children. The virus caused a disease called poliomyelitis, or polio for short. The virus loved summer, and polio epidemics reached their peak in July and August. There was no cure for polio, and since it was believed to be contagious, the parents kept children apart for safety. Parks, pools, and playgrounds were closed, and parents were told to keep their children home.

It is difficult to explain to later generations what an impact that silent, invisible killer had upon the quality of our lives. It is equally difficult to communicate the relief felt around the world on April 12, 1954, when it was announced that Dr. Jonas E. Salk had developed a safe and effective vaccine for polio.

People who lived through the polio epidemics of the 1940s and 1950s will never forget this dreadful and frightening disease. But for the ultimate in bad news, nothing can compare to Paul's conclusion about the human race, **"Therefore no one will be declared righteous in His sight by observing the law" (Romans 3:20).** God gave us His laws to live by; we cannot live up to them, and there is no way we can make up for our failure. So God has pronounced His verdict, "Guilty!" The penalty? **"The wages of sin is death" (Romans 6:23a).**

Paul has carefully brought his readers face to face with this grim reality so that when he gets to the good news **(verse 21),** we will hear it for exactly what it is, a reprieve coming from heaven. Humanity can breath a collective sigh of relief because God has provided a way we can be justified other than by keeping the Law. He reveals this plan in **verse 22: "through faith in Jesus Christ to all who believe."** Chapter 3 concludes with a clear and concise declaration of this doctrine.

You probably don't remember getting your polio vaccine, and you can hardly be expected to feel any deep gratitude toward Dr. Salk for freeing you from a danger you never had to fear. You are immune anyhow.

In similar fashion, you may not remember your baptism, and you may find it difficult to be very enthusiastic about a theological reality called justification, but you are cleansed just the same. A thoughtful reading of Romans can generate a new enthusiasm and a heartfelt gratitude in the soul of every reader for the wonder of God's plan of salvation.

Think about what you expect from your study of Romans in the days and weeks ahead. After giving it some thought, write a prayer expressing your desires. Consider sharing your prayer with your class. If you have never prayed for your teacher, please do so now. God answers prayer, and when students and teachers pray for each other, astounding things will happen in your classroom!

IN THE WORD
Verses 21–26
The Righteousness from God

"The righteousness of God" might be better translated "God's plan for making us righteous." The apostle now proceeds to detail the nature of the doctrine of "justification by faith," the main theme of Romans.

In **verse 21** Paul tells his Jewish readers that this was not a new teaching, but one clearly proclaimed in the Old Testament. In the following chapters Paul will offer proof of this from the Law and the Prophets. Wherever Paul went, he was careful to make this point. Before King Agrippa he said, " . . . **I am saying nothing beyond what the prophets and Moses said would happen" (Acts 26:22).**

1. Read **Psalm 32** and explain in writing how this psalm supports Paul's statement about God's gift of righteousness.

2. The first paragraph in this section of the lesson and the material you just wrote on **Psalm 32** is called *Bible commentary.* Continue this style of writing as you explain and comment on the key phrases in Paul's description of the righteousness of God:

- **Verse 22:** through faith in Jesus Christ to all who believe
- **Verse 23:** all have sinned
- **Verse 24:** justified freely by His grace
- **Verse 25:** God presented Him as a sacrifice of atonement
- **Verse 26:** to be just and the One who justifies

Verses 27–31: Conclusions

Try to imagine what God's family would be like if it were like your school. Not a very pleasant thought, is it? Not that your school is so bad, but it's full of people who are busy earning their way through it. Seniors who have worked their way through three years of school feel vastly superior to the lowly little freshmen. Athletes earn their varsity letters, and National Honor students earn their way into the society by their grade point average. In many aspects of high school life, people compete with one another (e.g., cheerleaders, homecoming court, class officers, valedictorian honors, prom king and queen). This competition may be healthy, and it may promote high achievement among the student body, but it can also separate and promote pride, cliques, and class distinctions. High school is hardly heaven!

Reread **verses 27–31,** and answer the following questions:

1. What is so unique about God's plan for making people righteous?

2. How do you feel about receiving something you could never earn and do not deserve?

LOOKING AHEAD

All this seems very clear, and yet many Christians find themselves confused about the relationship between faith and works. Read **Romans 4:1–5** before the next session. What is your understanding of the value of "good works"? Are works necessary? Or is faith alone enough? Think about these questions as you read.

But now a righteousness from God, apart from law, has been made known, to which the Law and the Prophets testify. This righteousness from God comes through faith in Jesus Christ to all who believe. There is no difference, for all have sinned and fall short of the glory of God, and are justified freely by His grace through the redemption that came by Christ Jesus.

Romans 3:21–24

SESSION 8

Faith and Works

ROMANS 4:1–5

Work is an important part of life. Most of us expect to get a job, earn a paycheck, and support ourselves in as grand a style as we can afford. We admire people who have good work ethics. We approve of the law of production-consumption which, simply stated, says we contribute as much to the society in which we live as we take from it. These were the values of our pilgrim and pioneer forefathers, and they are good ones.

A problem arises, however, when we try to apply these same principles to religion, or more specifically to salvation. Our entire upbringing says, "There is no such thing as a free lunch," "You get what you pay for," "If you want something then work for it." We are suspicious of anyone who offers something for nothing. So when God offers the priceless gift of salvation free and clear, He is met with skepticism more often than with gratitude.

In an ignorance born of pride, many people view God's plan of salvation as a form of divine welfare and want no part of it. They have the attitude that if God is not satisfied with what they are doing, then He can forget it. They are going to earn their own way to heaven, and they are not interested in receiving charity—not even from God.

Others are willing to accept the sacrifice of Jesus Christ as partial payment, but they want to contribute something, also. These people base their salvation upon a combination of faith and works.

Paul is very clear. Salvation comes from God to us as a gift, *never as reward*. If you earn a salary by the sweat of your brow, when that paycheck is put in you hand, you say, "I deserve this." If, on the other hand, you receive a sum of money you neither earned nor anticipated, it would be unthinkable to take any credit for it.

As you read **Romans 4:1–5** at the end of the last class session, what were your thoughts about faith and works? Take a few minutes now to organize your thoughts and write a definition of faith and another one for works.

IN THE WORD

Verses 1–3
What about Abraham?

Paul anticipates an objection from his Jewish readers. He has just stated that salvation comes not by keeping the Law, but by faith in Jesus Christ. So what about Abraham? He didn't know about Christ; and yet, God called him **"My friend"**(Isaiah 41:8). God promised, **"All nations on earth will be blessed, because Abraham obeyed Me and kept My requirements, My commands, My decrees and My laws" (Genesis 26:4–5).** This sounds like a clinching argument for justification by works.

Paul agrees that if Abraham was justified by works, he had something to boast about; Paul adds, however, **"but not before God" (verse 2).** As convincing as the argument sounds, it will not work where it really counts, and that is "before God." Paul turns to Scripture to support his case. He quotes **Genesis 15:6: "Abraham believed the Lord, and He credited it to him as righteousness."**

In **Romans 3:22** we learned that **"righteousness from God comes through faith in Jesus Christ to all who believe."** If you were witnessing to a Jewish friend and were asked to explain how Abraham, who lived 2,000 years before Christ, received righteousness, what would you say?

Verses 4–5: Works Do Not Produce Righteousness

The point has been made, remade, and will continue to be made that **"the man who does not work but trusts God who justifies the wicked, his faith is credited as righteousness" (verse 5).** This is not difficult to understand, but it does raise one last question. Is there any value in good works? To find an answer, do two things:

1. Think about the phrase, "God who justifies the wicked." Explain what this says to you and why it is important.

2. Read **James 2:11–16.** If it seems to you that James and Paul are in complete disagreement, you

should know a great many people think so, too. Write a paragraph on faith and works to explain how both James and Paul are correct in what they are teaching.

LOOKING AHEAD

Paul uses the words *blessed* or *blessedness* in each of the next four verses. Read **Romans 4:6–15** before the next session. What produces this happy state?

Abraham believed God, and it was credited to him as righteousness.

Romans 4:3

SESSION 9

Forgiveness

ROMANS 4:6–15

"I forgive you" can be the most comforting words in the human language. They can also be the most irritating.

Perhaps something like this has happened to you. Through no fault of your own, a friend begins a quarrel with you. Wishing to avoid trouble, you go to your friend and apologize for whatever it was you did to make him or her angry. Your friend's only reply is, "Well, then I guess I can forgive you." This sort of forgiveness does not produce comfort; in fact, it probably made you angry. Being forgiven for something for which you feel no guilt or responsibility does not produce gratitude. It produces wrath.

Strange as it may seem, many people subconsciously feel this same anger when they are told of God's forgiveness. They do not feel guilty of any serious wrongdoing, so they feel no need for forgiveness. Simon, the Pharisee, was like that. He invited Jesus to a dinner party at his home and found himself offended by a woman who crashed his party and washed Jesus' feet with her tears, and then wiped them dry with her hair. After telling Simon a story about debt and forgiveness, Jesus said, **"Therefore I tell you, her many sins have been forgiven—for she loved much. But he who has been forgiven little loves little" (Luke 7:47).**

True appreciation of forgiveness involves understanding why we need it. The woman knew; Simon did not. The woman worshiped her Forgiver; Simon criticized Him. Like Simon, we Christians have a tendency to think that because our actions aren't very bad, then we ourselves are not so bad. So far in Romans, the Holy Spirit has taken great pains to show us that we are indeed wrong, fundamentally wrong, and only the blood of the Lamb can make up for that wrong.

A person who understands forgiveness is willing to forgive. When we recognize how great God's forgiveness has been toward us, then we will be ready and able to do what God has commanded—to forgive one another.

Sometimes it takes an outstanding event to bring this truth vividly home to us. Not long ago, a three-year-old girl was struck and killed by a hit-and-run driver.

On the afternoon of their daughter's funeral, the parents said in a telephone interview that they were ready to forgive the driver. The father said, "We're not seeking vengeance of any kind. We don't feel that way. It was a tragedy, and maybe we can help this person. Maybe he was drinking or didn't have a driver's license or feels very guilty. We can help the driver by forgiveness—help him deal with it. I can feel for him. It could have been anybody. The worst is over for us. But the worst is happening to him."

(From "Family Wants to Tell Driver: We Forgive," *The Milwaukee Journal,* Friday, Aug. 1, 1986. Used by permission.)

Needless to say, these parents are Christians. They understand what it is to be forgiven. They are able to forgive, and even to reach out in love and concern to the person who took their daughter's life and ran away.

IN THE WORD

Verses 6–8: The Blessedness of Forgiveness

David also understood forgiveness. Paul used words from David's **Psalm 32:1–2** to prove that the Old Testament clearly teaches justification by faith apart from keeping the Law. In session 7 you were asked to do a study of **Psalm 32**. Do you remember David's expressions of guilt and his appreciation of forgiveness? Paul mentions three things to show how well David understood forgiveness. As you study these three things, your understanding of forgiveness will probably expand.

1. **"Blessed are they whose transgressions are forgiven" (verse 7).** The word *forgiven* here means *sent away*. God gave the Israelites a marvelous visual aid of what "transgressions sent away" really meant. Read **Leviticus 16:20–26** and explain the symbolism of the scapegoat.

2. **"Whose sins are covered" (verse 7).** Isaiah **44:22** and **Micah 7:19** are two more Old Testament verses that express the idea of sins being covered or put out of sight. Read these texts and find a 20th-century way of expressing the same idea.

3. **"Blessed is the man whose sin the Lord will**

never count against him'' (verse 8). David does not say that God does not count sins. God does, but He does not count it against the believer. Read Paul's Letter to Philemon (it's only one short chapter) and find a verse that relates to this aspect of forgiveness. (Helpful hint: Read **Luke 10:35.**)

Verses 9–15: Forgiveness Is for Everyone

1. Paul turns again to Abraham to demonstrate God's method of dealing with sins. The ritual of circumcision set the Jews apart from the rest of humanity. They came to regard circumcision as a way to receive justification, and they were deeply offended by the thought that an uncircumcised Gentile could be treated to the same forgiveness as a circumcised Jew. In your own words summarize how Paul proves them wrong in **verses 9–15.**

2. The people of God have always tended to rely too heavily upon ritual and tradition, often at the expense of faith (that is, trusting the practice of religion rather than trusting God). Can you think of ways in which this could be true in the church today? How does God deal with this sin?

LOOKING AHEAD

Even though Abraham may not have known as much about the God he believed in as is revealed to us in all of Scripture, he had a remarkable faith. As you read **Romans 4:16–22,** look for the things Abraham believed.

Blessed are they whose transgressions are forgiven, whose sins are covered. Blessed is the man whose sin the Lord will never count against him.

Romans 4:7–8

SESSION 10

The Faith of Abraham

ROMANS 4:16–22

What would you think of a teacher who always complained about how poorly you were doing and rarely if ever complimented you? Would you enjoy being taught by someone who never seemed satisfied, no matter how hard you tried? How would you like a class where the tests were so hard that everybody failed?

If you answered, "Not much," "No," and, "I'd hate it," to the above questions, you are normal; so, you may be surprised that those were Jesus' teaching methods.

Think of the disciples as the class and Jesus as the teacher. Jesus never said things like "you guys are really doing a good job" or "I appreciate the effort I see you making; keep up the good work." Even when they gave a correct answer, as they did on occasion, Jesus did not give them much credit for it. When Jesus said to Peter, **"Who do you say I am?"** Simon Peter answered, **"You are the Christ, the Son of the living God."** Jesus replied, **"Blessed are you, Simon son of Jonah, for this was not revealed to you by man, but by My Father in heaven"** (Matthew 16:15–17). In other words, Jesus said, "Correct answer, but you didn't figure that out by yourself, Peter, you had some help."

Jesus gave hard tests. On the day He fed the five thousand Jesus said to Philip, **"Where shall we buy bread for these people to eat?"** He asked this only to test him, for He already had in mind what He was going to do **(John 6:5–6)**. Philip, of course, failed the test. He said, "We can't; we don't have enough money."

Jesus never called His disciples men of great faith, but He often scolded them for weak faith. Even on Easter Sunday, His first words to the Emmaus disciples were those of an unhappy teacher **(Luke 24:25–26)**. Later He appeared to the eleven as they were eating. He rebuked them for their lack of faith and their stubborn refusal to believe those who had seen Him after He had risen **(Mark 16:14)**.

1. Just using one gospel, the Gospel of Matthew, let's look at four different occasions when Jesus was disappointed at the disciples' level of faith. Read:

  a. **Matthew 8:26**

  b. **Matthew 14:31**

  c. **Matthew 16:8–12**

  d. **Matthew 17:17**

Read the material surrounding each of these verses and note what the disciples said or did to upset Jesus.

Jesus knew He was teaching a course on survival. In a very real sense, His disciples' very lives and their effectiveness in ministry depended upon how deeply they were able to trust Him to deal with every aspect of their lives.

2. The disciples did learn, but it was not easy. They grew and learned. They graduated with the kind of faith that caused others to take notice.

Read about their "graduation day" in **Acts 2**. Skim the chapter and note the changes you can identify. What evidences of strong faith do you note? What had made this difference?

3. "What kind of faith do I have?" Have you ever asked yourself that question? As the disciples learned to stop relying on themselves and to trust Jesus without reservation, so must we.

What situations cause you to rely on yourself?

What situations cause you to trust other people?

What situations cause you to rely on human reasoning?

Having identified answers to these three questions, what specific changes would you like to see in your faith level? How can these changes become reality?

IN THE WORD

Verses 16–18: Abraham Believed God

Paul has been talking about faith from the very beginning of his Letter to the Romans. Since everything in our life with God depends upon faith, it is quite logical for Paul to use Abraham as an example of what constitutes genuine faith. What two things did Abraham know about God that created faith in his heart **(verse 17)**?

Reread **verse 18**. Put the idea of this verse into your own words.

Verse 19: Abraham Understood the Problem

1. Christians who live by faith are often called naive by the cynics of this world. The cynics claim that we just don't understand the problems. If we did, we would not be so calm and trusting. We would panic, like reasonable people!

Abraham was not naive. He understood that what God promised could not happen, at least, not according to normal biological laws. Read **Genesis 17:15–27** and explain in your own words why God's promise was totally unreasonable (humanly speaking).

2. Compare **Romans 4:19–20** and **Hebrews 11:11** with **Genesis 16:1–4a.** How can the New Testament writers repeatedly refer to Abraham as an example of faith in light of the facts of his life? Why is this so important for us as we think about our "faith-failures"?

Chapter 4:20—22: Abraham Was Strengthened

Faith grows as it trusts God to do the impossible. Abraham trusted God, and God strengthened his faith. Abraham received power to give glory to God for doing what He had promised to do even before He did it!

Think of a time in your own life when you had a problem or a crisis that only God could solve. As you trusted God to deal with the problem, what effect did this have on your faith? Read **Matthew 11:28.** Think about it for a moment, and then write a paragraph, explaining what the verse says to you.

LOOKING AHEAD

Abraham's faith was Abraham's; ours is another matter. Read **Romans 4:24–25.** What do these words say about your own faith?

Therefore, the promise comes by faith, so that it may be by grace and may be guaranteed to all Abraham's offspring—not only to those who are of the law but also to those who are of the faith of Abraham. He is the father of us all.

Romans 4:14

SESSION 11

Our Faith

ROMANS 4:23–25

Having faith is no big deal! Everybody has faith. In fact, everyone lives by faith of some sort or other. An atheist has enormous faith that there is no God. Some little children have a faith in Santa Claus that puts to shame the faith of many adult Christians.

From the moment we get up in the morning until we go back to bed at night, we exercise faith countless times. We believe the clock radio is correct, and we can afford to sleep for 10 more minutes. We have faith that the lights will go on when we flick the switch. We have faith that the chairs on which we sit will hold our weight. As we step into a car, an elevator, or an airplane, we are expressing our faith in their safety.

1. At any one time in life, though, any of these things can fail. The atheist will die and discover too late that God does indeed exist. The child grows up to find Santa Claus is in truth a fat impostor in a phony beard. Clocks stop; electricity fails; furniture breaks; cars and planes crash; elevators get stuck—no matter how much faith we have in them.

Faith is only as valid as its object. Having faith is important. But what we believe in, the object of our faith, is more important still.

2. What do you believe? What is the object of your faith? Peter encouraged believers, **"Always be prepared to give an answer to everyone who asks you to give the reason for the hope that you have" (1 Peter 3:15).** For many Christians this is easier said than done. They are not sure what they believe or why they believe it.

Abraham knew what he believed—or, rather, in whom he believed. It's healthy for us as Christians to set aside a few moments to think about what we believe. The last session ended with the thought that God considered Abraham righteous because he fully believed God was able to do what He promised **(verse 22). Romans 4:23–25** assures us that this principle works in the same way for us.

Of what are you fully persuaded? What is the object of your faith? Take a few moments to think about this and write a paragraph titled, "This Is What I Believe!"

IN THE WORD

Verses 23–25: We Believe in Him Who Raised Jesus, Our Lord

1. God treated Abraham with special favor (grace). Maybe that doesn't surprise us, because we think of Abraham as a special man. But many people are surprised that God is willing to deal with us in exactly the same way He dealt with Abraham **(verses 23–24).**

Compare your paragraph about your own faith with **Romans 4:24–25.** How close are you to what Paul wrote? List the three things Paul says we must believe in order to be considered righteous by God.

2. Think about these basic elements of your Christian faith. How would you explain them to someone who had never heard of them before?

Galatians 3:1–25: Justification by Faith

Paul's letter to the Galatian Christians is a mini-version of his letter to the Romans. In the first 25 verses of **Galatians 3,** Paul covers essentially the same content you have just studied in **Romans 1–4.** As a way of measuring your understanding of justification by grace, read these wonderful verses. Apply what you have learned so far in Romans to answer the following questions:

Verses 1–5

1. What seems to be the problem that causes Paul to call these Christians "foolish" **(verse 1)?**

2. What one question does Paul say he wants to ask of them **(verse 2–5)?** Answer this question as Paul expects the Galatians to answer it.

Verses 6–9

1. What illustration does Paul use to demonstrate the principle of justification by faith?

2. Why do you think he chooses this particular illustration?

Verses 10–14

1. Why can the Law only be a curse and never a means of just justification for us?

2. What is redemption, and how does it work?

Verses 15–18

1. What example from everyday life does Paul use to show justification comes by faith, not by obeying the Law?

2. Why is it important that the Law was given at Mt. Sinai 430 years after God made His covenant with Abraham?

Verses 19–20

1. Why, then, did God give the Law?

2. Who was the "Seed" of whom the promise spoke?

Verses 21–25

How does Paul show us that the Law and the Gospel of God's grace are not rival systems of justification?

LOOKING AHEAD

Read **Romans 5:1–11.** Look for the word *rejoice.* Paul uses this word three times. Each time, he talks about a different level of joy. Think about these three levels as you prepare for session 12.

Christ redeemed us from the curse of the law by becoming a curse for us, for it is written: "Cursed is everyone who is hung on a tree." He redeemed us in order that the blessing given to Abraham might come to the Gentiles through Christ Jesus, so that by faith we might receive the promise of the Spirit.

Galatians 3:13–14

SESSION 12
Rejoice!

ROMANS 5:1–11

A *masochist* is someone who enjoys being miserable. Unfortunately many people have the idea that Christians are masochists. Even many believers seem to think that following Jesus means being thoroughly miserable in this life so that God will make it up to us in the next. Sometimes Christians contribute to this misconception by our gloomy approach to worship and the idea that God doesn't want us to have any fun. Some sincere believers preach this "gospel of suffering."

Certainly Jesus did teach that His followers would not be exempt from problems. He told us that we would be treated no better than He was, that the world would hate us and persecute us. But He never commanded us to be miserable. In fact, He said just the opposite: **"I have told you these things so that My joy may be in you and that your joy might be complete" (John 15:11)**! Jesus spoke of joy in this life—a joy we can always feel, even in the most difficult of times.

Mature Christians "rejoice in tribulation." The New Testament repeats this theme again and again. James told some first-century Christians who were suffering persecution to **"consider it pure joy, my brothers, whenever you face trials of many kinds" (James 1:2)**. Peter, writing at about the same time, said, **"You greatly rejoice, though now for a little while you may have had to suffer grief in all kinds of trials" (1 Peter 1:6)**.

Rejoicing in tribulation seems to be a contradiction in terms. We feel happy when things are going well; we get depressed when we get into difficulties. Who in their right mind is going to rejoice in troubles? Christians can, and often do. Paul explains how and why in **Romans 5:1–11**.

Up to this point, the apostle has exposed the horrible helplessness of the human condition and the divine response to that condition in Christ, through whom we obtain justification and reconciliation by faith. Then Paul concludes this first portion of his letter with some appropriate remarks about how and why Christians can rejoice, even in the midst of very difficult circumstances.

IN THE WORD
Verse 1: Rejoice in the Present

Chapter 5 begins, **"Therefore, since we have been justified through faith . . . ."** Here Paul rests his case. He feels satisfied that he has proven this principle beyond any shadow of doubt. Next, he turns to the implications of this doctrine and our response to it.

The immediate blessing is peace with God. We had been God's enemies **(verse 10)**. But His just anger at human sin has been turned aside through Jesus' sacrifice for us. While we were controlled by our sinful nature, we were hostile toward God **(Romans 8:7)**, but now we have peace with Him. We can rejoice here and now because our war with God is over; our Lord Jesus Christ has won that war for us.

This peace with God makes other types of peace available to us—peace of mind, peace with other people.

Explain how peace of mind and peace with others are related to peace with God.

Verse 2: Rejoice in the Future

Because God's grace works in us, we "rejoice in the hope of the glory of God." Hope could be better translated as "confidence." We can have tremendous confidence in our future. God has unimaginable blessings in store for us, blessings so wonderful that no matter how we may be hurting right now, we can rejoice and wait in breathless anticipation for God to reveal them to us!

Read **1 John 3:2–3**. Explain at least one thing this passage says we know for sure about what our future glory will be like.

Verses 3–5: Rejoice in Problems

Finding joy in the glory God will give us in the future is only one kind of rejoicing. Many Christians seem to think this is all the joy there is. They practice a "suffer now, enjoy later" religion. They rarely, if ever, enjoy themselves. That makes a poor witness for the Christian life.

In **verses 3–5** Paul presents us a formula for joyful living that works, even when we encounter all sorts of difficulties. He says we can even rejoice in our sufferings because of what we know. The power to find joy in life, even when we find ourselves under pressure, depends upon knowledge and experience the Holy Spirit works in our hearts.

1. Paul elaborates on this "knowing" as he gives us four progressive stages of spiritual development that enable us to rejoice in suffering. Study this formula and explain each of the following steps:

    a. Suffering produces perseverance **(verse 3)**

    b. Perseverance produces character **(verse 4)**

    c. Character produces hope (that is, confidence) **(verse 4)**

    d. Confidence does not disappoint (produces courage) **(verse 5)**

2. Paul ends his formula with the words, **"because God has poured out His love into our hearts" (verse 5)**. What does God's love have to do with the process of rejoicing in our sufferings?

Verses 6–11: Rejoice in the Past

Paul saves the best kind of rejoicing for last. We rejoice in the hope of what is to come; we rejoice in suffering. But, most of all, we **"rejoice in God" (verse 11)**. We rejoice in what God has done, in what He is, and in what He will do.

The Christian faith is rooted in history. We believe in a God who acted in history to save us. Jesus' death and resurrection are historical facts. We can rejoice in the present and the future because of what Jesus did for us in the past.

1. How does **verse 6** help explain **verse 5?** What does **verse 6** add to your answer to 2 in the previous section of this lesson?

2. Read **verse 10**. Explain the difference between being "reconciled through Jesus' death" and "saved through His life."

3. **Verses 10–11** use the words *reconcile* or *reconciliation* three times. What does this word mean? Read **2 Corinthians 5:18–21** and explain how *reconcile* is a perfect word to explain what Jesus has done for us.

LOOKING AHEAD

Review **Romans 1–5** and look through the 12 sessions we have covered in this course so far. Organize in your mind the method Paul used to teach justification by faith.

Not only so, but we also rejoice in our sufferings, because we know that suffering produces perseverance; perseverance, character; and character, hope. And hope does not disappoint us, because God has poured out His love into our hearts by the Holy Spirit, whom He has given us.

Romans 5:3–5

SESSION 13

Concluding Activities for Unit 1

The 12 lessons of this unit have talked about the way God has dealt with our sins through the blood of Jesus Christ. We have seen and understood how God has rescued us from our sins. This review has been designed to help make the truths we have studied more memorable and more practical.

1. The 12 session titles are written below. Copy them into your notebook. Use your Bible, this lesson guide, and your own written work from the unit as you write down the central truth of each of these sessions as you remember it.

2. Discovering truth can be exciting. But knowing truth in our heads without applying it in our lives doesn't do us much good. Look back over the central truths you just wrote down. As you do so, look for helpful applications from each session. Explain your application as fully as you can, writing at least one paragraph for each session.

1. Paul, The Man and His Message, **Romans 1:1–7**
2. Profile of a Saint, **Romans 1:8–17**
3. The Wrath of God, **Romans 1:18–32**
4. The Judgment of God, **Romans 2:1–16**
5. The People of God, **Romans 2:17–3:8**
6. We Are All Guilty, **Romans 3:9–20**
7. Pardoned, **Romans 3:21–31**
8. Faith and Works, **Romans 4:1–5**
9. Forgiveness, **Romans 4:6–15**
10. The Faith of Abraham, **Romans 4:16–22**
11. *Our* Faith, **Romans 4:23–25; Galatians 3:1–25**
12. Rejoice, **Romans 5:1–11**

LOOKING AHEAD

Read **Romans 5:12–21** for the next session.

Therefore, since we have been justified through faith, we have peace with God through our Lord Jesus Christ, through whom we have gained access by faith into this grace in which we now stand. And we rejoice in the hope of the glory of God.
Romans 5:1–2

UNIT 2
Salvation Part 2

ROMANS 5:12—8:39

Humanity has a twofold problem; so divinity has provided a twofold solution. **Romans 1–8** contains the story of this two-part salvation. In unit 1 we saw how God dealt with the problem of our *sins*. **"The blood of Jesus His Son cleanses us from all sin" (1 John 1:7).** Thus, the first unit emphasized the justifying power of Jesus' blood to wash away every human sin—our sins are forgiven for Jesus' sake, no matter how great or how many those sins have been.

Unit 2 will concentrate on how God deals with the problem of *sin*—the inborn rebellion that lives within the best of every child of Adam's race. In **Romans 5:12–8:39** the word *sins* (plural) never appears. Instead, Paul uses the singular—*sin*—39 times. In unit 2 we will see how God has delivered us from sin. Jesus' sacrifice has taken care of the wicked things we do; it has also taken care of the wickedness that is a part of who we are by nature.

SESSION 14

Let Christ Reign by Grace!

ROMANS 5:12-21

Control is an interesting word. Think of all the different ways we hear it used. When our astronauts report back to earth from space, they call *mission-control.* If we are trying to break a bad habit, we use *self-control.* Hypnotists try to achieve *mind-control.* Someone having an emotional outburst is said to be *out of control.* And our televisions and video recorders have *remote control.* In every case control can be defined as "power to direct."

Denise is a young woman who needs Jesus Christ in her life. She resists all the witness attempts of her Christian friends. She understands that to acknowledge Jesus as her Lord and Savior would mean acknowledging His authority in her life. She wants to be free. But she doesn't understand the bondage she lives in right now. She is not truly free. Whether she knows it or not, sin controls her life.

In **Romans 5:12-21** Paul describes the two powers that grapple for control of the human race. He uses the word *reign,* which means to have royal power over someone or something. Sin or grace—which is stronger? Which has control in your life?

IN THE WORD

Verses 12-21: Sin and Death Through Adam; Life Through Christ

Paul has developed two major themes or teachings thus far in Romans.
- The condemnation and guilt specify wrong that acts (sins) have brought upon the human race
- The justification and righteousness available to all through Jesus Christ

In the concluding verses of **Romans 5,** the apostle contrasts the results brought about by the lives of two persons, Adam and Christ. One brought the reign of sin and death to all people; the other brought the reign of grace and righteousness.

Many brilliant theologians have found these verses confusing. To help us understand them, let's dissect this section just the way we would a specimen in biology class. Let's take it apart and examine it piece by piece to better understand the whole.

1. Quickly scan **verses 12-21.** As you do, keep the main idea in mind: the problem all human beings face and God's solution in Jesus, the Savior.

After your initial reading, reread the verses. This time, look for verses that speak about (a) sin entering, increasing, and reigning and (b) grace and righteousness entering, increasing, and reigning. Copy the chart below into your notebook and put the numbers of appropriate verses behind each phrase. **Verse 12** has been added to the chart below as an example.

From Adam sin and death
a. entered by one man **(verse 12)**
b. increased **(verse 12)**
c. reigned

From Christ grace and righteousness
a. entered by one man
b. increased
c. reigned

2. Now read verses you have listed behind each key phrase in your outline. Read each set of verses as a separate unit. For instance, read all the verses that refer to sin and death entering.

When you have finished, you will have looked at this section of Romans from six different angles.

3. Organize the information in your own mind. Then write a paragraph explaining in your own words how sin and death came to reign over humanity.

4. Now, think through what these verses say about grace and righteousness reigning. Organize your thoughts into a paragraph explaining how Christ freed the children of Adam from their bondage to sin.

5. Read **Genesis 3:17.** This account has often been called "The Fall of Man." Yet, it reads more like "The Fall of Woman." Only **verse 6** refers to Adam: **"She also gave some to her husband [Adam], who was with her, and he ate it."**

Why, then, do you suppose that Adam seems to get all the blame? Why does Paul keep stressing "one man sin's" instead of "one woman's sin"? (**First Timothy 2:14** may give you a clue.)

6. God's Word teaches the doctrine of original

33

sin—all people born since the fall of Adam are conceived and born in sin. By nature, all people are sinful and unclean before God. Many people rebel against this idea of hereditary sin. They reject it as unjust and unfair. What evidence does Paul give to prove the reality and power of original sin? (See **verses 13-14.**)

7. By now, you should have a fairly clear idea of Paul's main point in **Romans 5:12-21.** But you may be thinking, "What does this have to do with anything? How does this relate to me?"

These are valid questions. But only you can answer them. The Holy Spirit gives Christians the power to apply God's Word to their own individual lives. Take a few minutes to scan today's text one last time. Think about what you have learned and what impact it can have upon the way you think and act. Be ready to share with the class what God has brought home to you in this session.

LOOKING AHEAD

As you read **Romans 6:1-14** for the next session, note the importance Paul places upon knowledge. Each time he uses the word *know,* make a mental note of what Paul says we can know for sure.

For just as through the disobedience of the one man the many were made sinners, so also through the obedience of the one Man the many will be made righteous.

Romans 5:19

SESSION 15

What Do You Know?

THEY LOOK PRETTY TOUGH TO ME. MAYBE WE SHOULD FORFEIT.

ROMANS 6:1–14

Once a high school coach said, "I'm amazed how what we know affects how we perform. A few years ago while I was coaching junior varsity football, I had a team of fairly talented athletes. It was obvious from the start of the season that they would win more games than they lost, but they were not quite championship material.

"One Saturday, however, we were scheduled to play a team loaded with talent. Everyone agreed that this team would go undefeated, and we would do well just to avoid getting beaten up too badly.

"The first half went as expected. We were down by three touchdowns, but we were making our opponents work. The boys were not too ashamed of their performance, at least, not until one of their fathers came into the locker room at half time. He told us he had talked with some parents from the other school. The coach had taken his first and second stringers to scrimmage a public school team because he didn't think we could give his boys enough competition. We were playing against his third and fourth stringers!

"Needless to say, this changed my team's attitudes. They no longer felt satisfied with their losing effort. Now they ran back on the field to wipe out this insult to their athletic ability.

"We played well in the second half. We held the other team scoreless, and we scored two touchdowns of our own. But still we lost. In the locker room after the game, every boy knew that the team had lost because of what we didn't know."

Too many Christians live their lives the same way the losing coach's team played. Too many believers live defeated lives because of what they don't know. Let's explore that in this session.

IN THE WORD

Verses 1–2: Shall We Go On Sinning?

Paul begins **Romans 6** by asking, **"What shall we say then?"** To understand his question, we need to look at the last two verses of the previous chapter. Paul has just concluded that, **"Where sin increased, grace increased all the more."** The phrase "increased all the more" is one word in Greek. The word used earlier for *increase* is used again, but this time with the prefix *hyper* added. So the word for *increased all the more* means to *hyperincrease* or *superincrease.*

You have probably used the word *hyper.* When we say someone is "hyper," we mean that person is overactive. Paul says that one result of sin's increase in the human race is to make grace hyperactive. That grace is super abundantly great to cover *all* sin—no matter how deadly powerful.

People deceived and dominated by sin could draw a dangerously wrong conclusion from that truth, so Paul asks an obvious question, **"Shall we go on sinning** so that grace may increase?" Paul knew that some of his readers might conclude, "God's grace and forgiveness are so big; the more we sin, the more active grace becomes. So if I sin more, God will be glorified because He'll have more to forgive."

How does Paul answer his own question **(verse 2)?** What does he mean?

Verses 3–5: Alive in Christ!

Many Christians live all their lives ignorant of their spiritual condition. They know they disobey God, and they understand that the blood of Jesus cleanses them from all those sins.

They do not know, however, that sin's power has been destroyed. We need no longer live as though helplessly enslaved to a lifestyle of which we are ashamed.

Reread **verses 3–5.** What three changes happened in your spiritual condition at Baptism?

Verses 6–14: What Does This Mean?

1. Two thieves were crucified along side the Lord Jesus. But **verse 6** says they were crucified *with* Him. Why is that significant—what does it mean?

2. **Verses 8–11** spell out in more detail what Christ's death and our baptism means. If we died with Christ, we also live with Him. This monumental truth can change our whole attitude regarding the frustrating struggle with sin in our life. Our opponent is not an unbeatable foe; he is a defeated one! **Verse 11** spells out the victorious attitude God wants us to have. What does this verse say to you?

3. No Christian will be perfect in this life. We will all occasionally fall into disobedience. But sin can no longer control our lives. We can choose to allow sin to reign **(verse 12),** but we don't have to do that.

The words *know* and *no* are intimately related. We need to *know* that we can say *no* to sin **(verses 13–14).** Paul says, **"Do not offer the parts of your body to sin."**

Let's take just one part of our body, the tongue. Make a list of all the ways we offer this part of our body to the control of sin, and a second list of all the ways we can offer it to God as **"an instrument of righteousness"** (verse 13).

LOOKING AHEAD

Read the rest of **Romans 6.** Try to remember some of the things we learned about slavery in session 1. Think about the ways you offer yourself to sin's control. Ask yourself, "Can I stop doing this?" If your answer is yes, look for proof that you are right as you read **verses 15–23.** If your answer is no, do these verses change your thinking?

What shall we say, then? Shall we go on sinning so that grace may increase? By no means! We died to sin; how can we live in it any longer? Or don't you know that all of us who were baptized into Christ Jesus were baptized into His death? We were therefore buried with Him through baptism into death in order that, just as Christ was raised from the dead through the glory of the Father, we too may live a new life.

Romans 6:1–4

SESSION 16

Slavery

ROMANS 6:15–23

Think of all the ways you advertise your school and your faith. The fact that you attend a Lutheran high school is evident every time you wear a letter jacket or carry a school gym bag or drive a car with the school mascot affixed to the bumper. You identify yourself by your class ring, your book covers, or your homecoming pin. In these ways you proclaim loudly every day that you are Christian—whether you say a word or not.

The name *Christian* means *one who follows Christ,* or *one who emulates Christ.*

Imagine the confusion it might create in your neighborhood when little old ladies at the bus stop hear students from your school curse one another. Suppose people see Christian students write obscenities on the sidewalk, or trespass on the neighbors' lawns, or steal candy from the drug store.

Often, our actions shout messages we later wish no one had heard. But people do hear. They do see the contradictions in our life. We don't want to witness in these negative ways. It bothers us when we see classmates acting in these ways. But what's to be done? How can we help ourselves and other Christians live up to that name?

This problem is nothing new. Paul wrote about it in the first century. In **Romans 6** he describes the situation and begins to describe God's solution to our problem.

IN THE WORD

Verse 15: To Sin or Not to Sin?

Many of Paul's Jewish readers held the Old Testament Law in high esteem. These believers felt nervous about Paul's insistence upon justification by faith alone. They equated God's *free* grace with *cheap* grace. They believed God's grace would encourage Christians to disregard God's law completely and live any way they wanted.

This concern did not die in first-century Rome. One senior student at a Lutheran high school in Milwaukee is a Buddhist. She would like to become a Christian, but she is bothered by the same things Paul's Jewish readers were. She has attended worship services a few times, and she reports that all she hears about is forgiveness. She genuinely believes that if her fellow students had to worry a little more about forgiveness, they would act more responsible. Maybe there is some truth to her feeling. Unfortunately, bad behavior by Christians has offended her and has interfered with the work of the Holy Spirit in her life.

Think about the question Paul asks in **verse 15.** Have you ever known anyone who asked that question or one similar to it? How does Paul answer it? How would you answer the senior in the example above?

Verses 16–23: Whose Slave Are You?

1. Read **verse 16** and paraphrase it. Put in your own words what Paul is telling us about our lives. Is anybody free? What's the difference between being slaves to sin and slaves to righteousness?

2. Read **verses 17–23.** As you do, jot down five conditions that existed before we changed masters.

3. As you paraphrased **verse 16,** you should have seen that Christians are free to choose their own master. The Holy Spirit empowers us to be "slaves to righteousness" rather than acting as though we were slaves to sin.

God promises that if we choose to serve righteousness, two things will result. Read **verse 17** and tell what they are. Think about the relationship between the teaching you have received and the wholehearted obedience Paul talks about. What is the difference between knowing Biblical teachings and obeying God?

4. Maybe you've tried to stamp out sin in your life. Or, rather than all sin, maybe you've tried to free yourself from one particular sin that bothers you. Maybe you've given up in disgust after awhile.

Christians sometimes find themselves feeling frustrated at the sin that keeps popping up its ugly head in our lives, even though we choose to be slaves of righteousness. God knows we will never perfect our obedience as long as we live here on earth.

The accent in this part of Scripture lies on consistency: If we consistently give in to the influence that sin still has over our life, then we are slaves of sin. If, on the other hand, when we come to those frequent forks in the road labeled "right" and "wrong," we consistently obey God, then we are slaves of righteousness. Paul says in **verse 19** and again in **verse 22** that living in slavery to God produces a benefit called *holiness.* Explain what that means to you.

5. **Romans 5:23** explains the distinction between slavery to sin and the new life we have in Jesus. What main differences do you see? How could this encourage you in your obedience to God?

LOOKING AHEAD

Romans 7:1–6 is an analogy (an appropriate illustration to explain a similar thing or concept). Jesus used analogies frequently; the apostle Paul rarely does. This one, however, is very useful. As you read these verses, consider how Paul uses marriage to illustrate our relationship to the Law.

The wages of sin is death, but the gift of God is eternal life in Christ Jesus our Lord.

Romans 6:23

SESSION 17

Marriage

ROMANS 7:1–6

Can you imagine a marriage where the husband is perfect? He never makes a mistake. And he demands the same level of perfection from his wife. The wife, on the other hand, is far from perfect. Her husband gives her no help, only criticism. No matter how hard she tries, she can never get through a day without a mistake. The poor wife cooks, sews, cleans, washes, and makes her husband's favorite dessert; but if he finds even one lump in the gravy, he becomes angry. He gives her no credit for all the good things she has done.

No one can find any fault with the husband, but he and his wife are totally unsuited for one another. He can not bring himself to accept anything short of absolute perfection. And she, despite her best effort, cannot live up to his standards.

To make matters worse, there is another man, a man who loves the woman. While he is just as demanding as her husband, he is willing to do all the work for her.

The woman does not believe in divorce, so she knows she must stay with her first husband until he dies. Then she will be free to marry the other man. Imagine her horror and despair when she discovers that her perfect husband has no intention of ever dying or changing his standards! "Till death do us part" in this case has become an endless misery.

This may sound like a soap opera, but it's similar to the picture the apostle Paul paints for us in the opening verses of **Romans 7**. In his illustration the first husband is God's law, Jesus is "the other man," and we are the woman.

IN THE WORD
Verses 1–3: Married to the Law

Paul often uses marriage to illustrate spiritual relationships. Comment on the way the apostle uses the union between husband and wife in the following passages:

1 Corinthians 6:15–17
2 Corinthians 11:2
Ephesians 5:22–32

1. What do these passages teach?

2. The Gospel of Jesus Christ tells us what God has done for us. The Law, on the other hand, tells us what we must do to obey God. Just as marriage is a commitment, so we are committed— either to Jesus Christ or to Mr. Law. If we choose marriage to the Law, what two insurmountable problems do we face? (Hint: see **Galatians 3:10–11** and **James 2:10.**)

Verses 4–6: Married to Christ

1. God's law is not going to go away. It will never lie down and die. Jesus said, "Not the smallest letter, not the least stroke of a pen, will by any means disappear from the Law until everything is accomplished" (**Matthew 5:18**, paraphrased). How can we be legally united with Christ if our first "husband," the Law, refuses to die?

God gives us a remarkable answer: if the husband

won't die, then the wife must **(verse 4)**! This is the key point in this section from Romans. Read **verses 3–4** aloud and paraphrase their meaning.

2. A most obvious question now arises: "How do we die?" How does Paul answer that question in **verse 4**? (See **1 Corinthians 1:30** for more information.)

3. As you read through **verses 4–6,** find three things from which Christ has freed us.

4. What practical applications does all this have for your personal life?

LOOKING AHEAD

The rest of **Romans 7** has puzzled readers ever since Paul first wrote it. Read **verses 17–25** carefully. You will see that Paul is not giving in to the power of sin. Rather, he is accenting a truth about our daily struggle with sin and ultimate victory over it.

So, my brothers, you also died to the law through the body of Christ, that you might belong to another, to Him who was raised from the dead, in order that we might bear fruit to God.

Romans 7:4

SESSION 18

Our Struggle with Sin

ROMANS 7:7–25

Carla had never been very athletic. Back in grade school, she always chose to watch TV or read rather than take swimming lessons or join a softball league. In high school she avoided gym class whenever she could; she "forgot" her clothes; she begged her mother for notes excusing her from class. When she fell on an ice patch one winter and twisted an ankle, her first thought was one of joy at having a legitimate excuse to get out of dressing for gym.

If you had asked this reluctant athlete point-blank what she thought of gym class, she would probably have said, "I hate it." You might not have understood her attitude unless you had a chance to watch her play. Pick a sport. Any sport. As long as she sat on the bench, no one would spot her awkwardness. But as soon as she got out onto the court, her lack of coordination became embarrassingly obvious.

The gym teacher's demand that Carla participate was a legitimate one; the problem rested in Carla's court.

The story does not end there though. Sometime after Carla was graduated from college, she began taking long walks to relax after work. After six months or so, she noticed that she felt much better—more alert and energetic than ever before. She lost 12 pounds without even trying. Her clothes fit better.

One March afternoon while Carla walked along a sidewalk wet with melting snow, a thought suddenly struck her—it might be fun to run. Of course, it was a silly idea; she had never liked running in school. She always came in last. All the old excuses surfaced, but something inside whispered, "Go on. Try it."

Something happened that day. Carla ran 10 blocks without even breathing hard. The next day, she tried again. This time she went 15 blocks—a whole mile! That was the beginning. She started reading magazines about running. She learned about running shoes and bought a pair. She studied different training methods and began eating more fruits and vegetables. Eventually, she eliminated sugar from her diet almost entirely. Eight years later, she has logged nearly 8,000 miles in her running journal.

Now when someone offers her a piece of pie or a gooey fudge nut bar, she politely refuses it. If you were to ask her about that, she might say something like this, "I used to love desserts. The more sugar the better. When I first started running, I found that eating it kept me from enjoying my run as much as I might otherwise. Now, it really doesn't tempt me anymore—I'm a runner. In fact, not just my diet has changed. I feel like a different person. I hardly recognize myself as I was back then."

What changes do you see between the old Carla and the new one? Is it just her behavior, or is something else involved?

How does our picture of ourselves shape our behavior? Give some examples.

IN THE WORD
Verses 7–13: The Effects of the Law

God's law exposes sin in much the same ways as that gym class exposed Carla's clumsiness. Physical education in and of itself is good. God's law is holy, righteous, and good (**verse 12**). There is nothing wrong with the Law. The problem we sinners have with the Law is that it spotlights our shortcomings.

1. In **verse 7** Paul suggests that some might infer from his teaching that the Law is bad. The apostle's response to that mistaken idea is, "Certainly not!" Paul then goes on to explain several effects of the Law. What are they?

Verse 7

Verses 8–13

2. If the Law does these things, how can Paul say that it is good?

Verses 14–24: The Struggle with Sin

1. As you read over these verses, did the struggle Paul experienced sound familiar? Compare your thoughts with those of others in your class. Do all Christians find themselves struggling in this way?

2. Paraphrase **verses 14–25.** As you do, be sure to use the first person—so you might write something

like: "I want to do good, but I just don't do it." Reread your paraphrase when you have finished it. Share your feelings with your class.

3. At first reading, Paul makes himself sound as though he has a split personality. Are there really two equally powerful "me's" living inside us, each jockeying for power over our behavior? What is this "sinful nature" Paul writes so much about? Who is the real "me"?

To answer those questions, we need to look at a few other portions of Scripture. First, read **2 Corinthians 5:17–21.** As you do, jot down everything Paul says about Christians—those who have been born again into God's family.

Now, read **Galatians 5:17.** Paraphrase it to be sure you understand what this verse says.

4. Take your understanding of all three Scriptures you just read and answer these questions:

What is the "sinful nature" that lives inside all of us?

What happens to that "sinful nature" when we are born again into God's kingdom? Do all Christians have a problem with a kind of spiritual "split personality" complex?

Describe the "new you" and what it has to do with your struggle with sin. Compare your answer with the last part of **verse 24.**

5. Paul asks an important question in **verse 24.** How does he answer it? Explain his answer in a way a non-Christian friend might understand it.

LOOKING AHEAD

Chapter 8 begins with the words, "**Therefore, there is now no condemnation . . . .**" This chapter, a favorite among many Christians, brings a wonderful sense of release and freedom even as we continue to struggle with temptation. Read **verses 1–17** to find out why.

So, then, I myself in my mind am a slave to God's law, but in the sinful nature, a slave to the law of sin.

Romans 7:25

SESSION 19

Victory through the Spirit

ROMANS 8:1–13

Christians know they simply cannot keep God's law. No matter how hard we try, no matter how much effort we put into the task, no matter how hard we drive or punish ourselves, we will never be able to obey the demands of the Law. On the other hand, once we believe all that God has done for us in Christ, our Savior, we truly want to please God. That desire, placed in our hearts by the Holy Spirit, grows stronger and stronger as we read God's Word and use the Sacraments God has given us.

"I want to obey, but I can't"—what a dilemma! This statement pretty well summarizes Paul's frustration as he shared it with his readers in **Romans 7.** Chances are very good that it describes your own struggle as God's person, too. Paul concludes the chapter with a shout of relief: **"Thanks be to God through Jesus Christ our Lord!"** The Holy Spirit had led him to see God's solution to this terrible dilemma.

Think of it this way. We are not more able to keep God's law any more than we are able to flap our arms and fly; but, if we sit down in an airplane and allow the jet engines to do the work for us, we can defy the law of gravity. Through no effort of our own we fly. If, on the other hand, we get carried away with that experience and decide to step out of the airplane and try it on our own, the law of gravity will immediately reassert itself.

As long as we rely on God's power, we can live in victory over sin, Satan, and even death. If we try to go it on our own, we are doomed to frustration and failure.

IN THE WORD

Verses 1–4: No Condemnation

1. The word *law* can have different meanings. We talk about the "laws of nature," "traffic laws," "civil law," the "law of gravity," the "law of supply and demand," and so on.

Paul usually uses *law* to mean God's demands and requirements. In **verse 2,** however, the word *law* means something else. What?

2. Actually, **verses 1–4** can be read as a legal declaration. They deliver God's verdict for us who believe. Put this verdict into your own words.

3. Why does Paul so carefully word the phrase describing Jesus who came "in the likeness of sinful man"?

4. Is **verse 4** a description or a requirement God places on His people? Defend your answer. Compare **Galatians 5:13–26.** Why is this distinction important?

Verses 5–13: Delivered from the Power of Sin and Death

1. Paul now sets up a contrast between believers

and those who still live in bondage to the sinful nature. Reread **verses 5–13.** As you do, make a chart with two columns. In one column jot down Paul's description of the "natural man"; in the other, put down his descriptions of the "spiritual man."

2. In **Romans 1–7,** Paul mentioned the Holy Spirit only twice. In **Romans 8:1–13,** how many references to the Spirit do you count? What names does Paul use for the Spirit?

3. Why do you suppose the Holy Spirit suddenly has taken on such increased importance in Paul's letter to the Roman Christians?

4. In **6:12–13,** Paul first raised the question of what will happen to our physical bodies. Read those verses. Also read **7:23–25.**

Sin pays its wages—death **(6:23).** Because of our sin, we deserve eternal death in hell. We also have earned for ourselves physical death.

While our bodies in and of themselves are God's creation and thus "very good" **(Genesis 1:31),** we use our bodies to commit all kinds of sin. Give some examples. Can you think of any sins that do not fit this category?

Christ has redeemed us from the Law's curse. This includes the "sting" of physical death. How does Paul describe that part of the redemption in **8:11?** Compare Jesus' words in **John 6:38–58** and Paul's description of the resurrection in **1 Corinthians 15.**

Why might it be hard for a high school student to feel tremendously excited about these promises from God? Are they meaningful to you? Why?

5. The words from **verses 12–13** get to the nitty-gritty application of this part of the chapter for us. What do you notice about the way Paul contrasts *living* and *dying.*

After studying **Romans 7** and the first part of **Romans 8,** you should have a fairly good idea about what **verses 12–13** mean. Put them in your own words. Then write a paragraph to explain what they mean for your own life. Give specific examples.

LOOKING AHEAD

Paul goes on to explain the Holy Spirit's work for us and in us. Read **Romans 8:14–25.** As you read, look for statements explaining His work in our hearts and lives.

Therefore, there is now no condemnation for those who are in Christ Jesus, because through Christ Jesus the law of the Spirit of life set me free from the law of sin and death.

Romans 8:1–2

SESSION 20

Children of God

ROMANS 8:14–25

"As a young father, no words sounded more precious to my ears than 'Daddy.' Whether my children call to me in fear, joy, or pain, this word gives my life value and purpose. If one of my children is hurt, they come crying to me for comfort, sobbing my name— 'Daddy.' When I'm away on a trip, I can count on them welcoming me back with a big hug and the greeting, 'We missed you, Daddy.' If one of my little ones has a bad dream or wakes up frightened by a thunderstorm, I hear the cry 'Daddy!' through the darkness of the night."

1. What kind of relationship does this young father appear to have with his children? What leads you to that conclusion?

2. As important as the father considered the name Daddy, it was perhaps even more significant to his children. Why might this be?

3. Every language has a similar, familiar word for father. In Jesus' day, for example, children used the Aramaic word *Abba* to mean roughly what we mean when we used the word *Daddy*. The Jews never used *Abba* to address God. But when Jesus experienced His private agony in the Garden of Gethsemane, He prayed "Abba, Father" **(Mark 14:36).**

What does this tell us about Jesus' relationship with the heavenly Father?

4. Remarkable as it must seem, Paul uses the same expression in **Romans 8:15.** This name for God became common in the vocabulary of the Christian church. The early believers understood Paul's teaching that God had made them His children, and, as such, they were coheirs with Jesus Christ. God had made them "in Christ." They enjoyed a position of such intimacy with the Father, that to call the Creator and Sustainer of the universe "Daddy" was the most natural thing in the world. This lesson will explore these concepts further.

IN THE WORD
Verses 14–17: Members of the Family

1. Paul begins this session by again reminding us that we can live, led by the Spirit. The word picture he uses would have been very meaningful for his Roman readers. What contrast does he present?

2. **Romans 8:14–17** describes four facets of the Spirit's work in our lives as children of God. Find one aspect of His work in each of the four verses in this section.

3. Now spend some time thinking about how and why each one benefits you. Write a short prayer thanking God, your Father (Abba), for each of these rich blessings.

Verses 18–22: Present Suffering

Being children of God and coheirs with Christ is heady stuff, but Paul introduces a sobering thought at the end of **verse 17.** As long as we are in this life, there will be problems.

As Christians we face the additional prospect of suffering for the Gospel. We studied God's plan for helping us grow through our problems in **Romans 5,** so Paul doesn't go into that here. He simply states that whatever our problems are, they are as nothing compared with what God has in store for us.

1. In case you think Paul is a little too casual about this, that he dismisses problems too easily, read **2 Corinthians 11:23–33** and make a list of the suffering Paul endured for his Lord—problems he says are "not worth mentioning."

2. **Verse 18** deals with problems we face as individuals. **Verses 19–22** deal with problems everyone runs into, problems that came into God's creation when Adam fell into sin. Read this section carefully and tell in your own words the awful side effect of Adam's fall.

Verses 23–25: Future Glory

We have read about the groaning of the creation and maybe we have experienced much of it in our own lives. But now Paul turns our attention to the great glory God has promised us. The first stage begins right now! The apostle calls it the "firstfruits of the Spirit."

Read through the section once more, noting each time Paul uses the words *glory* or *glorious.* What glory is he talking about?

2. Notice the word *hope* in **verses 24–25.** Hope is a weak word as we use it most of the time in our daily conversation.

We *hope* it won't rain for Friday's picnic.

We *hope* Dad will loan us $20.00 for a date Saturday night.

We *hope* we'll get the job for which we've applied.

Read the definition of *hope* from a good Bible dictionary. Is hope merely a "weak wish," or is it something else?

Now write a paragraph explaining what Paul means in **Romans 8:24–25** and telling what difference the hope he mentions makes in your own life.

LOOKING AHEAD

Read **Romans 8:26–30** for the next session. These five short verses contain two of the most comforting thoughts in all of God's Word. Look for them and spend some time between now and the next class period thinking about how you could use these verses to confront family and friends.

For you did not receive a spirit that makes you a slave again to fear, but you received the Spirit of sonship. And by Him we cry, "Abba, Father." The Spirit Himself testifies with our spirit that we are God's children. Now if we are children, then we are heirs—heirs of God and coheirs with Christ.
Romans 8:15–17a

SESSION 21

The Power and the Promise

ROMANS 8:26–30

Mr. Meyer's class had come to a special section of Romans. After the teacher had read Romans 8:28 to his class, he told them that he considered this verse a very important one for every Christian to memorize and understand. "It's one of the most cherished verses in the Bible," he explained, "probably because Christians find such comfort in it. Whenever I have problems, I often bring this verse to mind. I know it has made my life more joyful."

As he talked, Jeffery van Dyke raised his hand. Mr. Meyer looked up. Jeffery had never volunteered a comment or asked a question all year. He answered point-blank questions only reluctantly. "Yes, Jeffery?" the teacher responded.

The student's question was brief and to the point: "Why don't you explain what possible good God can see in my mom's death?"

Then the bell rang.

Mr. Meyer stood in front of the classroom, stunned for a moment. The class had already begun to leave when the teacher caught Jeffery to ask, "Can I see you for a few minutes?"

As the two talked, Mr. Meyer learned that Jeffery's mother was in the final stages of a long battle with cancer. The teacher listened carefully as Jeffery began to explain the situation and as he began to express his doubts and fears, slowly at first, then with rising volume and the cadence of a rapid-fire machine gun. He spewed out his anger, grief, and bitterness.

"I can't explain those things," admitted the teacher when Jeffery had finished, "and I doubt that anyone else can answer all your questions. But even now, I still believe with all my heart that Romans 8:28 is true. And I believe that some day you will be able to answer your own question—if not on this earth, certainly in heaven."

How comforting do you suppose this might be to a high school student like Jeffery, who feels angry and confused? Why?

Would you have said something different if you had been Mr. Meyer? If so, what?

IN THE WORD

Verses 26–27: The Intercession of the Spirit

1. Paul has built a masterful description of God's incredibly costly, incredibly loving plan of salvation. He prepares for his dramatic conclusion by adding two promises of help for daily living from the Holy Spirit of God, who has worked the wonder of faith in our lives and who now works to sustain and complete it.

What promise(s) do you see in **verses 26–27?** What difference can this promise make in your life today?

2. How does the promise of **verses 26–27** lead into the promise of **verse 28?**

Verses 28–30: The Love of the Father

1. **Romans 8:28** sounds great in theory. But when the painful realities of life pop up, many of us have difficulty applying it to ourselves. It sometimes helps to see how God has worked in the lives of others to work all things for good. Review what you remember from the life of Joseph (**Genesis 37** and **39**) and list the times Joseph might have thought God had deserted him.

2. Read **Genesis 50:15–21.** How did Jospeh's life show that **"in all things, God works for the good of those who love Him?"**

3. Think of an event in your life that seemed like a disaster when it happened; now, though, you can see that God caused good for you or for others to come out of that event.

4. **Verses 29–30** contain just a few words. But in them Paul gives us a full review of what he has written so far. Five terms appear here, some of them for the first time. They all fit together, and the end result is the "ultimate good" God has always had in mind for His children.

Scripture interprets Scripture. Other verses from God's Word will help define the important terms Paul uses. Read the references for the following five words. Be prepared to explain each one and how they are related to one another:

a. *Foreknowledge*—**Isaiah 46:10; Romans 11:2; 1 Peter 1:2**

b. *Predestined,* to be conformed to the likeness of His Son—**1 Corinthians 1:25–31; Ephesians 1:4–7**

c. *Called*—**Isaiah 45:22; Matthew 11:28; 1 Timothy 2:4**

d. *Justified*—**Genesis 15:6; Acts 13:38–39; Romans 5:1**

e. *Glorified*—**Psalm 73:24; 2 Corinthians 3:16–18; 1 Peter 5:1; 2 Thessalonians 2:13–14**

LOOKING AHEAD

"What about all this?" In the next few verses of Romans, Paul steps back to take an almost breathtaking view of God's plan of salvation as he has presented it so far. Read **Romans 8:31.** Then skim **Romans 1–8** to review what you have studied in this course to this point.

And we know that in all things God works for the good of those who love Him, who have been called according to His purpose.

Romans 8:28

SESSION 22

What Shall We Say about All This?

ROMANS 8:31a

Paul asks a very significant question. It deserves a very significant answer. Paul does answer it—by asking a series of four more questions! We shall deal with them next time. For now, let's ask ourselves Paul's question, "What shall we say about this?"

Maybe you're puzzled. Maybe you're asking, "What shall we say about *what?*" To what does Paul want us to react? As we look back a few verses, it becomes clear that Paul actually expects us to remember what he has written in the entire first half of Romans. He is really asking, "What, then, shall we say in response to what I have written so far?"

We have studied this epistle verse by verse. We have examined each piece individually, and then carefully put it into its proper place. This has been a long and sometimes difficult activity. But now Paul asks us to step back and examine the whole picture. He challenges us to face the implications of what we have been taught.

IN THE WORD

Verse 31a: What Shall We Say about This?

Today you will work through a review of the four basic concepts Paul has presented so far. Go back over the first eight chapters of Romans. Use the main thoughts emphasized in each session. Try to develop an overview of the epistle in your mind. **Chapters 1–8** deal basically with the following four topics:

1. The guilt of humanity **(Romans 1:1–3:20)**
2. The grace of God **(Romans 3:21–5:11)**
3. The greatness of salvation **(Romans 5:12–8:17)**
4. The guarantee of glory **(Romans 8:18-30)**

As you scan these chapters, jot down references and notes to yourself to review how Paul deals with each topic. Then review the personal applications each of these has for your own life.

LOOKING AHEAD

Read **Romans 8:31b–39.** This has to be one of the most power-packed and beautiful passages in all of Scripture. Look for the four questions Paul asks but does not answer. What one response will correctly answer all four questions?

Those God foreknew He also predestined to be conformed to the likeness of His Son, that He might be the firstborn among many brothers. And those He predestined, He also called; those He called, He also justified; those He justified, He also glorified. What, then, shall we say in response to this?

Romans 8:29–31a

49

SESSION 23

Super Conquerors

ROMANS 8:31b–39

"It's always nice to have friends in high places," jokes Brian Nelson whenever he talks about his "second career." Mr. Nelson, like many teachers, works a summer job to supplement his income each year. One year, he landed a job working for a business owned by a millionaire. The millionaire's sister ran the business, and his college-age nephew worked for him.

Mr. Nelson noticed that the nephew always spoke politely, worked hard, and never took advantage of his privileged position. He had an air of confidence and security that Mr. Nelson seldom saw in the other employees.

The millionaire uncle had a habit of dropping in unexpectedly at odd times to check up on his workers. This habit made everyone nervous. Many of the employees spent a lot of time looking over their shoulder as they worked, but the young nephew never seemed bothered by it.

One day as the nephew and Mr. Nelson talked about it, the nephew said, "You know, it's really great to be related to a rich man. I don't mind working at these menial jobs because I know that, someday soon, I'll be running all this. I'm in training now, and I'm going to be ready when the time comes." The young man had job security, and he knew it.

Anyone who reads **Romans 8:31–39** can't help but be impressed with the confidence the apostle Paul preaches. The Holy Spirit wants us to have that kind of confidence in our "Friend in high places," too!

IN THE WORD

Verses 31b–37: More than Conquerors

Paul majestically concludes this section, "**In all these things we are more than conquerors through Him who loved us!**" He ringingly confirms God's faithfulness in dealing with His people. Notice, though, how the apostle began the section. He uses the almost timid words, "**If God is for us . . . .**" There seems to be a world of difference between the beginning statement and the concluding one.

Some Christians spend most of their lives in **verse 31b**, so to speak. They live in uncertainty and fear. They live with the worrisome question, "If God is for me . . . ," and stop right there. They don't know for sure whether God is for them or not! They have little confidence about what will happen when they die, and they aren't sure they want to find out.

On the other hand, some Christians use the power of God's Spirit to live out their lives as super conquerors—fully confident in the truths Paul shares in this passage.

In session 22, we reviewed what we have learned from Paul so far. This important information will help us draw the same conclusions Paul did—God *is* truly for us!

Maybe you noticed that Paul used a lot of questions in this particular passage. Here are four of the most important:

1. Who can be against us?
2. Who will bring any charge against us?
3. Who condemns us?
4. Who shall separate us from the love of Christ?

Paul follows each question with some thoughts and comments. Use the comments to write a paragraph in answer to each question. In your paragraphs, explain why we can answer every question with absolute confidence and authority, "No one!"

Verses 38–39: More than Confident

Paul pulls out all the stops when he contemplates the last question, "**Who shall separate us from the love of Christ?**" He covers 10 different things that might possibly come between a believer and the Savior. He names a wide range of powerful opponents and finally concludes that nothing can snatch us away from the wonderful love of God our Savior.

Think about the different forces that Paul mentions and be ready to discuss the meaning of each one in your own life. When have any of these threatened you? How did God protect you? Share with your classmates.

1. Death
2. Life

3. Angels
4. Demons
5. Present
6. Future
7. Any powers
8. Height
9. Depth
10. Anything else in creation

LOOKING AHEAD

Skim **Romans 1–8** in preparation for next time's review and unit evaluation.

In all these things we are more than conquerors through Him who loves us. For I am convinced that neither death nor life, neither angels nor demons, neither the present nor the future, nor any powers, neither height nor depth, nor anything else in all creation, will be able to separate us from the love of God that is in Christ Jesus our Lord.

Romans 8:37–39

SESSION 24

Concluding Activities for Unit 2

In the 10 sessions of this unit we have looked at the way God has dealt with the problem of human sin—through the death of His Son on the cross. In unit 1 we learned how **"the blood of Jesus . . . purifies us from all sin" (1 John 1:7).** God has forgiven all our acts of disobedience to His law.

Unit 2 has made us face the fact that sin itself—the rebellion that lies deep within the heart of every human born on earth—had a deadly contaminating effect upon our very nature before we became a member of God's family through His miracle of rebirth. **Chapters 5–8** describe how the Father has provided a deliverance from sin's polluting effect in our lives: **"If any one is in Christ, he is a new creation; the old has passed away, behold, the new has come" (2 Corinthians 5:17 RSV).**

Romans shouts the miracle of righteousness: God shares His righteousness with all who believe in the redemptive work of His only Son, Jesus Christ. God has declared us "not guilty" through faith in Jesus Christ alone. We have been freed from the penalty of sin. Now we have been enabled by the Holy Spirit to submit to God's will. This process of sanctification results in greater and growing freedom from the power of sin in our lives. We will never be perfect in this world. But God's Spirit helps us grow as He transforms us step by step into the image of Jesus.

1. Use your Bible, this lesson guide, and your own class notes to guide you as you write down what you believe to be the central truth for each session, 14–24, in this unit

14. Let Christ Reign by Grace! **Romans 5:12–21**
15. What Do You Know? **Romans 6:1–14**
16. Slavery, **Romans 6:15–23**
17. Marriage, **Romans 7:1–6**
18. Our Struggle with Sin, **Romans 7:7–25**
19. Victory Through the Spirit, **Romans 8:1–13**
20. Children of God, **Romans 8:14–25**
21. The Power and the Promise, **Romans 8:26–30**
22. What Shall We Say About All This? **Romans 8:31a**
23. Super Conquerors, **Romans 8:31b–39**

2. In session 22 you were asked to review the first eight chapters of Romans and think about the personal application you found in each session. Now look more closely at the portions you studied in unit 2. Write down what each session in unit 2 means for your personal life.

LOOKING AHEAD

Read **Romans 9:1–5.** Paul displays a remarkable attitude toward the Jewish people. What can you find in these verses that shows how deeply Paul felt about Israel's tragic rejection of their Messiah?

UNIT 3

The Righteousness of God Rejected

ROMANS 9—11

The first 8 chapters of Romans present the doctrinal foundation of the Christian church. As we read chapters 9 through 11, we enter an area of special concern to Paul: Israel's rejection of the Gospel.

Paul's heart broke over his nation's rejection of the true Messiah. Why did the Jews of Paul's day turn away from Christ? From **Romans 9—11** we can see that they had drawn wrong conclusions about the Messiah and about God's covenant with them. So Paul takes three more chapters to demonstrate the faithfulness of God to explain the tragedy in Israel's rejection of the Christian Gospel.

SESSION 25

The Tragedy of the Jews

ROMANS 9:1–5

During the last week of His life, Jesus summarized the tragedy of the nation of Israel in one sentence: "**O Jerusalem, Jerusalem, you who kill the prophets and stone those sent to you, how often I have longed to gather your children together, as a hen gathers her chicks under wings, but you were not willing**" (Matthew 23:37).

The love and compassion of the Lord Jesus flows through these words like the living water Jesus so often talked about. Even though Israel, as a nation, was often guilty of rebellion and worse, the Lord longed to give His people the gift of salvation. But they were unwilling. The people rejected Him, but that fact had no impact upon His love for them. His deep love and compassion drove Him to tears. He wept because He knew the lost opportunities and wasted privileges of His people would bring about the destruction of both the city and the people—the city and people He had come to redeem.

Paul feels the same kind of compassion and love for the Jewish people. His love for them is real. He had not, as some were accusing, turned against his own people in favor of the Gentiles.

What words and phrases in **Romans 9:1–5** reveal Paul's true feeling for his people?

Read **Acts 17:10–15**. What makes Paul's love for the Jews truly remarkable?

IN THE WORD

Verses 1–3: Paul's Attitude toward the Jews

Jesus said "**Love your enemies and pray for those who persecute you**" (Matthew 5:44). This sounds great in theory! When we read these words in a chapel service or a Bible class, no one ever disagrees.

Talk about Jesus' words. Share some experiences you have had putting this command into practice. What difficulties have you had? Does Jesus' command to love our enemies seem to you to be above and beyond the call of duty? Explain your feelings.

1. Since loving one's enemies is such an outra-geous idea, the first question has to be, "Was Paul sincere? Did he really mean what he was saying?" How did Paul attempt to prove his sincerity in **verse 1?**

2. Reread **verses 2–3.** What is the reason for Paul's sorrow?

3. Look carefully at **verse 3** and paraphrase what Paul is saying. Can he really mean that? Explain your opinion.

4. Can you find an occasion in your own life when you showed genuine love and concern for someone who didn't like you? If not, talk about an occasion when you had an opportunity to return good for evil (even if you didn't do it).

Verses 4–5: Paul's Pride in His Heritage

Although Paul was a Roman citizen and had been trained in Greek culture, he felt most proud of his Jewish heritage. At the end of **verse 3** the apostle Paul calls the Jews "**brothers, those of my own race, the people of Israel.**" To be a member of the people of God was, to him, an unparalleled privilege. Nothing in the human experience could be compared to the uniqueness of being an Israelite, for the name itself was a reminder of God's special intervention in the life of Jacob—intervention that led to the identification of Jacob's descendants as a unique people. (See **Genesis 32:22–32.**)

Much of Paul's grief was prompted by the fact that his people had wasted the special privileges God had granted them. In **verses 4–5** he lists eight privileges that set the Jews apart from all nations. Think about these and share with the class ways in which we as Christians today might be ignoring similar privileges.

a. Adopted by God

b. Shared God's glory

c. Received the covenant

d. Received the Law

e. Worshiped at the temple

f. Received God's promises

g. Claimed a godly ancestry

h. Received the Messiah

LOOKING AHEAD

With few exceptions, God's chosen and privileged people rejected Him and the salvation He offered in Jesus. This raised serious questions concerning the faithfulness of God. Read **Romans 9:6–18** to see how Paul answers this concern.

I could wish that I myself were cursed and cut off from Christ for the sake of my brothers, those of my own race, the people of Israel. Theirs is the adoption as sons; theirs the divine glory, the covenants, the receiving of the law, the temple worship and the promises. Theirs are the patriarchs, and from them is traced the human ancestry of Christ, who is God over all, forever praised! Amen.

Romans 9:3–5

SESSION 26

God's Chosen People

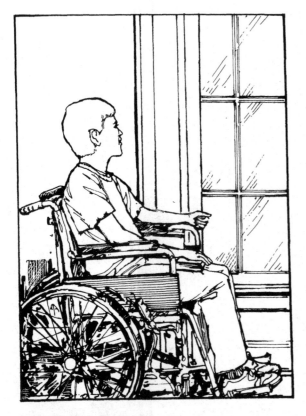

ROMANS 9:6–21

"It's not fair!" When did you last say (or think) those words? Have you ever thought about your relationship with God in those terms—have you ever wondered about God's fairness at any time? If so, share your feelings at the time and the circumstances that made you feel that way.

IN THE WORD
Verse 6: The True Israel

Clearly Paul felt his people might be crying, "It's not fair for God to reject our nation!"

Paul wanted to answer this objection, not only because he deeply loved his own people but also because of the profound significance of the questions themselves.

Romans 9:6 raises the first in a series of important questions: "Has the Word of God failed? Has God reneged on His promises?"

Paul has just described the glorious heritage of his nation. Despite this heritage, many in the nation had fallen into a grossly perverted view of who and what they were. They assumed that everyone born into the nation of Israel physically, could automatically presume to be a member of God's everlasting family as well. Paul quickly points out, **"Not all who are descended from Israel are Israel" (verse 6)**.

1. Read **John 8:31–41** to better understand what Paul means by that statement. When Jesus encountered the same twisted thinking in the Scribes and Pharisees, how did He respond?

2. In what ways might people today be guilty of the same faulty reasoning? Have you ever known someone personally who presumed to be a Christian based on faulty reasoning? Describe that person's reasoning.

Verses 7–13: Children of the Flesh; Children of the Promise

God's Word speaks powerfully about God's right to act as He chooses. He clearly demonstrates this in the lineage of Christ through Abraham, Isaac, and Jacob. God chose Isaac (not Ishmael) to be the branch of Abraham's line that would produce the Messiah. Scripture calls Isaac the "child of promise," and Ishmael the "child of the flesh." God chose Jacob rather than Esau while both were still in Rebekah's womb. God chose as He saw fit, not according to human considerations.

1. Paul's argument in **Romans 9:7–13** rests on the fact there had *always* been two Israels, distinguished not by blood, but by something entirely different. Read **Galatians 3:26–29**. How did one become part of the seed of Abraham?

2. In **Romans 9:13** Paul quotes **Malachi 1:2–3: "Yet I have loved Jacob, but Esau I have hated."** This language disturbs the casual reader. It seems to reduce God to an alarmingly arbitrary decision-making machine. Read **Malachi 1:1–5** and explain from the context what you think God is saying.

Verses 14–16: God's Mercy

In the process of election God chose Gentiles while most of the Jewish nation was rejecting Christ. This doctrine was totally unacceptable to the unbelieving Jews. They genuinely believed that if this were true, God was guilty of breaking His Word. In light of their interpretation of God's promises, God could not reject Jews and accept Gentiles. Paul refutes their argument by appealing to the Old Testament.

Compare **Romans 9:14–16** with **Exodus 33:12–23.** What point does Paul make by referring to the extraordinary dialog between God and Moses?

Verses 17–21: God's Sovereignty

Paul moves quickly to another illustration from the Old Testament showing the sovereign choice of God in a negative sense. Here again it may seem that God is using Pharaoh as a pawn in a game he neither understands nor controls. But our knowledge of God and His grace will not support such an interpretation. To better understand what Paul is teaching, scan **Exodus 7–11,** paying particular attention to **Exodus 9.**

1. Write a brief statement about the way God dealt with Pharaoh. Whose fault was it that Pharaoh was lost? Explain.

2. God is both merciful and sovereign. Why does Scripture emphasize His mercy?

LOOKING AHEAD

As you read through the rest of **Romans 9,** notice Paul's warning about challenging the righteousness of God. It is wisdom to allow God to be God. No matter how complicated it may sound, God is and always has been working on the same principle. Look for that principle at the end of the chapter.

[God] says to Moses, "I will have mercy on whom I have mercy, and I will have compassion on whom I have compassion." It does not, therefore, depend on man's desire or effort, but on God's mercy.

Romans 9:15–16

SESSION 27

"In Wrath, Remember Mercy"

ROMANS 9:22–33

People picture God in different ways. Some see Him as a partially senile old man who sits up in the sky somewhere rocking eternity away. Some see Him as a kind of celestial watchmaker who wound up our universe and then went His own way, leaving us to fend for ourselves. Someone once asked a little boy what God was like. The boy replied, "Well, He's the sort of guy who goes around to see if anyone is having any fun so He can stop 'em."

Yes, people picture God in many ways. Suppose someone asked you for your picture of God. In 30 words or less, what would you tell them?

IN THE WORD
Verses 22–29: A Two-Sided Coin

1. Read **Exodus 34:1–8.** Compare God's description of Himself **(verses 6–7)** with the description you wrote above. What do the two descriptions have in common? How are they different?

2. In the Exodus passage you just read, God stresses two main attributes. What are they?

3. Now reread **Romans 9:22–29.** At what points do you see evidence of God's just anger at human sin? What evidence can you find of God's mercy and grace? Which attribute seems to predominate? Defend your opinion.

4. Use a good concordance or topical Bible and a good Bible dictionary to do a word study on the term *remnant.* Write out your findings in a one- to two-page paper. Your study should include the meaning of remnant in the Old Testament. Compare and contrast this with its meaning in the New Testament. Also include

an explanation of why this concept is important for God's people today.

Verses 30–33: Pursuing Righteousness

1. Have you ever caught yourself doing the right thing but in the wrong way? (You had a good goal, but you were trying to accomplish it in a way that would never work.) Share your experience with your class.

2. Reread **Romans 9:30–33.** What good goal did the people of Israel have? What was so bad about the way many of them were trying to reach it? How did the Gentiles succeed in reaching that goal?

3. Think about the contrast between righteousness by works and righteousness by faith today. Why do you suppose so many pursue a righteousness-by-works life-style? What tendencies do you have toward that same life-style? What do you need to do in order to walk more consistently by faith?

4. Why is Jesus a "rock of offense" to those who want to attain righteousness by works? What difference does it make in your life that Jesus wants to be your "Rock of salvation"?

LOOKING AHEAD

Read **Romans 10:1–13.** The central thought of this session can be summed up in a single sentence. Which one of the 13 verses contains the central truth?

The Gentiles, who did not pursue righteousness, have obtained it, a righteousness that is by faith; but Israel, who pursued a law of righteousness, has not attained it. Why not? Because they pursued it not by faith but as if it were by works.

Romans 9:30–32

SESSION 28

Zeal, Truth, and Knowledge

ROMANS 10:1–13

Ralph Waldo Emerson once wrote, "Nothing important was ever achieved without enthusiasm." Why do you think he made this statement? Do you agree or disagree? Defend your opinion.

Another word for enthusiasm is *zeal*. Zeal can be very important. At a pep rally or in an athletic contest we might call zeal "school spirit." At times it can unite a student body and inspire athletes to perform beyond their capabilities.

But zeal has its negative side. For example, when students become abusive to athletes from competing teams or to fans or referees, ignorance, not zeal, is at work.

In today's section from Romans, Paul talks about a kind of religious zeal, zeal not based on knowledge. He warns his readers how very destructive such zeal can be. He contrasts zeal based upon error with a zeal for God's truth. Zeal grounded in truth, Paul concludes, results in an enthusiastic sharing of God's love with those who do not know their Savior.

IN THE WORD

Verses 1–3: Israel's Error

1. Have you ever seen a Christian friend, or perhaps a brother or sister, falling into error? Maybe they've started hanging around with new "friends" of questionable character. Maybe they've stopped wor-shiping regularly. Maybe you suspect them of drinking or of using other drugs. Did you confront that person? If so, what happened? If not, why not?

Pointing out another person's error is a thankless task at best. Few people like to be told they are wrong. Confronting someone carries with it the risk that that person will flare up angrily at us. Notice how gently Paul now eases into Israel's error.

In **verse 1** Paul demonstrates the very first principle of effective evangelism. Tell in your own words what you think that principle might be.

2. In **verse 2** Paul goes on to identify himself with his Jewish readers. He helps them see that he has had personal experience with their error, which he describes as enthusiasm or zeal without knowledge. Read **Acts 22:3–5** to find out what Paul means. What evidence does this passage reveal about Paul's zeal for Judaism?

3. Personalize the danger of having religious zeal without true knowledge. Have you yourself or has someone you know been deeply sincere but sincerely wrong? How many organizations, cults, or philosophies can you name that are guilty of the same error as the Jewish people to whom Paul wrote? Think especially of those groups that show remarkable enthusiasm for their cause.

4. Reread **verse 3**. Here Paul lists two characteristics common to people who have religious zeal without knowledge. What are they?

Verses 4–13: The Gospel Truth

As he writes to his people, the Jews, Paul quotes Moses more often than he quotes Jesus—probably because the people believed Moses and rejected nearly everything Jesus said. In **verses 4–13** the apostle refers to Moses twice.

In the first quote Paul focuses on the basic difference between the righteousness that comes from God and the counterfeit "righteousness" that comes from trying to obey the Law. Paul asserts that Jesus "**is the end of the Law**," the fulfillment or completion of the Law. Paul then quotes **Leviticus 18:5,** which says, "**The man who obeys them [God's decrees and laws] will live by them.**" This verse refers to human effort in keeping the Law. Take note of the present tense of the verse "obeys" **(verse 5b).**

1. What point is Paul making? Think about **verses 4–5** and try to summarize in one sentence the difference between the Law and the Gospel.

2. Next, Paul quotes part of Moses' farewell speech of encouragement to Israel. These words originally appear in **Deuteronomy 30:12–14.** Paul uses Moses' words to remind us that we do not have to rely on extreme human effort to find salvation for ourselves. We do not have to climb the highest mountain or plumb the deepest ocean. God has brought the Gospel of salvation through faith in Jesus conveniently near **(verses 6–8).** That Gospel, available to all **(verses 11–13),** is the basis of our Christian witness to the world.

Think about **verses 9–10.** Explain why you think Paul links salvation to confession of faith. What does this mean for you and how do you relate this to your life?

LOOKING AHEAD

Paul further develops the relationship between hidden faith in the heart and open confession of that faith with the mouth in succeeding verses. For next time read **Romans 10:14–21.** Note how Paul outlines both the process and the problem of evangelism.

If you confess with your mouth, "Jesus is Lord," and believe in your heart that God raised Him from the dead, you will be saved. For it is with your heart that you believe and are justified, and it is with your mouth that you confess and are saved. As the Scripture says, "Anyone who trusts in Him will never be put to shame." For there is no difference between Jew and Gentile—the same Lord is Lord of all and richly blesses all who call on Him, for, "Everyone who calls on the name of the Lord will be saved."

Romans 10:9–13

SESSION 29

Evangelism

ROMANS 10:14–21

As I think about how I became a Christian, I can get very enthusiastic about witnessing. As a young man I had never seen the inside of a church. I had never been baptized. And I certainly knew nothing about "the Lamb of God that takes away the sin of the world."

One day a Christian got hold of me and wouldn't let go. Of all the blessings God has poured out into my life, none was more wonderful than the blessing He sent when He caused my path to cross the path of that Christian friend.

Two things stick in my mind as I recall the event:

The first is that no one before or since ever asked me if I knew Jesus. Sometimes I wonder what would have happened to me if that stranger had not struck up a conversation and then followed it up over the next months. Would I be a Christian today? I don't know. Where would I be if my "spiritual father" had simply minded his own business instead of being about his Father's business?

The second is that I never thanked my Christian friend. No human being has been more important to me than that man. He cared. He taught. He persevered until I came to faith. He saw to it I was baptized, and he encouraged me to study for the ministry. Shortly after that, he died. Not until years later did I understand how rare a thing his witness was. That's the day I realized I had never said thank you. Many, many other people are important and dear to me. But when I get to glory, his is the first face (after Jesus') that I wish to see.

You may have been a Christian all your life. You may not be able to single out one individual who led you to faith in the Lord Jesus. But if you are a Christian, someone in your life taught you about your Savior. There may be many people (parents, grandparents, godparents, your pastor, teacher, friends, or neighbors) whom you can thank. Honor that person or those people right now by pausing for a moment and thanking God for them. Better yet, write notes letting them know how important they have been in your life.

IN THE WORD
Verses 14–15: The Process

In the closing verses of the last session Paul made two points:

- Paul wished, once again, to show that the Old Testament consistently reiterates the principle of salvation through faith and the intention of God to make His salvation available on a universal basis. Paul does this by quoting the prophet Joel, **"Everyone who calls upon the name of the Lord will be saved" (Joel 2:32).**

- Paul also wishes to demonstrate the relationship between the faith hidden in the believer's heart and the open confession of that faith with the mouth. He will further develop this latter theme in **verses 14–15.**

1. The last thing Jesus said before His ascension was, **"You will be My witnesses" (Acts 1:8).** This was not so much a request as it was a statement of fact. Witnessing is a privilege and a responsibility we all share. When we understand all our Lord has saved us *from* and saves us *for*, we can't help but shine as His witnesses—in what we say and in what we do.

Name some Biblical characters that simply overflowed with Jesus' love and concern for the lost.

Tell about a concern you have for someone who is lost.

2. Paul gives five steps of the process of witnessing in **verses 14–15.** The newly saved person calling upon God is the final result of that process. Prior to that, Paul lists four steps. Jot down a few thoughts as you think about each of these steps. Then discuss with your class how each relates to your life.
   a. Sending
   b. Preaching
   c. Hearing
   d. Believing

Verses 16–19: The Response

1. Witnesses for Christ will always have questions about the response of our listeners. Paul mentions three possible responses in **verses 16–19.** What are these?

2. Sometimes Christian witnesses are rejected. Think about why people resist the Gospel. Read **1 Corinthians 1:20–25** and **Isaiah 53:1–5** for clues about two of the most common reasons. What are those reasons?

3. In the face of this possible rejection, why do we keep on witnessing?

Verses 20–21: The Paradox

1. Find the word *paradox* in a dictionary and define it. Then explain the paradox in these two verses.

2. Think and pray together about what you have discovered in this session about witnessing to your Savior's love. Develop a personal plan that will make you a better witness for the Lord Jesus.

LOOKING AHEAD

Romans 10 concludes with a paradox that might lead some to believe God had rejected the entire Jewish nation. What does Paul have to say about this in **Romans 11:1–11**? For what reason did Israel not obtain what it was seeking?

How, then, can they call on the One they have not believed in? And how can they believe in the One of whom they have not heard? And how can they hear without someone preaching to them? And how can they preach unless they are sent?

Romans 10:14–15a

SESSION 30

Cast Away or Set Aside

ROMANS 11:1–15

Some years ago I bought a tie that I was very fond of. It was both stylish and attractive. People used to compliment me on my tie and say things like, "That's a great tie, where did you get it?" As time went by, my favorite tie went out of style. I didn't care. I kept wearing it anyhow, because I loved my tie.

I discovered, however, that people no longer complimented me. In fact, now they laughed at my out-of-style tie, and sometimes they even laughed at me for wearing it. My favorite tie had become a social and professional liability. People in my own family suggested I throw that ugly tie away. But I couldn't do that, because I loved it. So I put it in a box and stored it away on my closet shelf. A few more years went by, and I found that my old tie was back in style. Then, happy that I had not thrown it away, I took it out and wore it proudly.

In some ways the relationship between God and the Jewish nation is similar to the relationship between the writer and the tie. In **Romans 9** we learned that God chose Israel to be the recipient of great blessings. In **Romans 10** we discovered that, since Israel had become a liability to God's plan of salvation by their

rejection of Jesus, God appeared to have rejected the Jews. Now in **Romans 11** we will see that, in reality, God has set Israel aside; He has not yet finished with them, and He has not thrown them out.

IN THE WORD

Verses 1–10: God Preserves a Remnant

Israel's long history of rebellion against God and their abuse of His grace quite naturally leads to the thought that God might eventually say, "I've had it with these people!" He might at some point terminate His relationship with Israel. In **Romans 11** Paul declares that there is not the slightest possibility of such a thing taking place. Let's look at how Paul supports his case that God has not abandoned Israel. As you read through these 10 verses, remember the Jewish people's mistaken idea that to be a physical descendant of Abraham meant that one was a part of God's family forever. All people who claimed physical ancestry through the nation Israel were automatically saved. To those Jewish people it was unthinkable that God could reject any Jewish person.

1. A Jewish reader who had gotten this far into Paul's letter might be thinking at this point, "Well, *has* God rejected the nation of Israel?" Paul answers that question with a loud and clear NO!

Read **Romans 11:1–6.** As you do, find three pieces of evidence Paul uses to support this answer.

2. In **Romans 11:2–4** Paul recounts the lonely struggle and the deep discouragement Elijah felt as part of God's remnant people in Old Testament times. Read **1 Kings 19:1–18.** Why did Elijah feel the way he did? Was he really all alone? Write down some of the times when you felt depressed and alone like Elijah. Look at your list. What can you learn about the causes of your down times? How can you overcome these?

3. The situation in Israel in Paul's day differed little from that at the time of Elijah. A remnant of the people had their eyes and ears opened to God's grace in the Messiah. But many were blind and stumbling. Because of their own impenetrable stubbornness, God finished the hardening of their hearts that they had begun. (See

Romans 5:17–19 and session 26.) How does Paul explain this terrible conclusion in **verses 8–9?**

4. Paul makes it very clear that God does not draw people to Him by nationality. He does not call large groups of people to Himself. There may be safety in numbers from a human point of view, but in the realm of the Spirit only a remnant knows and believes the truth. What application for your life do you see in this principle?

Verses 11–15: Salvation for the Gentiles

1. At the time of Paul's ministry, the nation of Israel was stumbling, but had not completely fallen down. What was God's purpose in allowing Israel to openly reject His Messiah and live in the darkness that resulted from that rejection? Paul's answer is both striking and unexpected. Tell in your own words what that reason is.

2. In **verse 15** Paul suddenly introduces a thought of great significance without giving us any warning at all. What does he appear to be saying?

LOOKING AHEAD

A metaphor is a word picture. As you read through **Romans 11:16–25,** pay particular attention to the metaphors Paul is using, and consider what they might mean.

I ask then: Did God reject His people? By no means . . . . At the present time there is a remnant chosen by grace. And if by grace, then it is no longer by works; if it were, grace would no longer be grace. What then? What Israel sought so earnestly it did not obtain, but the elect did.

Romans 11:1, 5–7

SESSION 31

Baking and Botany

ROMANS 11:16–25

Sometimes it helps us understand God's method of dealing with His children if we think of them literally as children.

What will you expect to happen if one five-year-old child gets a cookie and the other one doesn't? Do you think the child with the cookie will break it in half and share it with the other? Probably not. More likely the one with the cookie will taunt the other child with words like, "Ha, ha. I've got a cookie and you don't!" The deprived child, of course, will sulk and pout.

Paul's earlier words could have produced the same kind of response in both Jewish and Gentile people. Paul knew that his reference of turning to the Gentiles to make the Jews jealous **(verses 13–15)** could offend Jewish people and give the Gentiles cause for arrogance. He heads off these improper responses by reminding the Gentiles of their relatively inferior position and the Jews of their privileged position. He lumps both Jew and Gentile together in two metaphors. Unfortunately, neither of God's "five-year-olds" seems to have paid enough attention to them.

IN THE WORD
Verses 16–17: The Metaphors

Paul uses two word pictures to illustrate his point. The first relates to baking. Under Mosaic Law a Jewish farmer gave the first fruit of his harvest as an offering to God. In this way the entire crop was then special in the eyes of the Lord **(Numbers 15:1–21)**. The people followed a similar procedure when baking. They gave the first piece of dough as a peace offering with the understanding that all after that would be baked to God's glory.

1. What do **"the part of the dough offered as firstfruits"** and **"the whole batch"** in **verse 16** symbolize?

Paul's second metaphor relates to botany. In one kind of grafting a gardener will graft vital, young twigs from one tree onto an older, well-established fruit-bearing tree ofter pruning off the dead branches. In this way an older tree, whose fruit production has fallen off, may

be recovered and again become valuable to the orchard and its owner.

The readers, who probably were familiar with the practice of grafting olive branches, likely understood Paul's metaphor. They also likely understood that this situation was "**contrary to nature**" **(verse 24)**, because a *wild* olive shoot was being grafted in; ordinarily gardeners would graft in a *domesticated* olive shoot, because they would not expect the wild shoots to bear much fruit.

2. Israel is obviously the domesticated olive tree, and the Gentiles are the branches of a wild olive tree being grafted in. You probably understand the picture "botanically" and as it related to the Jews and Gentiles of Paul's day. But what does it mean for our lives?

Even though not all parts of Paul's analogy fit, something a little like it happens in the church today. Think of your church as the traditional rich olive root, and yourself and other young Christians as the wild olive branches. Write a paragraph explaining how you might be of mutual value to each other.

Verses 18–25: The Warning

Paul directs the warning toward Gentile Christians. He cautions them not to be arrogant about being chosen for a transplant, but to recognize their dependency upon the root of Judaism. They owed a great debt of gratitude to the Jewish people. God warned that if they did not acknowledge this debt— if they became arrogant—they would suffer the same fate as the natural branches. God reserved the right to remove the initial branches, and He will not hesitate to do the same with those He has grafted in.

1. *The Gentile world has, for the most part, ignored this warning.* Give examples from history or your own experience to support this statement.

Paul demonstrates the power of God as He works according to His own righteous principles. As He works, we see both the "**kindness and sternness of God**" **(verse 22)**. He has shown kindness in bringing us into His church, even though we deserve punishment instead. He will continue to show His kindness as long as we do not reject His grace. If we do not "**continue

in His kindness" (verse 22), however; we will see God's sternness, and we will be "cut off." As you have seen many times during your study of Romans, God's grace is great and incomprehensible. If we, however, reject that grace, God will also reject us.

2. In **verse 25** Paul says he does not want his readers to be **"ignorant of the mystery."**

You probably understand the metaphor of the olive tree. If you learn more about grafting, you may understand it even better. But what about people today who know nothing about grafting? Can you make the lesson of this session clear to them?

Search through your own experience. Try to find a word picture that will explain Paul's mystery to a 20th-century reader. Look for something a Sunday school class of eight-year-olds could grasp and apply.

LOOKING AHEAD

These three chapters in **Romans (9–11)** contain concepts that are difficult (but not impossible) to understand. Paul seems to be conceding the difficulty in the doxology at the end of **chapter 11**. Read **11:26–36.** In your own words, what is Paul saying?

If you were cut out of an olive tree that is wild by nature, and contrary to nature were grafted into a cultivated olive tree, how much more readily will these, the natural branches, be grafted into their own olive tree!

Romans 11:24

SESSION 32

Mercy and Majesty

ROMANS 11:26—36

Do you remember how Paul opened **chapters 9 and 10?** He was deeply depressed about the spiritual condition of the Jews. **"I have great sorrow and unceasing anguish in my heart,"** the apostle exclaimed in **9:2.** He begins the next chapter with, **"Brothers, my heart's desire and prayer to God for the Israelites is that they may be saved" (10:1).** Now, as he nears the end of this section of his letter, he proclaims, **"And so all Israel will be saved."** If Paul knew in **9:2** what he was going to write in **11:26,** why was he so depressed? If he was aware of God's plans to restore Israel, what was his concern all about? As we consider this question, we should find some very real personal applications for our lives, also.

It seems that Paul's thoughts were operating on two levels. In **verse 25** he says that Israel was experiencing a **"hardening in part."** The apostle could rejoice that the hardening was neither total nor permanent. Paul knew that he was only one of many Jewish people at that time who had a genuine faith in God, and that in the future **"all Israel will be saved."** Through faith in Christ people of every generation, both Jew and Gentile, would receive the salvation Jesus has earned for us all.

At the same time, however, on an individual level, souls were being lost every day. People in the Jewish nation were for the most part languishing in spiritual darkness. Paul could take no pleasure in that, even though some Jewish fanatics frequently made his ministry difficult by their opposition.

In a similar way, we experience bittersweet elements in our own lives. We rejoice in God's accomplished plan of salvation. The love of God has been shed abroad, salvation is available to all through faith in Christ Jesus, and we wait for His promised return with eager anticipation!

But this joy must also be tinged with sadness for the countless souls being lost every day. Millions of co-inhabitors on planet earth—including friends, neighbors, and relatives—are living in sin-darkened blindness. Jeremiah expressed the anguish of the unsaved in the words, **"The harvest is past, the summer has ended, and we are not saved" (Jeremiah 8:20).** We have work to do while it is day; the time grows shorter, and the urgency grows greater!

IN THE WORD

Verses 26—32: All Israel Will Be Saved

1. We concluded our last session with **verse 25,** which Paul uses as a launching pad for these verses. The "hardening in part" will last **"until the full number**

of the Gentiles has come in. **And so all Israel will be saved.''** Interpret these words of Paul. What is he saying?

2. Upon what does Paul base this statement?

3. Sometimes we can better understand a section of Scripture when we put it into our own words. Look up **Deuteronomy 10:15** and **Numbers 23:19.** Incorporate the thoughts of those two verses into **Romans 11:28–29.** Write a paraphrase that will clearly explain what Paul is saying.

4. Read **verses 30–31** and explain in what way Jews and Gentiles were on the opposite sides of the same coin. Look up **Ephesians 2:1–2, 11–12** for a fuller explanation of the Gentile condition.

Paul concludes this section with the idea that, since the Gentiles have been disobedient and the Jews are disobedient, people in both groups can find hope only in the mercy of God. The whole concept of the mercy of God and the way He exercises it toward all people is overwhelming. Paul responds with a great doxology (hymn of praise). Let's examine it now.

Verses 33–36: Wisdom and Majesty of God

1. Paul begins his doxology with an exclamation that needs no proof: **"Oh, the depths of the riches of the wisdom and knowledge of God!"** He then continues with three questions that need no answer. Find the three questions and paraphrase them to bring out their meaning. Then explain what you think Paul is saying to us about God.

2. Paul concludes this portion of his letter with a statement about the majesty of God that is as profound as it is short. Dissect **verse 36** and jot down in your notebook a few thoughts for each of the following phrases:

> **For from Him**
> **and through Him**
> **and to Him are all things.**

If we can grasp the significance of **"from Him and through Him and to Him are all things,''** we will be better able to glorify Him. God grant it. Amen.

LOOKING AHEAD

Skim **Romans 9–11** in preparation for next time's review and unit evaluation.

And so all Israel will be saved, as it is written: "The deliverer will come from Zion; he will turn godlessness away from Jacob. And this is My covenant with them when I take away their sins.''

Romans 11:26–27

SESSION 33

Concluding Activities for Unit 3

We have just completed the third major section of Romans. The first eight chapters presented the doctrinal foundation of Paul's letter. Your review sessions (13 and 24) were "Salvation, Parts 1 and 2." In **Romans 9–11** we discovered an area of special importance to God—the relationship of the Gospel to His chosen people, the Jews. We have learned that God's plan for Israel is consistent with His character. In mercy He called them—made them His special people. When they turned from Him, He used their rejection as an opportunity to begin a massive ministry to the Gentiles, but He still loves the Jewish people and is calling them back into His fold.

1. Use your Bible, this lesson guide, and your own class notes to guide you as you write down what you believe to be the central truth for each of the eight sessions in this unit.

25. The Tragedy of the Jews, **Romans 9:1–5**

26. God's Chosen People, **Romans 9:6–21**
27. "In Wrath, Remember Mercy," **Romans 9:22–33**
28. Zeal, Truth, and Knowledge, **Romans 10:1–13**
29. Evangelism, **Romans 10:14–21**
30. Cast Away or Set Aside, **Romans 11:1–15**
31. Baking and Botany, **Romans 11:16–25**
32. Mercy and Majesty, **Romans 11:26–36**

2. Now change your focus from central truth to personal application. Page through the material in this unit and jot down the most memorable application you discovered in each lesson.

LOOKING AHEAD

Romans 12:1–2 contains some of the most profound thoughts for Christian living ever written. Just consider the words *living sacrifices, conform, transformed,* and *renewing.* Be prepared to share your thoughts on their meanings for next session.

UNIT 4

The Righteousness of God Applied

ROMANS 12–16

In his first 11 chapters, Paul has firmly established the foundational truth of the Christian faith—the doctrine of salvation by grace through faith in Jesus Christ alone. Because of the powerful way Paul has arranged his argument, believers down through the centuries probably have turned to this portion of Scripture more often than any other when doctrinal clarification was necessary.

Now, beginning with **chapter 12,** Paul begins to make the exciting transition from doctrine to practice. The powerful truths he has established have concrete, practical implications for the daily lives of believers. In the last five chapters of Romans, God makes it very clear that He wants to use His people to their full potential. And He tells us how He releases that potential through our loving service.

Therefore, I urge you, brothers, In view of God's mercy, to offer your bodies as living sacrifices, holy and pleasing to God.

SESSION 34

Therefore . . .

ROMANS 12:1–2

The writers of the New Testament epistles frequently use the word *therefore*. While we might be inclined to overlook it, we need to remember that this word is often key in interpreting what follows it. Whenever we see it, we need to ask ourselves, "What is the *therefore* there for?"

To help answer that question in this case, look back over **Romans 1–11.** Jot down what you think are the most significant truths Paul has in mind as he begins to write **chapter 12.** Note the chapter and verse in which you find each. Be ready to defend your choices.

IN THE WORD

Verse 1: Offer Your Bodies

1. "In view of God's mercy," Paul writes, "offer your bodies as living sacrifices." Even though his *therefore* reminds us of all he has just written about our Lord's grace, Paul chooses to remind us of God's mercy once again. What point is the apostle trying to drive home for his readers? Why do you think he makes this point again and again?

2. We are justified by grace. But we are also sanctified by grace. What is the difference between sanctification by grace and "trying hard to be good"? Why is this distinction so important?

3. What kind of animal sacrifices did God's Old Testament people offer? What differences do you see between those offerings and the kind of offering for which the Lord asks in **verse 1?**

4. We know that by our own efforts we could never dedicate ourselves so totally to God that our lives are holy and pleasing to God. How, then, can we accomplish what this verse asks of us?

Verse 2
Have Your Minds Transformed

One Bible scholar paraphrases this verse:
Don't let the world around you squeeze you into

its own mould, but let God re-make you so that your whole attitude of mind is changed. Thus you will prove in practice that the will of God's good, acceptable to Him and perfect (Phillips).

1. In what ways does the world around you try to squeeze you into its mold?

2. Human beings are incorrigible conformists. The temptation to fit in with those around us can be incredibly seductive. Paul asks us to resist this temptation by letting **"God remold [our] minds from within."** How does this remolding take place? (See **2 Corinthians 10:3–5**; **Ephesians 4:22–24**; and **Colossians 3:1–3** for clues. Then write two or three paragraphs explaining this process as you understand it.)

3. The Greek word translated *transformed* in **verse 2** is *metamorphouthe*. Biology students will readily see the English word taken almost directly from the Greek—metamorphosis. The word means "to change in bodily form." The most dramatic example of this in nature occurs when caterpillars almost mysteriously change into butterflies. How does this word help identify and explain the change our Lord wants to make in both our ways of thinking and in our life-style?

4. It's tough to swim upstream. When we fail to conform, when we do not fulfill the expectations others have of us, we can expect some pressure from those around us—maybe even outright ridicule or persecution of one kind or another. But what benefit does Paul hold out for all who allow God to transform their minds and their lives?

LOOKING AHEAD

Read **Romans 12:3–8**. Here Paul asks us to look inside ourselves and think about the gifts God has given us to use in His service. Spend some time between now and the next class period thinking about what your gifts might be.

Therefore, I urge you, brothers, in view of God's mercy, to offer your bodies as living sacrifices, holy and pleasing to God—this is your spiritual act of worship.

Romans 12:1

SESSION 35

Evaluate and Activate

ROMANS 12:3–8

There is a difference between talents and gifts, at least in a Christian's life. *Talents* are the abilities with which we are born. They are genetically transmitted from parents to their children. Our intellect, musical ability, artistic skill, and athletic coordination, or lack of them, are ours as a matter of birth. *Gifts,* on the other hand, are special skills or abilities that God gives to His baptized children for the express purpose of building up the body of Christ.

Sometimes, however, human pride short-circuits God's intention. Christians sometimes forget the reason God gives His children talents and gifts. We sometimes push others down by pushing ourselves up. How often our human nature likes to take credit for our talents, "Look! I got an *A* on that test!" "Hey! I scored the winning point for the team!" How easily we fall into a feeling of self-importance or superiority over others! In our sin-fallen world, that attitude is common.

Many people do not recognize that their talents come from God, which is bad enough. But if Christians do not recognize that their special gifts also come from God (to be used for God's purposes), those gifts can become destructive, not constructive, in the church. God is the Giver of both gifts and talents, and He should get the credit. As Jesus put it, **"Let your light shine before men, that they may see your good deeds and praise your Father [not you] in heaven"** (**Matthew 5:16,** with parenthetical addition added by author).

IN THE WORD
Verse 3
Use Sober Judgment

The first thing Paul asks us to do with our renewed minds is to use sober judgment. He means that out of our faith in Christ, we can now evaluate our talents and gifts properly, in the way the Holy Spirit guides us, not for self-promotion (as the world does) but for the good of the whole people of God.

The apostle begins with a negative note: **"Do not think of yourselves more highly than you ought."**

Take a moment to reflect on Paul's advice. At what times are we very tempted to think "more highly" than we ought? When we try to impress our peers? our teachers? a cute member of the opposite sex? When we pant for a position on the student council? the team? the honor society? Do we sometimes even try to impress God?

Simon Peter once thought **"more highly than [he] ought."** The incident is recorded in **Mark 14:17–31** and **66–72.** Read it, and answer the following questions.

1. In what way did Peter think more highly of himself than he should have? Why might it be easy to fall into the same kind of bragging as Peter?

2. Why, do you think, was Peter trying to impress Jesus?

3. Later, Peter would become a dynamic instrument in God's kingdom, but only because the power of Christ's love worked the miracle of repentance in him. Scan **John 21:15–19.** Why, do you think, would Peter never forget this seashore breakfast incident? What made Peter such a dynamic disciple after that meeting with Jesus? Did his natural talents or his God-given gifts make the difference? Defend your opinion.

4. Without Christ, Peter was nothing. You probably feel the same way at times. Read **2 Peter 1:3–4.** Even if we are uncertain about our talents, why is there joy in sharing our God-given gifts with others?

It is common in our world to think more highly of ourselves than we should. Yet it is also very common for some people to look at themselves so negatively, feeling so inferior, that they feel worthless. Both views fail to qualify as "sober judgment," for both fail to recognize how much we have from God and that we have received everything we do have as a gift of grace. Superiority or inferiority complexes can be healed when the Holy Spirit moves us to look to Jesus Christ instead of to ourselves.

Verses 4–5
One Body, Many Members

The church is the body of Christ, and Christians are the different members, or body parts. The reason Christ's people are so different should be as obvious to us as the reason the parts of the human body are so different: **"not all have the same function" (verse 4).**

Compare, for further insight: **1 Corinthians 12:12–31.**

1. Why should no Christian feel either superior or inferior to others in the church? How can we help one another overcome these feelings?

2. Read **verses 24b–26.** List some ways you have seen the whole church suffer when one part of the body of Christ suffers. List some ways the whole church can rejoice when one part is honored.

3. If this shared suffering and shared rejoicing took place at your Christian school or church, what would happen to feelings of envy, jealousy, inferiority, or superiority?

4. Our value comes from the fact that we are loved by God and redeemed by Christ and have been called by the Spirit to be His body, the church. But how might the world's standards obscure our view? Reread **Romans 12:2** and apply it to the message of television commercials, magazine ads, etc. Does the world even know about the special gifts God gives His people? Explain your answer.

Verses 6–8: Different Gifts

Jesus Christ gave us everything He had, including His life. That gift gives us our true self worth. God also gives us everything else we have and need, including special gifts for the welfare of the church. Paul lists seven of these gifts as examples.

1. Write one or two sentences on each of the seven gifts. What is your understanding of each of them?

   a. Prophesying ("proclaiming")

   b. Serving

   c. Teaching

   d. Encouraging

   e. Contributing

   f. Leadership

   g. Showing mercy

Share your thoughts with your class.

2. Select one of the above gifts and write a short paragraph explaining why it can be a great help in the overall building up of the body of Christ.

LOOKING AHEAD

Read **Romans 12:9–13** before the next session.

Just as each of us has one body with many members, and these members do not all have the same function, so in Christ we who are many form one body, and each member belongs to all the others.

Romans 12:4–5

SESSION 36

Love, the Real Thing

ROMANS 12:9–13

In the last session we learned about gifts God gives to His people, and how those gifts may be used to serve Him and the church. In this session we will discover that our attitude about serving is as important as our gift for serving. Many gifted Christians are aware of their abilities and use them regularly but still find no joy in their service. They work, instead, out of a sense of duty or obligation. They severely resent other, lazier Christians who are not "doing their share." Like Martha **(Luke 10:40),** who resented her sister, these people allow resentment to take hold of their hearts. Obviously, something is missing. This segment of Romans shows us that the missing element is love.

Just as St. Paul also pointed out in **1 Corinthians 13,** all the other gifts from God add up to nothing without love behind them. But Paul is speaking of a special love—the *agape-love* of God. Self-giving-up, self-sacrificing-for agape-love is precisely what moved Jesus to His cross for us. Unlike Martha, the Son of God did not bear the cross out of a sense of duty or obligation. He did not complain from Calvary that others were not doing their share. Jesus simply loved us into His kingdom of grace. This is the kind of love that God now asks of us, His people.

Immediately, however, we see the utter impossibility of our loving others as Jesus loves us. And if we read this segment of Romans as simply Paul's marching orders, ordering us to love others, we would fail. Instead, we need to read and study this text as though it were an invitation to try out a new gift from God: the gift of agape-love. "With God," the angel told Mary, "nothing is impossible."

IN THE WORD
Verses 9–13: Be Sincere

A. The Dilemma

If people imagined they could either fake or crank out love, this statement stops that notion cold. We can fake or manufacture love, but not for long. Sooner or later, love created by us will wear thin, and the disguise will be over. The harder we try it—the more we crank ourselves up to do it on our own—the sooner people will see how faked our love has always been.

God, therefore, expects sincere or genuine agape-love. Nothing less will do. Understandably, many Christians realize that they simply do not have the ability or capacity to love this way, especially when Christ tells us that this agape-love must also reach out to our enemies! Loving those who love us is hardly unique to Christians; even unbelievers can accomplish that **(Matthew 5:44, 46–48).** Many Christians find this troubling. They know what God's will is. They wish they could love as Christ does. They don't know what to do.

B. The Definition

Before we see the solution our Lord has worked out for us, we should arrive at a working definition of what this genuine, sincere agape-love is.

IMAGINE!

You are an archaeologist from A. D. 3249. You have been working at a dig on the site where you now sit. Painstakingly, you have lifted and sifted through strata of dust and debris, until you have reached a layer which, you determine, must be from North American culture of the A. D. 1980s.

Among the debris you find packages of celluloid ("Ah, video cassettes, I believe," you say to your colleagues), long strips of a plastic-like material ("Humm! Wonder if this was an audio tape," your colleague says to you), and piles of bound pages of brittle paper ("Magazines?" you ask).

You and your colleague take your finds to your laboratory and cautiously, using the highest quality instruments of the 33d century, examine the contents. You are particularly interested in what North American culture of the 1980s thought, felt, and philosophized about love. Since you are writing your Ph.D. thesis on this very subject, you take notes.

Your Research

As an archaeologist of the 33d century, you will be copying stanzas of music and summarizing contents from videos, movies, magazines, and books (fiction and nonfiction) that people may have enjoyed during the 20th century. As specifically as possible, take careful notes, using the helps below:

On the subject of love, as viewed by the 20th century, select one or two of the following, and write out

- a stanza from your favorite music;
- a remembered line from your favorite movie or video;
- a favorite scene from a favorite novel;
- a favorite thought from a nonfiction book;
- a favorite saying from a favorite celebrity;
- a favorite point from a major magazine.

Your Observations

You have just gathered the data. Now jot down your conclusions. Describe the view of love held by people in the North American culture of the 20th century!

Previously, you prepared some initial statements. Now complete them, based on the observations you have reached. You ponder for a while, then finish these sentences:

1. The 20th-century North American culture viewed love as mostly—
2. People of that century loved if—
3. People of that century loved because—
4. Sometimes love ceases because—
5. The most worthwhile quality I see in this concept of love is—
6. The least worthwhile quality I see in this concept of love is—

Now, Some First-Century Conclusions

Now turn the tables. Take the same data you gathered but give it to the apostle Paul. Based not only on **Romans 12:9–13,** but also on the agape-love that Christ Jesus has for us, how would the apostle Paul complete the sentences 1 through 6? (Remember, Paul's time frame is different than yours. Does this make any difference?)

This may be a roundabout way of coming to a definition of God's agape-love, but you have almost arrived!

My Conclusions about Agape-Love

You have gathered data and recorded some of your observations. Now write down some conclusions about agape-love as contrasted to the ideas about love which were so popular in the 20th century. To get started, use (but do not limit yourself to) the helps that follow:

God's Agape-Love
  Conditions?
  Commitment?
  Self-giving?
  Time Limits?

Society's Idea of Love
  Conditions?
  Commitment?
  Self-giving?
  Time Limits?

After completing the chart, give your overall conclusions.

C. The Delivery

Obviously you have reached the conclusion that God's agape-love is infinitely higher and harder than human society's ideas about love. Perhaps you have even come to the conclusion as you read **Romans 12:9–13** that it's impossible to even attempt to love one another with agape-love. We will eventually fail when we try to love one another with agape-love. Why even attempt it?

First of all, the point is not that we can agape-love each other, but that God, in Christ Jesus, agape-loves us. Look again at the chart above. If yours was accurate, every item under the "God's Agape-Love" tells about the love that Christ Jesus has for you. Instead of nailing us for not loving as we ought, God lifts us with His love. He delivers us from the sin of failing to love. God loves even the unloving, the unlovable, and the unlovely.

Read **Romans 12:9–13** once more, but this time read it as though God is telling you that this is a description of His agape-love for you. How does God make it possible, then, for us to carry this same love to others?

LOOKING AHEAD

Read **Romans 12:14–21** before the next session.

Love must be sincere. Hate what is evil; cling to what is good. Be devoted to one another in brotherly love. Honor one another above yourselves.
Romans 12:9–10

SESSION 37

Good Swallows Evil

ROMANS 12:14–21

Brett may have been small for his 16 years, but he did not lack strength—at least, not any longer. He breathed in and felt the cloth of his shirt stretch, giving way to his chest muscles. That satisfied him. That was the payoff for 10 months' sweat, rigorous discipline, and pumped iron. Strength felt good. Muscles felt good. And so did power. And as he walked to the track of St. John's High, Brett felt good. With a look that none of his closest friends had ever seen on his face before, Brett smiled. But his best friends did not. Including Julie.

"This isn't just a track meet for you, is it?" she asked, eyes forward as they walked. "This is your own private vendetta against Jack. It's your way of getting even."

"I'm not going to do a thing that hasn't been done before," Brett said, his voice lower than a year ago. That, too, gave him satisfaction. He was a different man now than he was last year. At least this year he was a man. Jack and his gang of upperclassmen would be wise to stay out of Brett's way this year, but Brett hoped they wouldn't. "It's all been done out there before," he repeated.

"Done to you, you mean!" Julie said. "Please, Brett! Let it go. Why can't you just let it go?"

"Let it go" was the one thing Brett would not do. A year ago as an underclassman, Brett had still been one of the swiftest cross-country runners for St. John's High. He had edged Jack out of first place, but never thought much about it—until the day when Jack and his cohorts converged on Brett near the course's end. They were fresh; Brett was not. They were built like football players; Brett was not. They were muscular; Brett was not. When they finished with Brett, there was little left of him that wasn't bruised or broken. "Accident," they told the coach, and the coach believed them. Brett spent the next two months with a cast around his leg, bandages around his ribs, and humiliation wrapped around his ego.

No, he would not just let it go. His strength was tremendous, and he knew it. His plan for Jack was flawless, and he loved it. Just another accident, coincidentally at that same dangerous curve near the creek

bank. Why, just where Brett "slipped" on gravel last year.

"Brett? Are you listening to me?" It was Julie. "You've got to change your mind."

"Nothing's changed." Brett's voice was low, his eyes were steel, and his smile was cold. "Nothing's changed."

"Oh, yes." Julie stopped him, turned him around to look her in the face. "Something has. You've changed, Brett. You have."

IN THE WORD

Verses 14–21
Overcoming Evil with Good

A. The Danger: Evil Overcoming Us

A year ago, Brett was the innocent victim of a cruel attack. No one could justify the evil Jack and his friends had done to him. Brett had simply, honestly beaten the upperclassman in a fair race. Out of pride and utter greed (and with a little help from his friends), Jack eliminated his competitor. At least Jack thought so. But for a year, Brett's outraged hurt drove him to plan, plot, and build for this moment of revenge. Physically, there was no doubt that Brett would succeed. Jack would be paid back, measure for measure, eye for eye, tooth for tooth.

What in the world could be wrong about that? It's a classic case of the underdog finally getting the upper hand, isn't it? Or is it? Jot down a few notes, using the questions below. Be ready to share your thoughts with others:

1. Was Brett's plan for revenge justified? Defend your opinion.

2. What did Julie mean when she said that Brett had changed? Has the desire for revenge ever made you or someone you know change?

3. Reread **verses 17** and **21**. In a paragraph write what you think it means to be overcome by evil. Why doesn't it simply mean to be hurt as Brett was when he was beaten up?

4. The warning is clear: victims can easily become evil, too. If the evil done to us is not forgiven, it can take over— our thoughts, our ideas, our very selves.

The Hitlers of the world believed that they (or those they "represented") were victims once and that they had "good justification" for their violent plots and schemes and for their revenge.

If Brett were suddenly thrust into a position of power that affected the lives of millions, what real difference would there be between him and someone such as Adolph Hitler? *That* is what vengeance can do to us. What other cases do you know (stories, news accounts, movies, history, or personal accounts) where the victim turned into a victimizer?

5. Discuss: "If you do not forgive and love your enemies, you shall inevitably become just like them." Explain why you agree or disagree.

B. The Dilemma: Unstoppable Evil?

So, unless we "bless our persecutors" and "repay evil with good," we may end up being consumed by that evil. We may turn into the very thing that hurt us. Victims can become victimizers! That is what Paul warned about when he wrote, "Do not be overcome by evil." Brett allowed evil to eat its way into him, and Brett was overcome. We likely have allowed evil to do the same in us.

Imagine that you, like Brett, were also victimized and received no justice. You may have felt helpless and angry because evil seemed unstoppable. It might also make you angry that God forbids you to return evil for evil. Imagine that you are not at all convinced that evil would overtake you. Discuss:

1. Many feel that following God's answer here would be cowardly, that His solution would simply allow evil to run freely. Reread **verse 19**. What phrase clearly shows that God is not deaf to people's cries for justice?

2. God is not speaking to governments here (**Romans 13** will show us government's role). He is speaking to those who follow Jesus. What would happen if everyone acted as if it was up to each individual to execute justice as that individual happened to see fit?

C. The Defense: Only Christ's Undefeatable Good

Evil can be stopped, really stopped. But we must admit we cannot stop it on our own, or else it will infect us, too. Brett tried to stop it, but it took him over instead. As difficult as it is to accept, we simply are not good enough to stop evil.

1. Only Jesus Christ is good enough to stop evil. He stopped the worst kind of evil in the most surprising way. Look up one of the following texts:

Mark 15:3–5
Luke 22:47–51
Luke 23:33–34

In a few of your own words jot down some notes to show how Jesus swallowed evil with good. Share

your thoughts with your class.

2. Obviously, Jesus did not even attempt revenge, or else He would never have saved His enemies. But by forgiving them, their evil simply had no place else to go! Jesus took it on to Himself and nailed it to His cross. Of course, it cost Jesus greatly. What did Jesus feel for His enemies that He was willing to pay that cost? (For help, refer to **Romans 5:6–8**.)

3. Forgiveness takes power—superhuman power which our world cannot understand! Why is it easier for our world to get even with evil (revenge) than it is to forgive (send away) evil? How can the unbelieving world see Christ Jesus' kind of forgiveness-power today?

D. Cross Purposes

We cannot understand **Romans 12:14–21** without seeing Jesus and His death on the cross. Without His action, this segment of Romans sounds like a lesson in moral laws which are impossible for us to keep. God's Word simply goes against our human nature. Someone may as well order us to jump over the World Trade Center as to tell us to overcome evil with agape-love and forgiveness!

But God gives us His Son's superhuman power so that we can do the impossible!

1. Review **Romans 6:1–7**. Look back at your notes from this book. What gift did God give us so that God's purposes can be accomplished in and through us?

2. Our vengeful "old self" was crucified and killed with Christ. Now what can the "new (Christ) self" in us accomplish with God's power? Why aren't we enslaved to evil vengefulness any longer?

3. It's still hard—but not impossible—for us to overcome evil with Christ's goodness. The "old self" still wants to dominate and to get even with those who wronged us. But God freely gives us the gift of His agape-love. With that free gift in mind, review **Romans 12:20**. Share some practical ways God's purposes can be fulfilled by

a. feeding and giving drink to your enemies;

b. heaping burning coals on their heads.

Read **Romans 12:14–21** once more, but this time read it as though this is a description of God's love for you, even if you, too, have given in to revenge, and have been overcome by evil. How does Jesus' love-cry in **Luke 23:34** make you feel?

LOOKING AHEAD

Read **Romans 13:1–7** before the next session.

Do not be overcome by evil, but overcome evil with good.

Romans 12:21

SESSION 38

Citizenship

ROMANS 13:1–7

Most of us would like to live in a society where no conflict exists between our Christian faith and our government's laws. Yet sometimes conflicts happen, despite our wishes. What would you do in the following situations?

CASE 1

You are 17-year-old William Kent, living in Philadelphia in 1775. News has just arrived that armed rebellion has broken out in Massachusetts. American colonists have battled at Lexington and Concord with British troops stationed in Boston. The news greatly upsets you.

On one hand, men you admire, like Benjamin Franklin (whom you recently met), urge the American people to exert their freedoms. You have always respected the governor and legislature of Pennsylvania and appreciate the orderly way they have governed your commonwealth.

But on the other hand, you have always thought of yourself as a loyal subject of King George III of England and never imagined that the tensions between the American colonies and Great Britain would ever lead to a rebellion.

Now, however, it appears that a rebellion has begun. Your family believes they are still British subjects and that armed rebellion is sinful. But many of your friends believe they are American citizens and want to enlist you in the Pennsylvania militia to fight the British.

Based on your reading of **Romans 13:1–7,** you must reach a conclusion. Which government is indeed the authority over you—the British king or the Pennsylvania legislature? Which course of action would you take—support for the king or support for complete independence from Britain?

What are you going to do?

CASE 2

You are 16-year-old Sölveg Segezha, living in Leningrad, the Soviet Union. Only this morning, some of your favorite cousins, who are visiting you from nearby Finland, asked your help for a most dangerous project. They requested that you allow them to visit you frequently because, they tell you, your home in Leningrad is most strategic in their efforts to smuggle Bibles into your country.

You are a Christian. For that reason you understand your cousins' very risky mission. You, too, want to see the Gospel of Jesus spread in your country. But you are also a loyal Soviet citizen, and you have always loved your nation. You realize fully that if you are discovered, you will be arrested, for smuggling Bibles in the Soviet Union is illegal. You would be tried in court, found guilty, and perhaps imprisoned. You certainly would lose your privilege to attend school, and any hope of attending the university would be shattered.

Your choice is terrible. Should you break Soviet law and help your cousins smuggle Bibles and take the risk and the sacrifice if necessary? Or should you tell your cousins they have no idea what they are asking of you and decline their request so that you may continue with your life?

What are you going to do?

IN THE WORD
Verses 1–7

A. Called to Honor and Obey

William and Sölveg are both caught in a conflict. Their faith in Christ calls them to make a decision about citizenship and the authority of government. Any decision they make will neither be simple nor easy to follow.

Read **Romans 13:1–7** and answer the following as thoughtfully as you can:

1. The Case of William Kent

a. If I were William Kent, God's Word would lead me to—

b. **Romans 13** would lead me to make this choice because—

2. The Case of Sölveg Segezha

a. If I were Sölveg Segezha, God's Word would lead me to—

b. **Romans 13** would lead me to make this choice because—

3. The early Christians, too, had hard choices to make. While confessing Jesus Christ as Lord and King, they also recognized that God had placed earthly rulers over them. Many of these rulers were pagans, corrupt, and no friends to God's people. Still, that did not give the Christians the right to disobey or rebel; for rebellion against earthly rulers was rebellion against God as well **(verse 2).**

a. Does **Romans 13** apply to us only if our rulers are Christians? good? upright? Why or why not?

b. By God's permission and authority, government exists to promote civil harmony and to protect good conduct **(verse 3).** If a government is not doing its job well enough, does that give a Christian grounds to rebel against it? Explain your answer.

c. Paul wrote this letter just before the outbreak of some imperial persecution against the Christians in Rome. Later, Paul himself would be imprisoned by the emperor's command. Eventually he would be executed. If a government is blatantly anti-Christian, does that give Christians the opportunity to rebel? Defend your opinion with Scripture.

B. Caesar or God?

All governments exist by God's authority. Today, however, many religious-political groups call for the overthrow of a government, claiming that it is God's will. Their reasons sound convincing: a certain government may be corrupt, suppressive, and intolerant of its people's faith.

Many Pharisees in Jesus' day also sought justification to rid their land of their Roman overlords. They questioned whether it was even lawful according to God's law to pay taxes to the emperor (or Caesar).

Read how the Pharisees tried to trap Jesus into this debate in **Matthew 22:15–21.**

1. The Roman emperor, Tiberius, did not believe in God. Many of his laws were repugnant to the Jews, and they (carefully!) questioned his authority. Their loyalty, they said, was to God, not Caesar. Why would Jesus not involve Himself in this debate?

2. Explain what Jesus meant by **"Give to Caesar what is Caesar's, and to God what is God's" (verse 21).**

3. Christians can take strength and comfort in the fact that God is still in control, even if an evil or corrupt ruler governs. The ruler is still God's servant, whether the ruler knows it or not. Perhaps in a way neither we nor the ruler recognizes, the ruler still carries out the will of God, although he may oppose it!

Think of an example from Scripture which shows that God is still in control, using the civil authorities for His divine purposes even though the ruler may be unaware of God. How does your example show that God is still in control, even if a ruler is corrupt and evil? How does this help explain why **"all governments are established by God" (verse 1)?** How does trusting God on this promise help us honor and obey our government?

C. When Caesar Plays God

Government has God's sanction and authority behind it, even though it is a human institution. We owe respect and honor to rulers even though they (like us) are sinful humans. If rulers, however, forget they are merely rulers, they sometimes grab for themselves authority which belongs only to God. Forbidding what God commands and commanding what God forbids is an inexcusable abuse of authority.

The apostles Peter and John found themselves in that very situation. The leaders of the Jewish senate commanded the two men to stop speaking or teaching about Christ Jesus. Read about it in **Acts 4:18–21** and **5:25–29.**

1. Sölveg Segezha's government prohibited the distribution of the Bible. Explain ways in which Sölveg faced the same opposition as did Peter and John.

2. Here, to keep human law would mean breaking God's law. When facing such a situation, what is the faithful response of a Christian? Does the Acts text contradict or support the **Romans 13** text? Explain your answer.

3. Christians are not to be like the Pharisees, simply looking for trouble and artificial conflicts between the laws of God and men. Nevertheless, list some ways Christians today may be faced with having to break human laws in order to remain faithful to Christ Jesus.

a. How can we be sure that we do not (like the Pharisees) merely look for trouble?

b. When clearly convinced by the Word of God alone that we must disobey civil authorities, how may we receive God's assurance, strength, and comfort?

4. List some ways Christians today may have to go against the current of popular opinion and obey the government when it is unpopular or unprofitable to do so?

LOOKING AHEAD

Read **Romans 13:8–14** before the next session.

Everyone must submit himself to the governing authorities, for there is no authority except that which God has established. The authorities that exist have been established by God.

Romans 13:1

SESSION 39

Wake Up

ROMANS 13:8–14

Some of us simply are not morning people. It's a struggle for us to open our eyes and focus our minds on the business of the day. If we have been in a sound sleep, dreaming deeply, we may have difficulty distinguishing reality from fantasy when the alarm goes off. It takes several minutes to sort out what day it is, what we have to do, and (sometimes!) who we are.

What is true about physical sleep may also be true when it comes to spiritual sleep. When Paul wrote in **Romans 13:11: "The hour has come for you to wake up from your slumber,"** he was not concerned about his readers dozing off. He was very much concerned about them (and us) never coming out of a spiritual daze. Certainly some Christians are spiritually wide awake. They're alert, expecting and anticipating our Lord Jesus' return. They're ready for that Day. But many of us drift along in spiritual slumber, hardly able to distinguish between God's reality and the world's dreamy fantasy.

The apostles' message to us in this section is not pleasant—unless we actually like the jolting sound of the alarm clock or the blaring notes of a bugle. He calls us to wake up and arm ourselves for discipleship to Christ. Our natural selves want to drift back into the cozy comfort of our daydreams. But Paul is not appealing to our natural selves. He's calling that new self, the new creation born in our baptism.

So stretch those muscles; enjoy one final yawn. Then dig into this text from Romans. It's not just the Christian's marching orders of the day. It's an invitation from Christ to shake off the sleepy fog of this world and see, instead, the kingdom of God.

IN THE WORD

Verses 8–10
Love, the Fulfilling of the Law

In the previous section, Paul wrote about our obligation to pay taxes and give respect to those to whom it is due. Now he turns our attention to private financial matters and says simply, "Pay your debts!" Interestingly, he links paying our debts to loving our neighbor.

The apostle is not necessarily saying that we should not have debts. But he is saying that we, as Christ's people, should faithfully pay them. If we use credit, we should be good credit risks. Why? God's love for us motivates us to love the creditor, and we will want to show that love by repaying the debt.

The only debt, therefore, that we should not be able to pay back is the debt of love.

1. Based on Paul's words in this section of Romans, how would you define love?

2. Love whom? Is Paul speaking here of loving other Christians or loving even the nonbelieving people who live around you? For further definition of whom we are to love, read **Luke 10:25–37.**

3. Paul states that if we love other people, we fulfill the Law. The apostle is not forcing us to go back and live under the demands of the Law. Rather, he is simply showing that the law of God consists also of loving our neighbor as ourselves. What commandments does Paul cite? What reasons can you offer for Paul citing these commandments here?

Verses 11–14
The Day Is Near. Wake Up!

Christians are blood bought. We now belong to Christ, not to this world. Yet many of us struggle, because we still live in this world; we are daily bombarded with the world's values, philosophies, and life-styles. Quite often, we fall into the same thinking as the worldlings. We want, desire, and long for all the same pleasures, comforts, and ego trips as the worldlings. The more we set our eyes on worldly goals, the more our zeal for Christ and what He has in store for us withers.

Bluntly, Paul compares this weakening state of a Christian to slumber. It is very much like a trance; we can hardly distinguish between reality and fantasy. In order to discover why Paul is sounding an alarm here, discuss the following:

1. Apparently many of Christ's people have slipped into a trancelike spiritual slumber. In your own words, why is there every cause for urgency? In other words, what is approaching that will usher in reality?

2. In **verses 11–12** Paul runs through a series of contrasts, listed below:

a. slumber   wake up
b. night   day
c. put aside . . .   put on . . .
d. deeds of darkness   armor of light

Select one of the contrasting statements. Use the items to head two columns (e.g., "deeds of darkness" and "armor of light"). In one column list aspects of the "old life" that you see in people your age. In the other column list aspects of the new life God has given you—attitudes and behaviors you see in other Christians as the result of their faith in God. You will not be asked to show your lists to anyone, so you may be very personal. You may have an opportunity, however, to share some items during class discussion.

3. In the world, but not of the world, is one description of Christ's people. Yet sometimes we want what the world offers even at the risk of losing what Christ offers. In your own words write out why the world's promises seem more appealing at times than Christ's promises. When this happens, how do we know there is the danger of falling into a spiritual trance or slumber (see **verse 14**)?

4. Like a fog, our episodes of spiritual slumber make the reality of Jesus and His promises hazy to us. Although Paul says, **"the hour has come for you to wake up from your slumber" (verse 11),** we may not have the power or desire to do so. What power is there, then, to pull us out of our spiritual fog, and how do we know our Rescuer will use that power? (See **John 15:16, 19.**)

Verse 14
Clothe Yourself with Christ

Christ Jesus never stood around waiting until we had the desire or power to choose Him. He chose us even when we were in a spiritual fog. Therefore we belong to Him. He never forgets those who are His.

That is why when Paul says, **"clothe yourself with Christ" (verse 14),** he is not telling us to do the impossible or unattainable! We have already been clothed with Christ, dressed up to be like Jesus.

Read **Galatians 3:27.**

1. When were you clothed with Christ? You may not remember the day, but somebody (your parents or guardians) probably has recorded it.

2. What does this gift of being clothed with Christ mean to you? Especially at those times when the "fog" or trials hit you, how does this gift give you Christ's power to go on?

3. You were clothed! It was (and is) God's action done for you. It makes you a "son of God."

Refer to session 18 of this book and review the story of Carla. How did her image of herself shape her behavior? How does our image of ourselves as God's "sons" help shape our behavior? Do Paul's words here **(Romans 13:8–14)** now seem more like a command or an invitation?

LOOKING AHEAD

The first 12 verses of **chapter 14** are titled "The Weaker Brother." Read them for the next session and try to discover just what a "weaker brother" is, and how we are to deal with that person.

Clothe yourselves with the Lord Jesus Christ, and do not think about how to gratify the desires of the sinful nature.

Romans 13:14

SESSION 40

The "Weaker Brother"

ROMANS 14:1–12

Paul begins **chapter 14** by telling us not to "**pass judgment on disputable matters.**" In other words, never let anything trivial or nonessential cause divisions or produce disharmony among Christians. The church has lumped all these disputable matters into a category called *adiaphora,* which refers to issues in the church that God has not addressed in Scripture.

The church at Rome had two such matters, neither of which seems particularly important to us, but both apparently were sore points to the Christians there. The first had to do with food and the second with holy days. The problems arose because Gentile Christians tended to have a more relaxed attitude about some issues that became deeply ingrained in the Jewish consciousness, and Hebrew Christians were very uncomfortable with their New Testament freedom from the ceremonial law.

A word of caution may be needed when we talk about nonessentials or adiaphora. Whenever Christians disagree over the essential truths of Christianity—such as Christ's deity, the virgin birth, reality of miracles, His bodily resurrection, and the inerrancy of the Bible—then the issues must be resolved quickly, without compromising Scripture. Here we are discussing matters that are not prescribed in Scripture, matters where compromise is a better alternative than division.

IN THE WORD
Verses 1–6
Who Is the "Weaker Brother"?

When Paul speaks of Christians whose faith is weak, he means they are not yet mature in their relationship with Christ. This was particularly evident in those who taught rules and limits that Jesus did not teach and applied them to their lives. This is not wrong, but neither is it Biblical. And applying human rules becomes wrong when we impose those rules on others.

One point of contention in the church at Rome rose up between those who believed that it was permissible to eat all things and those who followed strict dietary laws **(verse 2).** Although Paul does not identify the two sides in the dispute, most Bible students assume that they were Christian Jews and Gentiles. In pagan societies the meat of sacrificial animals was sold (as a matter of economics) to the neighboring butcher shops. For Gentile Christians meat was meat, but the Jewish Christians were appalled at the thought that they might be eating meat that had been sacrificed to some heathen god. Many preferred to become vegetarians rather than to risk becoming unclean in this way.

The same kind of conflict rose up over what day of the week was best for worship. The Jewish Christians revered the Sabbath so much that they were troubled over observing a day other than Saturday as the holy day. The background of the Gentiles, on the other hand, brought no such bias. The early church could easily have divided into two churches, Jewish and Gentile, each going its own way.

Discuss: Paul could accept no solution that divided the body of Christ over non-Biblical issues. He was committed to a higher, although more difficult, solution. In your own words list at least three guidelines for getting along with the "weaker brother." Use **verses 1–6** as your resource.

Verses 7–12
Harmony for the Lord's Sake

1. **Verses 7** and **8** tell us that all Christians are interrelated. Since we are bonded together by the in-

dwelling Lord Jesus, our actions affect one another. We should be supportive of one another rather than tearing each other down. In **verse 10,** against what does Paul warn the "weaker brother"?

2. The "weaker brother" tends to confuse convention with conviction. Paul urges those who have no such problem to deal with controversial issues based upon their commitment to the Lord Jesus rather than upon their rights. He does not mind, personally, whether or not they eat meat, provided they base their decision upon what they understand the Lord's will to be. To eat or not to eat, worship on Saturday or some other day— these are probably not problems that keep you awake at night. But you probably know Christians who disagree over some issues. List some issues on which Christians disagree, even though Scripture has no hard and fast rules about them.

3. Which of the issues that you listed troubles you the most? Discuss ways you and others work to resolve that issue. What enables you to act in loving ways instead of sitting in judgment on others?

LOOKING AHEAD

Paul continues the theme of the weak and the strong brother for the rest of this chapter. For the next session, read **verses 13–23.** Here Paul speaks of confusing two sins: the sin of offense and the sin against conscience. What do you understand these to mean?

If we live, we live to the Lord; and if we die, we die to the Lord. So, whether we live or die, we belong to the Lord.

Romans 14:8

SESSION 41

The "Stronger Brother"

ROMANS 14:13–23

Paradoxes. Frustrating to some. Fun to others. Fascinating to others still. They look like falsehoods, but sometimes they are the only way to express the truth.

In a paradox two seemingly contrary statements are both true. Discuss how some of the following paradoxes can be resolved:

1. You are poor, but you are rich.
2. You are a kid, but you are an adult.
3. He's so dumb; he's smart.
4. She's so smart; she's dumb.

Scripture is full of paradoxes. That should not surprise us, because paradoxes can be such a good way to explain a truth. You worked with one paradox in session 29.

Look at the paradoxes that follow. Who said them, what is the context, and how can they be resolved? Some are spoken by Jesus, others by Paul, and some are paraphrases of one or the other. Who said which, and how would you resolve them?

1. When I am weak, then I am strong.
2. Blessed are those who mourn, for they will be comforted.
3. Whoever wants to save his life will lose it, but whoever loses his life for Me will find it.
4. He who believes in Me will live, even though he dies.
5. I am a sinner, but I also am a saint (paraphrased).
6. The foolishness of God is wiser than man's wisdom.

Virtually every major action of God recorded in Scripture, any major teaching of Jesus, the prophets, or apostles is a paradox!

Out of nothing, God created everything.

The Son of God became human so that humans could become children of God.

The King of kings was born in a stable.

The sinless Son of God died the death of a common criminal.

The Father treated the Sinless One as the only sinner and treats sinners as though they are sinless.

Jesus Christ was dead, but lives.

This list is incomplete. What other paradoxes of the Christian faith can you add?

BACKGROUND

This segment of Romans is packed with paradox. Here Paul declares that Christians who look like the strongest believers (to themselves as well as to others!) may actually be the weakest. The "weak brothers" often come across as strong, especially when they are defending a tradition in the church—but a tradition that is neither commanded nor forbidden by Scripture. Scripture is silent on the point, but the weak Christian sounds off!

In Rome, some weak Christians were apparently sounding off about other Christians who were eating nonkosher foods and drinking wine. The weaker Christians believed that these foods and drink were harmful to themselves and, therefore, they must also be harmful to everybody else. They wanted rules to forbid the others from this free-style eating and drinking and undoubtedly spoke out strongly about it.

But Paul is not speaking to the weak Christians here; he is speaking to the strong—the authentically strong Christians. They have freedoms they are entitled to enjoy, yet they should not flaunt their freedoms in the face of the weak.

IT'S NOT SIN JUST BECAUSE SOMEONE ELSE CALLS IT SIN

1. For many Jewish Christians, eating meat offered to idols (most nonkosher!) was a horrendous sin. They took great offense if they saw a fellow Christian purchasing meat at pagan temples. Discuss what you would do if you were a strong Gentile Christian who enjoyed meat very much. Would you discontinue eating this kind of meat? Give reasons for your actions.

2. List some activities which some people today consider to be a sin, but which Scripture neither forbids nor commands. Share your list with your class.

a. What on your list do others consider as a sin? What on others' lists do you consider as a sin?

b. Examine each item. What does Scripture say about it, or is Scripture silent?

3. Imagine that pogo-stick jumping became very popular at your school. First, a few individuals competed. Eventually, teams and entire pogo-stick jumping

leagues were formed. Then, because of some rowdiness among some participants, a backlash against pogo-stick jumping developed. Many of your Christian friends at your school and church were scandalized and called the sport violent. Eventually, they began calling pogo-stick jumping a sin.

You, a pogo-stick jumper par excellence and captain of your team, now face a dilemma. You love pogo-stick jumping. You know it is not a sin. You resent others imposing their private definition of sin on you. Unlike some other freedoms, playing in the St. John's High School Pogo-Stick League is not something you can do out of the sight of the weaker brother.

a. Faced with this situation, what would you do? Give reasons for your answer.

b. Obviously, this is a ridiculous example. Nevertheless, use this example to think through and develop some guiding principles for more serious (and realistic) situations.

WHEN NO ONE SAYS IT'S SIN BUT IT IS!

1. Reread **verses 14** and **23.** If we consider something wrong for ourselves, then it is wrong, even if Scripture does not say it is wrong. Plowing ahead into some action, or partaking of some food or drink, which we just "felt" wrong for ourselves (although no one in authority, not even Scripture forbade it) would be a "sin against the conscience." This is a case where no one says it's a sin, but it is!

Give examples from your own life or from a friend (anonymously, of course!) which illustrate the sin against one's conscience. Discuss whether or not the day may come when this sin may no longer be a sin for a person.

2. Imagine: Mary Jane was raised in a congregation where members frowned upon dancing and called it sin. At the wedding of her sister's friend, Mary Jane was asked to dance. Everyone else, including her sister, danced. When a young man asked Mary Jane to dance with him, she blushed, apologized for her clumsiness, but consented. Later, she felt tremendously guilty about it.

When she asked her sister about it, her sister said, "I don't think dancing is a sin, because I just don't see the Bible calling it that. And I refuse to let others tell me what is and what isn't a sin, based on their own home-grown ideas that do not come from the Bible. But in your case, Sis, if you feel it's wrong, don't do it."

a. Would you agree or disagree with Mary Jane's sister? Give reasons for your answers.

b. Is it possible that a time may come when this "sin" for Mary Jane is no longer a sin? Explain.

c. "If it's not really a sin, how did it become one?" is a question Mary Jane asked her sister. How would you explain to her on the basis of this segment of Romans?

d. Terrible things can happen when we make unnecessary rules and laws where Scripture does not speak. These regulations become burdens on the consciences of others. Would you agree or disagree that these kinds of laws create sin where there is none? Defend your answer.

FREED OR ENSLAVED? THE PARADOXICAL ANSWER

"You can't tell me what to do!" may be a true statement for believers who are exerting their Christian freedoms, but if acting out our freedoms hurts or offends a weak brother, we are not acting out of God's love. On the other hand, we are not faithful to the Gospel if we submit to rule after unnecessary rule and then give the impression that our relationship to God depends upon how well we obey.

Therefore, what are we? We are freed by Christ's perfectly obedient life, suffering, and death from the curse of the Law. We are God's, living under His grace and no longer the Law. Not only can we not become righteous on our own by doing the Law (or rules!), we are not even supposed to try becoming righteous by doing the Law. Paul, writing to the Galatian Christians when they forgot the Gospel and returned to the Law, said, **"I am astonished that you are so quickly deserting the one who called you by the grace of Christ and are turning to a different Gospel"** (Galatians 1:6).

Yet Christ's freed-by-the-Gospel people still desire to act in love towards others. While they do not wish to offend the weaker brother with their Christian liberty, neither do they wish to submit to another form of slavery: to be afraid to do anything, lest it offend the weak.

What's the answer to this dilemma?

Read the following statements from Luther's essay, "The Freedom of the Christian." Note the enormous paradox.

A Christian is a perfectly free lord of all, subject to none.

A Christian is a perfectly dutiful servant of all, subject to all.

1. Compare Luther's paradox with **1 Corinthians 9:19** and **Romans 13:8.** Which statements in the paradox come from which texts?

2. Explain in your own words why both, seemingly contradictory statements, are actually true.

3. How does this paradox help us minister Christ's love to the "weaker brother" while, at the same time, stand on our own Christian freedom? Give some examples how this may work in your own situations, or apply this paradox to the pogo-stick conflict.

LOOKING AHEAD

Read **Romans 15:1–13** before the next session.

For the kingdom of God is not a matter of eating and drinking, but of righteousness, peace and joy in the Holy Spirit.

Romans 14:17

SESSION 42

God-Given Unity

ROMANS 15:1–13

Up to this point Paul has given some very helpful principles governing how the body of Christ is to function together in each local congregation. He has chosen examples of issues that have, at times, divided believers into rival camps—each group believing it has a monopoly on the truth. What examples has he used?

Romans 12:3–8

Romans 14:1–23

In many ways, the various ideas of which Paul writes in **Romans 12–15** might be grouped under the heading "Christian Unity." In these chapters, the apostle answers questions about where this kind of unity comes from, how it is maintained, and what kinds of problems can sever it.

Before going on with today's verses, find the word *unity* in a good dictionary (perhaps an unabridged one). Write out the definitions you find. Which definitions and synonyms come closest to describing your ideas about the unity our Lord wants for His church? Base your choices on what you have read in **Romans 12–14.**

IN THE WORD

Verses 1–7
The Responsibility of the Mature

In any family unit, the adults must act like adults if there is to be any sense of family unity. Likewise, in the church, those who are spiritually stronger or more mature shoulder more of the responsibility for fostering the congregation's oneness in Christ.

Keep in mind the importance our Lord places on this oneness as you think through the following questions based on **verses 1–7.**

1. How does Paul describe the responsibility of the strong in **verses 1–2?** Which words or phrases stand out for you? Why?

2. To what example does Paul point in **verse 3?** What idea does the quotation from **Psalm 69:9** add to Paul's example?

3. From all we've seen in Romans to this point, we know that we cannot drum up inside ourselves the kind of strength and courage we need to carry out the commands Paul has given in the first two verses of this chapter. How, then, will we receive the humility and power we need in our hearts and in our actions to foster unity with other believers? (See **verse 4.**)

4. Reread **verses 5–7,** aloud if possible. When we use the endurance and encouragement given to us by our Lord, what results can we expect?

Verses 8–13
Unity Produced by God

Paul brings his message home to us by reminding us of the role Jesus played in laying the foundation for Christian unity: Christ became a servant so that both Jews and Gentiles might come to know God's mercy and praise Him for it.

1. Paul quotes from **Psalm 18:49; Deuteronomy 32:43; Psalm 117:1;** and **Isaiah 11:10.** What similar thread runs through all these quotations? Why did Paul, inspired by the Holy Spirit, choose these particular verses?

2. Paul concludes his counsel with an exhilarating benediction. The oneness of which he has written will not come through human effort; but as Paul has so often pointed out, we serve a God who specializes in producing the impossible in the hearts and lives of His children. What are the promises and what is the power Paul includes in **verse 13?**

WHEN THE RUBBER MEETS THE ROAD

Perhaps all this talk about unity sounds appealing as we sit in our Christian classroom, isolated from the sticky questions of how to apply the truths to our everyday lives. But what does our Lord's call for unity mean in our relationships with other believers in our school and congregation?

To explore that a bit further, read the situations described below. Talk about them with two or three classmates. Decide what actions you might take that would lead to more *disunity* and what actions you might take to bring increasing *unity.*

Case Study A. You belong to a small but active

youth group at your church. After their confirmation, the new ninth-grade class joins your group for the June meeting. Since last February, you and your friends have been planning a weekend float trip for July. You've carried out several fund-raising projects to get enough money to rent tents and canoes and to buy the other supplies you will need.

As you're putting the final touches on your plans, the freshmen begin to question the activity. It seems they want to spend the money on a day at a nearby amusement park instead. You and your friends have already been there a dozen times. In fact, the president of your group groans, "Oh, come on, you idiots! What a boring suggestion!"

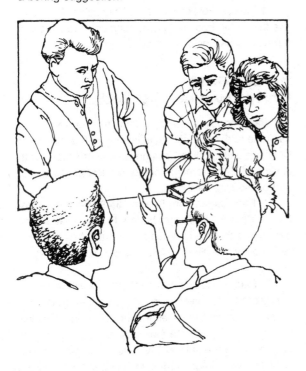

Case Study B. Your high school religion class has developed a series of chancel dramas that you feel will help other young people understand the message of salvation through faith in Jesus. The dramas incorporate some original songs written by the members of your group. The series of brief dramas are set in contemporary situations. You feel positive that they will be meaningful to other teenagers—especially those who are unchurched.

Several congregations have invited your class to give your presentation during one of their Sunday morning worship services. Late Thursday afternoon, just before the weekend of your first scheduled performance, the pastor of the first host congregation calls your director. He has heard that you will be using drums and acoustical guitars in your presentation. He lets your director know, in no uncertain terms, that if this is true, you are no longer welcome.

Your best friend, the main song composer, responds, "Well, that's one less performance we have to give!"

Case Study C. You have followed in Michael's shadow ever since grade school. Everyone looks up to him and admires his "spirituality." He's your class president and heads up the chapel service planning committee for your school. He's also quarterback for the varsity football team and has been in the honor society since your sophomore year. Whenever you get into trouble, it seems, your parents and principal say to you, "Why can't you be more like Michael?"

Now you scarcely believe your eyes! You're taking a trigonometry test and lo and behold: Michael, the perfect, is cheating! "Well, Mr. Perfection," you think, "I've got you now!"

LOOKING AHEAD

Good leadership encourages the kind of unity we've been talking about in this lesson. As you read **Romans 15:14–33,** look for specific leadership qualities Paul stresses:

1. A supportive, encouraging attitude **(verse 14)**
2. A humble emphasis on the Gospel and on God's sanctifying power **(verses 15–21)**
3. Competent leadership that plans ahead **(verses 22–28)**
4. Faithful intercession for God's people and dependence on God's willingness to answer specific prayers **(verses 30–33)**

May the God who gives endurance and encouragement give you a spirit of unity among yourselves as you follow Christ Jesus, so that with one heart and mouth you may glorify the God and Father of our Lord Jesus Christ.

Romans 15:5–6

SESSION 43

Personal Notes

ROMANS 15:14–33

Our last session ended with a striking benediction that sounds suspiciously like the end of a sermon. Paul seems to conclude his major thoughts to the Roman Christians with **chapter 15, verse 13.**

In the remaining portion of the letter Paul writes personal notes to a church he knows only by reputation. Nevertheless, the apostle has felt a deep sense of ministry for them, as demonstrated by this letter, and sincere appreciation for their mature witness.

Paul's epistle to the Romans endures as the outstanding doctrinal statement of the Christian church; but if you skipped all the material between **1:15** and **15:13,** you would read, in essence, a pleasant personal letter full of tender expressions of affection and personal information. In these verses the apostle allows us a rare opportunity to peer into his mind and catch a glimpse of his zeal, his plans, and his dreams. So let's approach this autobiographical passage expecting to learn much from the life of a man so deeply committed to the Lord. Even though it was written long ago, it remains refreshingly relevant for us today.

IN THE WORD
Verses 14–22
Personal Care and Ministry

Paul opens this section with "**I myself am convinced.**" To find out how Paul had developed such a positive concept of a church he had never visited, turn back to **1:8: "I thank my God through Jesus Christ for all of you, because your faith is being reported all over the world."** The apostle had heard about the Roman Christians and their acts of faith. Now, near the end of his letter, he again compliments them on their Christian character.

1. In **verse 14** Paul comments on three characteristics he was confident were present in the Roman Christians because they are commonly found in mature believers. Write a brief paragraph on each of the three and think about their presence or absence in your life:

    a. Full of goodness

    b. Complete in knowledge

    c. Competent to instruct one another

2. Paul now proceeds to another characteristic—one he views as a responsibility for himself and for all believers. What is this "**priestly duty" (verse 16)?** What is your role in carrying out this duty? What is God's role?

3. As an active evangelist, Paul had many achievements. What was his perspective on them? What two things does Paul mention about his accomplishments in **verses 17–18?** Suppose God moves you to follow Paul's example. How will you react after your achievements?

4. As an aging evangelist, Paul could have been content to rest on his achievements and do the things he had been unable to do, such as visit Rome **(verse 22).** In fact, he states that he fully proclaimed the gospel of Christ from Jerusalem to Illyricum **(verse 19).** If the apostle had been referring to the United States, he could have communicated the same idea by saying he had evangelized every state east of the Mississippi. What motivated Paul to be such a prolific missionary **(verses 20–21)?**

Verses 23–29
Personal Planning

Not only was Paul not planning to retire, he was enthusiastically considering a missionary endeavor four times as long as anything attempted before.

1. As you think about Paul's zeal and optimism, also consider our own commitment to the spread of the Gospel. Spend a few minutes thinking about your future. Have you talked to the Lord about it? What concrete plans do you have for contributing to the expansion of God's kingdom?

2. If this is a new line of thought for you, compose a prayer asking God to give you a missionary heart.

3. Someone has said that there are only two kinds of human beings—missionaries and mission fields. Do you agree? If so, how does that truth affect you?

Verses 30–32
Personal Prayer

1. Paul was very aware of the difficulties facing him both in Jerusalem and on his proposed trip to Rome

and Spain. He does a very wise thing. He asks for prayer support. What does Paul's request teach you about prayer?

2. Think for a few minutes about your prayer life:

a. List items you could place on a prayer list. Think of yourself, but also think of your family, your classmates, your school, your congregation, etc.

b. Discuss your prayer list items with others in your class. After hearing their ideas, consider adding items to your list. Perhaps you will also want to delete some items.

c. Next, divide the items into groups. Many people, for example, prepare one list for Mondays, another for Tuesdays, etc. If you prepare a weekly plan, be sure to decide how many days per week you will use your prayer lists. Some people prefer to have only five lists, and others use six or seven.

LOOKING AHEAD

As you read **Romans 16** for your next class, look carefully at the three areas with which the apostle chooses to finish his letter:

1. His loving concern for people **(verses 1–16)**

2. His awareness of the potential for problems **(verses 17– 20)**

3. His always giving the glory to God **(verses 18–27)**

I glory in Christ Jesus in my service to God. I will not venture to speak of anything except what Christ has accomplished through me in leading Gentiles to obey God by what I have said and done.
Romans 15:17–18

SESSION 44

Warm Regards and a Strong Warning

ROMANS 16

How do people in your congregation greet one another? If it's a typical American church, nothing more than a nod or hand motion accompanies a word of greeting. Touching, primarily with a handshake, occurs in other churches. Our society tends to frown upon stronger displays of affection, such as a hug or a kiss, though this practice is common in a few churches.

Romans 16 says a lot about Christians showing affection for one another. Readers are tempted to skim over this chapter, particularly the first 16 verses. At first glance we do not think these verses contain much of spiritual value, but as Paul told Timothy, **"All Scripture is God-breathed [inspired] and is useful" (2 Timothy 3:16a).** God has seen fit to inspire this example of Paul's devotion to fellow believers; so let's see what pearls of wisdom the Lord has in store for us!

IN THE WORD

Verses 1–16
Greet One Another

As you read over these verses, you can begin to feel the sort of affection that existed, and still can exist, among brothers and sisters in Christ. Although Paul had never visited the Roman church, he had a remarkably large number of friends there. He mentions 27 people by name. The fact that Paul remembered all of these individuals implies that he cared deeply about them.

Paul does more than just remember names of people he had met. In many cases he mentions acts of service and love they had performed within the body of Christ. Paul also records 21 titles (such as "sister," "fellow workers in Christ," "beloved," and "fellow prisoners"), and 19 times he makes a reference to greeting or commending a person. In short, these are people who have made a difference, and they live in Paul's memory.

1. Paul concludes this section with the directive to **"Greet one another with a holy kiss" (verse 16a).** Do you think this is still a good idea? Does a physical display of affection demonstrate a healthy caring attitude? What would happen if members of your class (including your teacher) would hug one another? Someone has said that as we grow in the Word we also grow together in the Word and that hugging is the most natural reaction we have to all this growing. Do you agree? Talk about these questions. Include discussion about other ways we can express our love for other Christians.

2. Write a paragraph to tell how each of the following directives from Paul applies to you:
   a. Accept one another's differences.
   b. Be willing to become a servant of others.
   c. Demonstrate your love to one another.

Verses 17–20
Look Out for Troublemakers

Whenever the love of Christ is alive and active among His people, Satan immediately begins to sow

seeds of dissension. So it is very appropriate that Paul injects a warning against false teachers in the middle of this last chapter.

Maybe this was already happening in the Roman church, or maybe Paul is just giving them a timely warning. That question, however, makes little difference. The fact is that this was an all-too-common experience in the early church **(Acts 14:26–15:35)**, and it still happens today. This very problem prompted Paul's letters to the Galatians and the Corinthians.

1. Let's assume that trouble was brewing in the church at Rome and see what Paul was concerned about. Answer the following questions:

    a. What was happening **(verse 17)?**

    b. Why was it happening **(verse 18)?**

    c. How was it to be handled **(verses 17–18)?**

    d. How could it be overcome **(verse 19)?**

2. Paul warns about those who cause divisions and put obstacles in our way that are contrary to the teaching we have learned. They use smooth talk and flattery to deceive us. Give examples of those kinds of individuals or groups in today's world.

3. Paul advises, **"Keep away from them"** (verse 17b). How can you follow that advice?

Verses 21–27
To God Be Glory Forever

1. Paul appropriately ends this landmark document of the Christian faith with a doxology to the grace and glory of God. It contains significant truths about God.

Let's pull together all that we have learned and focus on this great passage of praise. The largest portion of this benediction concentrates on five truths concerning God and His plan for humanity. Think about them and write down your thoughts as you contemplate the eternal God. He

    a. establishes us by the Gospel **(verse 25);**

    b. proclaims the mystery of Jesus **(verses 25–26);**

    c. makes His will known to the nations **(verse 26);**

    d. produces faith and obedience **(verse 26);**

    e. receives glory through Jesus **(verse 27).**

2. Which of the above truths means the most to you? Why?

The epistle ends with the word *Amen.* "Amen" expresses the deep conviction of every true believer that this is most certainly true. It is an expression of faith in our God and the truth of His eternal Word. May you believe it, too! Amen.

LOOKING AHEAD

Skim **Romans 12–16** in preparation for next time's review and unit evaluation.

Now to Him who is able to establish you by my gospel and the proclamation of Jesus Christ, according to the revelation of the mystery hidden for long ages past, but now revealed and made known through the prophetic writings by the command of the eternal God, so that all nations might believe and obey Him—to the only wise God be glory forever through Jesus Christ! Amen!

Romans 16:25–27

SESSION 45

Concluding Activities for Unit 4

In this unit we have examined the last major section of Romans. You have examined not only the factual knowledge but also the practicalities of relating our faith to our own lives and the lives of others. As has been our custom during our study of Romans, we will use this final session to review and condense what we have learned.

1. Use your Bible, this lesson guide, and your own class notes to guide you as you write down what you believe to be the central truth for each of the eleven sessions in this unit.

34. Therefore . . . , **Romans 12:1–2**
35. Evaluate and Activate, **Romans 12:3–8**
36. Love, the Real Thing, **Romans 12:9–13**
37. Good Swallows Evil, **Romans 12:14–21**
38. Citizenship, **Romans 13:1–7**
39. Wake Up, **Romans 12:8–14**
40. The "Weaker Brother," **Romans 14:1–12**
41. The "Stronger Brother," **Romans 14:13–23**
42. God-Given Unity, **Romans 15:1–13**
43. Personal Notes, **Romans 15:14–33**
44. Warm Regards and a Strong Warning, **Romans 16**

2. Now change your focus from central truth to personal application. Page through the material of this unit and jot down the most memorable application you discovered in each lesson.

UNIT 5

Faith Battles Pride

FIRST CORINTHIANS 1–11

"We're number one!"
"When you've got it, flaunt it."
"Sometimes I'm so good, it's scary."

Human pride has been around a long time. We recognize it immediately by its air of superiority and its arrogant mannerism. Like the proverbial rooster with its head held high, it struts and swaggers as if on parade. No wonder people with inflated egos turn us off. They're really trying to put us down.

It's easy for Christians to talk about the way human pride infects non-Christians. But Christians, too, struggle with this problem of pride. If you look closely, you will see that pride is behind most of the problems we deal with in the church. Such things as spiritual boasting, quarreling among members, and loveless behavior are symptoms of the pride that lurks in Christian hearts.

Are you surprised that the church often limps along like a cripple instead of victoriously running the race of faith? You shouldn't be. *All* of us struggle with the heart problem of pride.

In this unit we will be examining some of the major problems God's church faces because of human pride. We will also discover how God comes to rescue His church. He shares with us the healing love of Jesus Christ and empowers us to run the great race of faith.

SESSION 46

When Christians Quarrel

FIRST CORINTHIANS 1:10–17

"Who does she think she is, bossing everyone around like she does? I'd like to tell her a thing or two."

"This was a nice church until he joined it. He ought to take his weird ideas and go somewhere else."

"I'm not going back to church until she apologizes. She's nothing but a troublemaker."

Do statements like these sound familiar? Life in the church is not all harmony and unity. Sometimes the church resembles a battleground with quarreling factions hurling barbs of criticism at each other. Fellow members refuse to speak to each other. Feelings are hurt. Tempers flare up. In such a situation, spiritual growth may slow to a snail's pace.

Maybe you have experienced some of these disagreements in your own group of Christian believers. Do you remember how you felt? How did you react? How did this affect your spiritual life?

Why do you suppose believers in Christ bicker and quarrel? This is not a topic we should hide under the carpet and pretend that it does not exist. Let's come to terms with it and discover God's solution to our human failings in the church.

DISSENSION IN THE CHURCH AT CORINTH

1. Look carefully at a problem in a congregation of the early church. The apostle Paul was upset with the behavior of the Corinthian Christians. Read **1:10–17** and discuss the following questions:

a. Describe the unloving manner in which the Corinthians were behaving **(verses 11–12)**. What do you suppose they were saying to each other?

b. Identify the various factions in the Corinthian church **(verse 12)**. Why do you think the members were choosing different spiritual leaders to follow? Is this still a problem in the modern church? Explain.

c. How were the Corinthians distorting the meaning of Holy Baptism by the divisions in their church **(verses 13–17)?** What does Baptism mean in terms of our fellowship with other Christians (see **Galatians 3:26–28**)? Why was Paul thankful he did not baptize many of the Corinthians?

d. Read the important passage in **1 Corinthians 3:1–4** in which Paul tells the Corinthians that they are behaving like "infants" because of their pride. Then discuss this question: *Why are fighting and quarreling marks of spiritual immaturity, signs that we need to "grow up" spiritually?*

2. The apostle reminded the Corinthians of the *unity* Christ gives to His church. He pointed these quarrelsome Christians to a higher calling. Read **1:10**.

a. Why do you suppose Paul made his appeal "in the name of our Lord Jesus Christ"? Describe what Christ means to genuine Christian fellowship. How *should* members of Christian congregations behave toward each other?

b. What does it mean to "be perfectly united in mind and thought"? Debate: Christians can never disagree with one another.

c. Look at **verses 5–9**. What spiritual truths do you find here that clearly state how Christ gives the church the power to remain a strong, unified fellowship?

d. Examine **verse 17**. In what ways are Paul's words to the Corinthians more than a simple "pep talk" to patch up their differences? Why is Christ's power so essential to Christian unity?

AM I A PART OF THE CHURCH'S PROBLEM?
A SELF-DISCOVERY EXERCISE

To help you find out what areas of your Christian behavior may need improvement, rank yourself from 1 to 5 in the following categories of unloving behavior (5 means that this is a big problem in your life; 1 means that this is not a big problem for you). Be honest and candid. You don't have to share your findings with anyone else.

Argumentiveness. I like things to go my own way, and I get angry if they don't. I don't like to give in to opinions of others.

Exclusiveness. I spend most of my time with my special friends. I never have fellowship with anyone in the church except my own group.

Neglectfulness. I am only concerned about my own problems, not the problems of other Christians. I

take care of myself and let them take care of themselves.

a. Reflect a moment about that area of unloving behavior in which you scored your highest mark. Ask yourself, "Why am I keeping God's church from the unity Christ desires?" Share your thoughts with God and tell Him how you feel. Also ask Him to forgive you your unloving behavior. Remember, He restores you in the grace of Jesus Christ (see **Psalm 51:7**).

b. Jot down a couple of ways you can improve the unity of God's church by changing your behavior.

HIS LOVE MAKES US WHOLE AND COMPLETE

1. Here's some Good News! Christ's love can heal the broken relationships we have through our pride. He empowers us to build bridges of friendship to those we have alienated. Read **Ephesians 4:29–32.** Discuss with one another some concrete ways to put His love to work.

2. Is there a fellow Christian with whom you are not on speaking terms? What do you suppose Christ's love is urging you to do? How would you go about doing this?

3. Suppose a couple of your classmates, once very close friends, have had a serious misunderstanding and now avoid each other. Their squabble is ruining the fellowship in your youth group. On the basis of this lesson, what strategy would you use to mend this broken relationship?

4. Rosita has recently joined your church but cannot seem to be accepted by the youth because of her ethnic background. Suggest a Christ-like way to include her in the fellowship of God's baptized people.

5. Share with your classmates a personal experience of how Christ's healing love changed an antagonistic relationship into an harmonious one.

A PRAYER TO PRAY TODAY

Show me Your way, O Lord. Fill me with Your love so I can be the Christian person You want me to be. Help me to contribute to the unity of Your church by being an example of compassion and kindness. In the name of Jesus, who died that His church might be holy and righteous. Amen.

Blest be the tie that binds
Our hearts in Christian love;
The unity of heart and mind
Is like to that above.

From sorrow, toil, and pain
And sin we shall be free,
And perfect love and friendship reign
Through all eternity.

Lutheran Worship 295:1, 4

I appeal to you, brothers, in the name of our Lord Jesus Christ, that all of you agree with one another so that there may be no divisions among you and that you may be perfectly united in mind and thought.

1 Corinthians 1:10

SESSION 47

Trying to Be Wiser Than God

FIRST CORINTHIANS 1:18–2:5

If you ever visit the United Nations building in New York City, you will discover a small chapel set apart for meditation. The chapel itself is unpretentious, actually only a tiny room. But the decorations inside the room soon catch your eye. There are only curtained walls, a potted plant . . . and silence.

This is a chapel dedicated to all the nations of the world. However, there is no cross, no statue of any kind, and nothing at all to remind you of the world of the spirit. The authorities of the United Nations believed that placing a religious symbol in the chapel might offend people of other religions; it might even offend those who were atheistic. So they decided to build a chapel in which no one would be offended. They built a room with curtained walls, a potted plant . . . and silence.

Spend a few minutes thinking about what you just read. Discuss with your classmates the following questions.

- What impressions would this chapel at the United Nations give you of the power and majesty of God? Would you feel "turned on" by meditating here to the God who is in control of the world?
- What could you discover in this chapel about God's great love and concern for you? about your salvation in Christ?
- What does such a chapel say about human efforts to define God in terms that will please everybody? Is it possible to have a religion that will be completely inoffensive?

CAN HUMAN PHILOSOPHY LEAD US TO GOD?

1. The church at Corinth was struggling over a similar problem. Many of the members were ashamed of the *cross* of Jesus Christ. They wanted a Christ who appealed to their interest in philosophy and matters of the mind, not a Christ who died on the cross for their sins. For them the cross symbolized weakness, shame, and contempt. So they tried to "correct" the Christian faith. They turned Jesus into a great moral philosopher who simply died for His teachings.

By changing the meaning of the cross, the Corinthians were emptying the cross of all its spiritual power. They did what many have tried to do since—*"tried to be wiser than God!"* In trying to *avoid* foolishness, how did the Corinthians become foolish?

2. Let's look more carefully at the situation at Corinth and understand this important topic.

a. Read **verses 18, 23,** and **25.** What word describes how the Corinthians felt about the Gospel message of Christ's death on the cross? Have you met people who share this same view? What was your response to them?

b. In contrast, what does Paul say about the message of the cross **(verses 18, 23–24)?** What blessings do all believers in Jesus Christ receive because of His death on the cross? (Compare **Romans 1:16**.)

c. Why do you suppose so many people are offended at God's way of salvation? What are they lacking in their lives? See **1 Corinthians 2:13–14.** Discuss the necessity of the Holy Spirit and faith in Jesus Christ.

d. Notice how the Corinthians sought after wisdom and philosophy as the way to God **(verses 20–25).** Can you give examples of people today who believe that salvation is only a matter of living by moral principles, "right living," the Golden Rule, and the like? Share your thoughts on this.

e. What is God's opinion of those people who think that they are wiser than God, who substitute human philosophy for the salvation won for us on the cross? See **verses 18–19.** How would you present the Gospel message to them?

f. Examine **verse 25.** Then reflect on this question: Can human philosophy lead us to God? Give a reason for your answer.

THE WAY TO GOD THE CRUCIFIED CHRIST

1. The apostle presents the matter of salvation in terms of a road going in two opposite directions. Look at **verse 18.** Describe the two directions of the road and where each is leading. How do those who are being saved view the message of the cross?

2. Examine **verses 23–24.** How *important* does

Paul make the message of the crucified Christ? Would you say he makes it very important? important? somewhat important? not very important? Explain your answer.

3. Notice how God's plan of salvation makes use of the things the world considers "weak" and "foolish" **(verses 26–28).** Can you think of what Paul might be referring to? Discuss this point and share your thoughts.

4. Look at **verses 28–31.** Why did God deliberately choose the weak and lowly rather than the strong and mighty in His plan to save the world? What statement was God making about human philosophy and human wisdom?

5. In whom only do believers in Jesus Christ *boast* in regard to their eternal salvation? (See **verse 30.**) Give a reason for your answer.

SHARING GOD'S PLAN OF SALVATION WITH OTHERS

1. After examining **1 Corinthians 2:1–5,** try to understand how the apostle Paul presented the Gospel to unbelievers. See if you can identify Paul's approach. How does Paul *not* attempt to convince unbelievers about the claims of Jesus Christ? What approach does he use?

2. Why does God always bless the simple but powerful preaching of Jesus Christ crucified for our sins? What is in the Gospel that is so persuasive?

3. What is your opinion? Should Christians use their intelligence when speaking to others about Christ or should they not? (Paul himself was a very intelligent man, a Ph.D. in his day.) Explain Paul's statement, **"I did not come proclaiming to you the testimony of God in lofty words or wisdom" (1 Corinthians 2:1 RSV).** Discuss this important point.

4. Suppose you were in a discussion with a friend who was seeking after God. Your friend said she wants to find a religion that really challenges her mind. How would you answer her?

5. Many people today believe that science supplies us with all the answers to the problems of life. Some even arrogantly say that science has made God unnecessary. How would you respond to such mockers of the Christian faith? Do some scientists believe in Christ? Can a person be both a scientist *and* a Christian? Explain.

6. Share with members of the class a personal experience in which a friend or acquaintance became a Christian through the preaching of the Gospel.

In the cross of Christ I glory,
Tow'ring o'er the wrecks of time.
All the light of sacred story
Gathers round its head sublime.

When the woes of life o'ertake me,
Hopes deceive, and fears annoy,
Never shall the cross forsake me;
Lo, it glows with peace and joy.
Lutheran Worship, 101:1–2

I resolved to know nothing while I was with you except Jesus Christ and Him crucified.
1 Corinthians 2:2

SESSION 48

The Pleasure Principle

FIRST CORINTHIANS 6:1–20

"Why can't I do what I want? It's my life!"

"You live by your rules, and I'll live by mine. Don't tell me what to do."

"Eat, drink, and be merry. Tomrrow we may be dead."

We have all heard statements like these. They express the pleasure principle of the human race. Sigmund Freud, a famous psychologist, believed that each of us possesses strong impulses to do the things that give us pleasure. He called this the pleasure principle. Freud also said, however, that our parents and society in general prohibit us from doing the things we desire most. They give us rules and guidelines that govern our behavior. Freud called this the reality principle.

What do you suppose life would be like if everyone pursued the pleasure principle? Would we live like lustful animals?

What if no reality principle monitored human behavior? Would social life be possible at all? Would life have any purpose or meaning?

Our lesson today discusses the theme of an abundant and meaningful life designed by God to give us maximum pleasure. But let's be honest! Sometimes we want to follow our own pleasure principle rather than God's well-designed plan. That's when God has to remind us of who we are and what a great new life He has planned for us.

FOLLOWING THE WORLD'S PLEASURE PRINCIPLE

1. Many members of the Corinthian church had adopted a strange understanding of the Christian faith. They believed that they could serve Christ in their minds, but they also could do anything with their bodies that they pleased. They felt that they had absolute freedom to live life on their own terms. Read **verses 1–18.**

a. Notice the clever pleasure principle the Corinthians had devised (**"Everything is permissible for me"—verse 12**). Compare **10:23–24** for another reference to the same principle.

b. Study **verse 13.** In what two activities in particular did the Corinthians believe they had absolute free-

dom to do anything they pleased? (See also **10:23–30.**)

c. The Corinthian pleasure principle was really a license to sin. What are some other pleasure principles that people use to rationalize their behavior? Try adding to the list of popular sayings that follows. (Talk about this with your classmates. Do we rationalize sin?)

"But everybody's doing it."

"Enjoy yourself; it's later than you think."

"I live only for number one."

d. How does Paul make it clear to the Corinthians that their behavior is offensive to God and to the high standards of their calling in Jesus Christ (**verses 9–10**)?

e. What has Christ done to deliver us from a lifestyle that is dominated by human sin and a lust for personal pleasure (**verse 11**)? What special meaning does the word *washed* have for you?

2. The pleasure principle causes a tragic consequence: people become loveless toward one another. Notice the behavior of the Corinthians. They were engaging in lawsuits against fellow believers. Study **verses 1–8.**

a. In what way is taking a fellow Christian to court creating a scandal to the Christian Gospel (**verses 1 and 6**)?

b. How should Christians attempt to resolve the differences they have with one another (**verses 2–5**)?

c. Why is it better to be wronged than to sue a fellow Christian in a court of law (**verses 7–8**)?

3. Another scandalous consequence of the Corinthian pleasure principle was their involvement in sexual promiscuity, especially with prostitutes. Study **verses 13–18.**

a. What does Paul mean when he says that the body was not made for sexual immorality but for the Lord (**verse 13**)? How are we treating our bodies when we engage in sexual sins (**verse 18**)?

b. Explain how the dignity with which we treat our bodies today is related to the future resurrection of our bodies (**verse 14**).

c. In what way is sexual union with another person the same thing as marrying that person (**verses 15–**

16)?** Why is this more than a simply momentary pleasure?

d. Our society today is saturated with sexual activity and general sexual permissiveness. How does **verse 17** give you a higher view of how we should use the bodies God has given us?

e. Discuss the topic of pornography with your classmates. Do you feel that the government should make laws restricting the type of sexually explicit materials sold to the public? Defend your opinion.

FOLLOWING GOD'S PLEASURE PRINCIPLE

1. Here's good news! God has designed our bodies for pleasure—Pleasure with a capital P. It's a design that allows us to use our bodies for a high and holy purpose. When the Holy Spirit leads us, we are able to feel good about our bodies. What is more, we can use them as God originally intended. Read **verses 19–20.**

a. **Verse 19** states that your body is a temple of the Holy Spirit. Share with one another what this means. How does the presence of the Holy Spirit influence the way you treat your body?

b. Explain this important truth: We do not own ourselves; Christ owns us! What has Jesus done to make a claim on everything we are—our bodies, our minds, and our spirits **(verses 19–20)?**

c. Why is it true that you can feel good about your body? From what has Christ freed you so that your body now counts for something important?

2. God's pleasure principle leads us to use our bodies for a high and productive purpose. Because of Christ we can now honor God with our bodies **(verse 20).** List some ways God could make maximum use of your body.

3. A very important way to honor God with our bodies is to take care of our bodies. Look at the examples below. Suggest some God-pleasing ways a Christian might respond to these examples:

—drugs	—stress
—smoking	—not feeling well
—obesity	—being out of shape
—driving a car	—alcohol

4. When we use our bodies in ways that honor God, we often feel good. Our bodies have a way of telling us that they like being treated well. What would be a suitable Christian response you might make to God if your body felt super?

Take my life, O Lord, renew,
Consecrate my heart to you;
Take my moments and my days;
Let them sing your ceaseless praise.

Take my hands and let them do
Works that show my love for you;
Take my feet and lead their way,
Never let them go astray.

Take my love; my Lord, I pour
At your feet its treasure store;
Take myself, Lord, let me be
Yours alone eternally.

Lutheran Worship, 404:1, 2, 6

Do not be deceived: Neither the sexually immoral nor idolaters nor adulterers nor male prostitutes nor homosexual offenders nor thieves nor the greedy nor drunkards nor slanderers nor swindlers will inherit the kingdom of God. And that is what some of you were. But you were washed, you were sanctified, you were justified in the name of the Lord Jesus Christ and by the Spirit of our God.

1 Corinthians 6:9b–11

SESSION 49

To Marry or Not to Marry

FIRST CORINTHIANS 7:1—41

Some high school students found themselves in a heated debate about marriage. Mrs. Carver, their sociology teacher, had just informed them that remaining single had become a popular option among many modern young adults. She mentioned that young adults are not only delaying marriage; many are choosing lifelong singlehood.

Sheila and Tom were opponents in the debate. "Marriage is the normal way to live," Sheila claimed. "Staying single is selfish and abnormal. Besides, how would any children be born if everyone remained single?"

"You're wrong," countered Tom. "Staying single will allow me the time to get a lot more worthwhile things done in my life than if I had to worry about a family."

Sheila: "But what about love and romance?"

Tom: "St. Paul wasn't married, and who knew more about love than he?"

No one won the debate, although team members made good arguments for both points of view. How do you feel about the subject? Share some opinions before we examine the Scriptural teaching about marriage and singleness.

MARRIAGE AS GOD'S CALLING

1. Marriage is a *gift* of God just as singleness is God's gift. Read **verse 7.** How does Paul express this truth?

a. What meaning does it have for you that God calls some of us to be married and some of us to remain single?

b. Do you feel our American culture pressures men and women to become married whether they have this gift or not? If so, in what ways? Discuss this point.

c. Why is it unloving for married people or those who intend to marry to judge those who don't become married? See **Matthew 7:7.**

2. Sexual desires for members of the opposite sex find their natural fulfillment in marriage. Read **1 Corinthians 7:2, 8–9.** What do these passages say about the person with strong sexual desires?

a. Study **Hebrews 13:4.** What does this passage tell us about our God-given sexual desires and fulfilling them in marriage?

b. On the other hand, what does God tell us about fulfilling our sexual desires outside of marriage? See **1 Corinthians 6:18.**

c. Many couples today are cohabiting rather than becoming married. Should this be tolerated as an acceptable life-style in the modern world? Explain your answer.

3. In God's design for marriage, we are to give lovingly of ourselves to our marriage partner. Read **verses 3–5.** Discuss what Paul says here about the duties and expectations of marriage.

a. Why do you suppose the emphasis here is on *self-giving* rather than on *personal rights*? Is there a difference? Explain.

b. What do **verses 10–11** tell us about marriage being a lifelong commitment? Should all marriages be for life? How does God feel about divorce? (Compare **Matthew 19:3–12.**)

c. Discuss this statement: *If a person does not intend to commit himself or herself to the other person for life, he or she ought not to become married.*

d. Suppose you were to fall in love and marry the person of your dreams. In what ways would you be honoring God by this calling of marriage?

4. Should a Christian marry a non-Christian? (This was a weighty problem in Paul's day. It still is today.) Look at **verses 12–16** and reflect on these questions.

a. What spiritual benefits does the nonbeliever receive when married to the Christian? What about the children of such a mixed marriage? Do they receive spiritual benefits as well?

b. On the other hand, what are the potential problems of a mixed marriage? Try to picture how difficult such a marriage might be.

c. Do you believe it is preferable to marry a Christian? If so, why? See **verse 39.**

d. Why is it wise for every Christian to insist on premarital counseling before becoming married?

SINGLENESS AS GOD'S CALLING

1. Remaining single is also a gift of God. Singleness, like marriage, is honorable, and many Christians

pursue this life-style as a calling of God. Examine **verses 7, 8, 17,** and **40.**

a. What does Paul say here about his preference to remain single rather than becoming married?

b. What does Jesus say about the desirability of remaining single? See **Matthew 19:10–11.**

2. Let's look at some of the benefits of being a single person in a society in which most people become married:

a. Read **verse 28.** What "troubles" of the married life do you suppose single people are spared?

b. Read **verses 32–35.** Paul mentions some distractions to the service of God that married people must endure but which single people are spared. What are some of those distractions?

c. Do you think single people are mostly lonely and depressed? Do you think some spend as much time with other people as those who are married? How might they use this time in God-pleasing ways?

d. Is every person gifted with the capacity to be a good husband? a good wife? a good father? a good mother? If a person does not believe he or she has the qualities for married life, should the person be encouraged to remain single? Why or why not?

e. If you were single rather than married, how could you give more of yourself to the Lord's work? List some examples of how you might spend your time.

f. Picture yourself working as a missionary in another culture. What would be most advantageous, to be single or to be married? Why?

THINKING ABOUT MY LIFE'S DECISION

1. At this moment in your life, do you feel God is calling you to become married or to remain single? Write down the reasons why you feel the way you do.

2. Think of the *vocation* you might want to pursue during your lifetime. What are the advantages of pur-

suing this vocation as a married person? as a single person?

3. Suppose you are strongly attracted to becoming married but prefer not to have children. Discuss this possibility in view of your desire to serve God with the full commitment of your life.

4. Write a prayer asking God to make your life a blessing to the world whether as a married person or as a single person.

> Let us ever walk with Jesus,
> Follow his example pure,
> Through a world that would deceive us
> And to sin our spirits lure.
> Onward in his footsteps treading,
> Pilgrims here, our home above,
> Full of faith and hope and love,
> Let us do our Father's bidding.
> Faithful Lord, with me abide;
> I shall follow where you guide.
>
> *Lutheran Worship,* 381:1

(From *Lutheran Book of Worship,* copyright © 1978. Concordia Publishing House representing the publishers and copyright holders. Used by permission.)

You were bought at a price; do not become slaves of men.

1 Corinthians 7:23

SESSION 50

When Temptation Strikes

FIRST CORINTHIANS 10:1–13

"Should I or shouldn't I?"

"Do you think anyone will find out?"

"I really shouldn't do this, but . . . ."

All of us have experienced the pangs of temptation, perhaps more than we care to remember. At the time we were swayed back and forth. But later on we regretted the decision that led us to do what we really knew was wrong.

Our lesson today focuses on the problem of temptation. Now's your chance to talk about some of the most important decisions that face you as a Christian.

Try the following exercise as a way of getting started. Tell whether each statement is true or false. Be prepared to give a reason for your answer. Then share your opinions with your classmates:

1. Teenagers face more temptations than adults.

2. The most dangerous temptations are physical ones, such as alcohol, drugs, and sex.

3. It is impossible for a strong Christian to fall into temptation.

No doubt you have concluded that there is a lot to learn about this subject. God has some important truths to share with us today—the manner in which temptation comes, the heart attitude that is susceptible to it, and the spiritual resources we have available to overcome it.

The church at Corinth provides a good setting to use to discuss these truths. Let's examine how these Christians dealt with the problem. Then we will look more closely at temptation in our own lives.

PRIDE COMES BEFORE THE FALL

1. By now you are aware that the Corinthian church was a "proud" church, one whose members were infected with sinful pride and arrogance. Paul writes like a pastor to these proud Christians and warns them of the temptations to sin that result from pride.

a. Look at **verses 11–12.** These are key passages. What does Paul warn the Corinthians to be careful about?

b. Has anyone close to you (for example, a father or mother) warned you about something that could happen unless you changed your attitude? If so, what was it? What was your response to this warning?

c. Why do you suppose "proud" people are particularly open to temptation? What attitude makes them such easy victims to the power of temptation?

d. Have you heard this old saying: "The bigger the ego, the greater the fall"? Talk about it.

2. Paul teaches the Corinthians a vivid lesson about another "proud" people who were undone by temptation. He gives them the example of the children of Israel, who tested God severely in the journey through the wilderness. Examine **verses 1–12.**

a. The Israelites were the covenant people of God, His chosen nation. What do you think the "cloud" and the "sea" refer to in **verses 1–2.** (Consult **Exodus 13:21–22** and **14:10–31.**)

b. See **verses 3–4.** God supplied the Israelites with *food* (**Exodus 16:13–15**) and *water* (**17:1–7**). He especially provided them with His spiritual blessing and divine presence. In what way can it be said that Christ Himself was with them on their journey **(verse 4)?**

c. Look at **verses 5–6.** What terrible tragedy happened to God's chosen people? Note the point Paul is making: *if God's special people fell into temptation, it can happen to Christians as well.* Talk about this important truth.

d. Notice how the Israelites tested God with proud and rebellious behavior **(verses 7–10).** Describe some of their sinful activities. How did God judge these proud people? (Compare **Hebrews 3:16–19.**)

e. Does God tempt us to sin against Him? What important truth do you learn from **James 1:13–15?**

f. Examine **verses 11–12.** What lesson does Paul intend for the Corinthians to learn from the example of the Israelites?

UNDERSTANDING TEMPTATION

1. Temptation is a common human occurrence. It happens to all of us, male and female, rich and poor, godly and ungodly. To be tempted is a sign of our common human experience in the world of sin.

a. Read **verse 13.** How does Paul explain temptation's universal occurrence?

b. Does it help you to know that the temptations you face are those faced by other people as well? Explain your answer.

c. Even Jesus was tempted. See **Hebrews 4:14–15** (and **Luke 4:1–13**). What comfort do you receive from knowing that Jesus endured the same temptations you endure?

d. How did Jesus deal with temptation? Why was it necessary for our salvation that He successfully overcome all temptations to sin?

2. **A self-discovery exercise.** Examine the various types of temptations listed below. Rank them in order according to the severity of their influence in your own life:

- temptations of the flesh (sex, drugs, alcohol, food)
- temptations of worldly pride (money, clothing, possessions)
- temptations of the mind or emotions (anger, moodiness, self-pity)
- temptations of the spirit (despair; denial of God's love and goodness)

a. Discuss these temptations with your classmates. Which type of temptation (if any) is more severely felt by teenagers? by young people? by middle-aged people? by older people?

b. What truths about temptation did you learn from this exercise?

DEALING WITH TEMPTATION

1. God promises to come to our aid when temptation strikes. *He assures us that we will not fall into temptation if we depend on His grace.* Look again at **verse 13.** What two promises does God make to us?

2. Are there temptations so severe that, even with God's help, you could not stand up against them? Explain your answer.

3. Explain how God provides "a way out" when temptation comes. Give some examples. You might compare **Luke 22:46** and **Philippians 4:6–7.**

4. Examine **Ephesians 6:10–18.** What spiritual resource is especially mentioned in this passage to help us overcome temptation?

5. Suppose by God's grace you have resisted a particular temptation. One of your friends tried to resist but eventually fell to the same temptation. What should be your attitude towards that friend?

6. Share with members of the class the most important truth about temptation that you learned in this lesson.

> Lead not into temptation, Lord,
> Where our grim foe and all his horde
> Would vex our souls on ev'ry hand.
> Help us resist, help us to stand
> Firm in the faith, armed with Your might;
> Your Spirit gives your children light.
>
> *Lutheran Worship,* 431:7

(Copyright 1980 Concordia Publishing House. Used by permission.)

God is our Refuge and Strength, an ever-present Help in trouble. Therefore we will not fear, though the earth give way and the mountains fall into the heart of the sea .... The Lord Almighty is with us; the God of Jacob is our Fortress.

Psalm 46:1–2, 7

SESSION 51

Worship That Does More Harm than Good

FIRST CORINTHIANS 11:17–34

Imagine the surprise of the congregation when they read the pastor's sermon topic for that Sunday. The bulletin announcement said in large, bold letters: "THE DANGER OF GOING TO CHURCH."

Some of the members were upset and fidgety. "How can going to church be *dangerous?*" whispered one woman to her friend. "I thought going to church was always a blessing to us."

"Well, that sermon topic sure got my attention," came the reply. "By the way, did you see that family that just walked into church? They look like they just got off the boat."

"Quiet!" said a voice from the pew behind them.

"Maybe we had better wait and hear what the pastor has to say," concluded the first woman.

That Sunday the pastor preached about a topic that relates to our lesson today. He asked the congregation to examine their worship attitudes as they came into the house of God. He challenged them to think about these questions: *Are there times when God is displeased with our attitudes when we worship? Are there times when our worship does us more harm than good?*

What is your reaction to these questions? Have you ever thought about what God sees when you come to church? What would you consider to be the "danger zone" in Christian worship?

Let's examine this important truth and grow in our understanding of worship that truly honors God. Let's also find out how worship can be a blessing to our faith and to our fellowship with other believers.

THE DANGER OF GOING TO CHURCH

1. Look briefly at these two examples of church-going. Notice how God is quite disturbed at the manner in which these people worship.

a. **Isaiah 1:11–17.** How are these worshipers making a mockery of God's temple? In what ways could such behavior take place in the modern church?

b. **Luke 18:9–14.** What is wrong with the Pharisee's prayer? How does our attitude toward other people affect our worship of God?

2. The church-going behavior of the Corinthians was especially disturbing to God. Read **verses 17–22.** Then discuss these questions.

a. What do you suppose these people were doing when they came to church **(verses 17–19)?** Describe in your own words their loveless behavior toward others in the congregation.

b. Notice the behavior of the Corinthian Christians when they came together to eat the Lord's Supper **(verses 20–22).** What was happening to the poorer members of the congregation? How did this affect the people's closeness to one another? to Christ?

c. How does Paul react to the loveless attitudes of the Corinthian Christians **(verse 22)?** Whom does he accuse them of "despising"?

d. Look at **James 2:1–4.** Describe what was happening in this congregation. Do you feel this emphasis on the "proper" clothing when attending church is still a problem? In your opinion, can rich and poor Christians worship comfortably together in the same congregation? Discuss this.

e. Review and discuss this spiritual truth: *if we despise our fellow Christians in worship, we are also despising God.*

WORSHIPING IN A "WORTHY" OR AN "UNWORTHY" MANNER

1. The Lord's Supper is a central feature in Christian worship. In this Sacrament God comes to unite us in fellowship with Himself and other believers. As we eat and drink this holy Supper together, we celebrate our *common salvation* in Christ. Study **verses 23–26.**

a. Explain how Christ is present in the eating of the bread and the drinking of the wine. What words in particular reveal that Jesus Christ Himself is present?

b. Look back to **1 Corinthians 10:16.** How does this passage demonstrate the "Real Presence" of Christ in the Lord's Supper?

c. What event does the Lord's Supper cause us to "remember"? How is this event related to our salvation?

d. Look carefully at **verse 26.** What does this passage tell us we are doing every time we partake of the Lord's Supper? How does this relate to our worship together as Christians?

2. Since Jesus Christ is present in the Lord's Supper, it is important to examine the *manner* in which we worship. Worship in a "worthy" manner honors God. Worship in an "unworthy" manner dishonors God. Examine **verses 27–32.** Then answer these important questions.

a. What does eating and drinking the Lord's Supper in an "unworthy" manner mean? What does such an approach to worship fail to recognize (see **verse 27**)?

b. In contrast, what do you suppose worshiping in a "worthy" manner might mean? Describe those worshipful attitudes that bring honor to God.

c. Why does Paul advise that we examine ourselves before partaking of the Lord's Supper **(verse 28)?** What should be the purpose of such a spiritual examination?

d. Describe the tragic consequences of worshiping in an unworthy manner **(verses 29–31).** What do you think Paul means by the words *weak, sick,* and *fallen asleep?*

e. What blessings does God freely give those worshipers who worship in a "worthy" manner? Compare **Ephesians 3:16–19.**

WORSHIP THAT HONORS GOD

1. Worship of the living God is one of life's most treasured experiences. By means of worship we are brought close to Christ and our fellow Christians. Worship creates *true spiritual fellowship.*

a. Look at **verse 33.** How would you rewrite this passage to make it apply to worship in a modern congregation?

b. An important passage on worship is **Ephesians 5:19–20.** What does this passage say about building up our fellow Christians during the worship service?

2. Read the following example of a modern worship situation and write your reaction to it on a sheet of paper. You may want to discuss your answers with your classmates.

You are attending services in your church. Your congregation is all white, is mainly middle class, and primarily of European ancestry. This morning a black student from your school comes into the church and sits in the back pew. You notice that many church attenders greet him with "ugly" stares. He finds himself sitting alone. Afterward, during the coffee fellowship, you hear some older members making derogatory comments about his presence.

What would you do in this situation? Would you deal with the problem or ignore it? What suggestions might you make to the congregation in the light of this problem?

3. Suppose a stranger attends worship at your church and sits next to you. He seems bewildered by the hymnal and the order of worship. How would you include this person in the unity of your church?

4. On the basis of this lesson, what important truths impress you about worship and participation in the Lord's Supper?

A PRAYER TO PRAY TODAY

Lead me to truly worship You, O Lord, in both word and deed. Help me to seek a closer experience with You and my fellow Christians as I praise and honor Your name. Empower me to strengthen the faith of others as I worship, even as You strengthen me. In the name of Jesus, whose body and blood assure me of forgiveness, life, and salvation. Amen.

Whenever you eat this bread and drink this cup, you proclaim the Lord's death until He comes.
1 Corinthians 11:26

SESSION 52

Concluding Activities for Unit 5

Several activities are listed below to help you review the major truths of this unit. Following your teacher's directions, complete one or more of these activities.

"TEN YEARS FROM TODAY AT MY CLASS REUNION, I . . ."

On a blank sheet of paper write the "futurology" of your life. Do this by imagining yourself 10 years from today at your class reunion. Will you be married or single? Will you be a parent or not? What will be your vocation? Where will you be residing (in what city and in what type of home)? What especially will be the focus of your activities in God's church? Finally, what kind of person do you imagine (hope) that you will be?

Start your "futurology" with the topic sentence above. Then write down all the dreams about your future that come to mind.

When you have completed the exercise, discuss this assignment with your classmates. Talk about what you have written. Take turns sharing your dreams about marriage or singleness, about your discipleship in God's church, and about your progress in the Christian faith. You may also want to discuss the importance of making plans for one's life and how necessary it is to ask God's guidance in this process.

SKITS

Divide your class into about four groups. Each group should prepare and present a skit on the theme:

"A Divided Church Vs. a Unified Church."

In preparing the skit, work with the themes of "Argumentiveness," "Exclusiveness," and "Neglectfulness." Be prepared to act out the behavior that such themes portray in a divided church. Especially show how this applies to the harmful worship practices that were discussed in session 51.

The second part of the skit should present what a church unified in Jesus Christ appears like in the eyes of the world. Deal especially with the themes of "love" and "forgiveness."

Take ample time to prepare for the skits. After you present them, you and your classmates may want to discuss the importance of Christ-like behavior in the church.

HIGHLIGHTING

Choose a session from unit 5 that was especially meaningful. Spend a few minutes reviewing that session.

Write down two or three highlights of that session to share with other members of the class. Be prepared to explain why these highlights are personally meaningful to you.

You and your classmates should take turns sharing your highlights with the class. If it appears that many of the highlights are the same, discuss these truths in more depth. Ask your teacher to help you schedule a time when you will have the opportunity to do so.

UNIT 6
Faith Uses God's Gifts

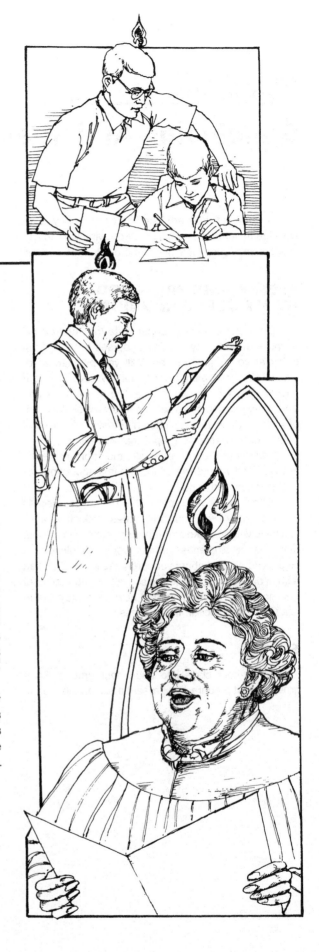

FIRST CORINTHIANS 12–15

"What a superb dancer. She's pure grace in motion."

"He's a natural. Best shooter I've ever seen."

"He's a born teacher. Watch how the children hang on to every word he says."

"Talk about being gifted as a leader. She has just the right qualities for it."

Gifts . . . skills . . . talents! God has distributed them to people in abundance. Everyone has some gift from God that makes him or her unique. What matters is not the particular talent a person may have. What matters to God is whether that person is using the talent to honor Him.

What would life be like if each of us were the same? The fact that God gives out so many different gifts enriches our lives and stimulates us to share our lives with one another.

This topic of gifts and talents is especially important for life in the Christian church. In the church the Holy Spirit gives out special gifts called "spiritual gifts" to all believers in Christ. Think of what that means for each one of us. With the unique gift that every Christian possesses, *each of us plays an essential role in God's plan for building His church!*

This unit on spiritual gifts opens up a whole new dimension in how we can express our faith in Jesus Christ. As we explore how the Holy Spirit distributes blessings within the church, we stand in awe at the marvelous love God has for every one of His people.

SESSION 53

Finding My Spiritual Gift

FIRST CORINTHIANS 12:1–31

At a spiritual gifts workshop held at their church, several young people were discussing the discoveries they had made about themselves.

Andy was enthusiastic: "I think I've found my spiritual gift. I have a knack for communicating the truth of Scripture to others. I believe God has given me the gift of *teaching*."

Tamdrika was no less excited: "I believe I have the gift of helping people who have problems. I'm sure God has given me the gift of *service*."

It was Karla's turn to share her discovery: "I can't wait to use my spiritual gift," she said. "Whenever there is an 'impossible' challenge that has to be met, I find that I can overcome it with God's power. I believe I have the gift of *faith*."

"What about you, Victor?" asked the others. "Have you found your spiritual gift?" Victor was thoughtful for a moment. Then he replied: "I think I have two gifts. Learning the Scripture comes easy for me. It just kind of sticks in my head. But I also find that I can apply it to real-life situations so that it makes sense to others. Maybe I have the gifts of both *knowledge* and *wisdom*. What do you think?"

Discovering one's spiritual gift is not only exciting in itself, but it also awakens within each of us an important spiritual truth. *Every believer in Jesus Christ has a significant role to play in God's church!* Let's study how this divine plan of the Holy Spirit and spiritual gifts works.

WHAT ARE SPIRITUAL GIFTS?

1. The Holy Spirit first creates the spiritual foundation necessary for the distribution of His gifts. He gives these gifts only to those who call Jesus Christ "Lord." We receive the gifts for service to Christ in His church. Study **verses 1–11.**

a. What words in **verse 1** suggest that the teaching of spiritual gifts is an important teaching of the church?

b. Explain how it is possible for you to confess that Jesus Christ is your "Lord" **(verses 2–3).** Compare **2:12–15.** Why can this remove all doubts that you are indeed a true believer in Jesus Christ?

c. The Holy Spirit distributes a wide variety of spiritual gifts to believers **(verses 4–6).** What reasons can you suggest to explain why so many different gifts are given throughout the church?

d. **Verse 11** is an important passage in the teaching of spiritual gifts. How can we be certain that every believer has been given one or more gifts by the Holy Spirit? What selection process does the Holy Spirit use in the distribution of gifts?

e. What is the entire purpose for the distribution of gifts to members of the church **(verse 7)?** Can you explain God's plan? See also **Ephesians 4:11–13.**

2. Notice the listing of spiritual gifts in this chapter. Several gifts are mentioned in **verses 8–10** and **verse 28.** This does not exhaust all of the gifts the Holy Spirit gives to the church. Paul refers to other gifts in **Romans 12:6–8; Ephesians 4:11; 1 Corinthians 13:3;** and **Hebrews 13:2.** Read **verses 8–10** and study carefully the gifts discussed below:

a. *The message of knowledge.* An exceptionally thorough knowledge of the great truths of divine revelation, particularly the mysteries of the Gospel.

b. *The message of wisdom.* The ability to expound such mysteries in a clear and convincing manner as well as to apply them to individual cases in life.

c. *Faith.* Not saving or justifying faith, but a heroic, unwavering trust and confidence in the power of God to reveal Himself in extraordinary deeds that seem impossible to us.

d. *Healing.* May refer to those remarkable deeds performed in the early Christian church to heal the sick without medication, to cast out unclean spirits, and to cure the lame.

e. *Miraculous powers.* A broader term that may include the many wondrous deeds performed by early Christians through the almighty power of Christ.

f. *Prophecy.* Does not refer primarily to the gift of declaring coming events in advance but rather the God-given ability to interpret Scripture correctly and to apply its message of Law and Gospel to human needs. It is the gift of expressing the will of God in a given situation.

g. *Ability to distinguish between spirits.* A God-given power by which certain individuals in the early church were able to test the prophets to determine

whether they were true or false and to judge whether a doctrine was of God or not.

h. *Different kinds of tongues.* Refers at times to a "language," unintelligible to others as well as to the speaker, by which a Christian praised God. At other times to the ability to speak a foreign language without receiving training, as in **Acts 2:4–11.** (See the discussion of this gift in **1 Corinthians 14.**)

i. *Interpretation of tongues.* The ability to transmit the content and message of such "language" for the benefit and edification of the speaker and other members of the body of Christ.

j. *Pastor-teacher.* The ability to take on the responsibility for the spiritual welfare of the community of God's people and to communicate the truths of God's Word so that others learn.

k. *Encouragement.* The ability to stand alongside fellow Christians in need and bring them counsel and encouragement.

l. *Serving.* The ability to seek out needs of people and implement plans to meet those needs.

m. *Leadership.* The ability to motivate God's people, delegate responsibilities, and direct and inspire so that the church's work goes on effectively.

n. *Giving.* The ability to offer material blessings for the work of the church with exceptional willingness, cheerfulness, and liberality.

o. *Showing mercy.* Possessing an exceptional measure of love and compassion, and moved to devote large amounts of time and energy to caring for the suffering.

p. *Hospitality.* Possessing a willing heart, thus enabling you to cheerfully open your home to others, offering them lodging, food, and fellowship.

God gives the church the gifts we need for our time. Therefore we do not receive all the gifts that He gave to the early church. For example, we may not receive the gifts of healing and miraculous powers.

3. As you ponder these spiritual gifts as well as others mentioned in the Scriptures, here are some suggestions to think about in finding your spiritual gift:

a. Examine your feelings about any one of them.

b. Experiment with as many of them as possible.

c. See how effective you are with any one of them.

d. Ask others in the church if they believe you are effective with any one of them.

e. Pray that the Holy Spirit will lead you to the proper spiritual gift.

HOW THE BODY OF CHRIST WORKS

1. God gives spiritual gifts to make His church strong in its mission to the world. The church may be compared to a human body in which each part has a useful function. We see God's plan at work as every believer contributes his or her spiritual gift for the functioning of the church. Study **verses 12–26.**

a. Explain how you have been made a member of God's church through Holy Baptism **(verses 12–13).** How do these verses make clear that all believers have been given the Holy Spirit through water baptism?

b. Notice how each part of the human body serves a useful function **(verses 14–19).** There is diversity, yet there is unity. What would be the result if every member of the church had the same spiritual gift? Discuss the importance of diversity in the church.

c. By the same token each part of the human body needs the contribution of the other parts **(verses 21–26).** In your own words explain why each believer's spiritual gift is essential for the unity of God's church.

d. How does **verse 25** make it clear that a Christian should not use his or her spiritual gift for selfish purposes? How can a "Lone Ranger" complex destroy the whole purpose of spiritual gifts in the church?

2. Although all spiritual gifts are helpful to the church, some are more vital for the effective functioning of the church than others. Read **verses 27–31.**

a. How does **verse 27** encourage you to find your own spiritual gift?

b. Notice how the spiritual gifts listed in **verse 28** are arranged in a priority of importance. Explain why the first three gifts listed here are more vital to the ministry of the church than the others.

c. Why do you suppose the gift of speaking in

"tongues" is mentioned last in this list **(verse 28)?**

d. Tell why Paul urges believers to desire the greater gifts **(verse 31).**

3. Spend some time sharing your thoughts about the teaching of spiritual gifts. What are some of the good things that might happen in Christian congregations if every member used his or her spiritual gift? What especially excites you about the teaching of spiritual gifts?

Now to each one the manifestation of the Spirit is given for the common good. . . . God has combined the members of the body and has given greater honor to the parts that lacked it, so that there should be no division in the body, but that its parts should have equal concern for each other. If one part suffers, every part suffers with it; if one part is honored, every part rejoices with it.

1 Corinthians 12:7, 24b–26

SESSION 54

Using My Spiritual Gift in Love

FIRST CORINTHIANS 13:1–13

A young man was discussing his vocational plans with his pastor. During the conversation the pastor mentioned the young man's considerable talents. He said, "You are a very gifted person."

Immediately the young man began to blush and move nervously in his chair.

"Why are you blushing?" the pastor queried. "I only said that you were a gifted person. I wasn't admiring *you*. I was admiring the *gifts* that God has lent you."

This story reveals a profound truth. We have difficulty separating the gifts God gives us from our own self-serving nature. Our sinful pride seeks to take credit for the talents we possess. We assume that God's gifts are our gifts. No wonder we often fail to use those gifts in the proper way.

Have you ever noticed how the careers of some exceptionally talented people end in tragedy? For example, a brilliant baseball pitcher is washed out because of drugs, or a promising actress fails to get a part because of unreasonable demands. How do you suppose such people perceived the gifts that God gave them?

In our lesson today we will discover a "more excellent" way of using God's gifts. The way of God is the way of love. Only when God's love touches our hearts can His gifts find their rightful purpose.

(People often use the term *gifts* to describe various talents God has given us, as was done in the examples above. Paul wrote **1 Corinthians 13** in response to the abuse of *spiritual gifts,* the kinds of gifts we discussed in session 53. We can, however, apply Paul's words to all the gifts and talents God has given us.)

THE MOST EXCELLENT WAY

1. When we use our spiritual gifts without love, we become useless in the service of God. In a figure of speech, we are behaving like "strutting peacocks." Read **verses 1–3.**

a. Notice how the Corinthians prized the gift of speaking in tongues over any other gift **(verse 1).** What does Paul mean by **"a gong or a clanging cymbal"**?

b. What spiritual gift is referred to by **"surrender my body to the flames" (verse 3)**?

c. Paul repeatedly says that if I **"have not love, I am nothing" (verses 2–3).** What does he mean by that? Share your thoughts about this important point.

d. Frequently in a congregation's life some members threaten to stop contributing their gifts because no one appreciates them. What do you think about this kind of behavior? Have you ever volunteered some service to the church for no other reason than to draw attention to yourself? How much satisfaction did you receive from the experience?

2. Only God can provide the spiritual power that enables us to use our spiritual gifts to benefit others. He shares with us the gift of love. Study the qualities of love found in **verses 4–7.**

a. Which of the qualities in these verses remind you of Jesus Christ? Mention some specific examples from the life of Jesus. Compare **Ephesians 4:32; 1 Peter 2:23; Luke 23:34;** and **1 John 3:16.**

b. The word *not* appears eight times in this list of the qualities of love. This use of the negative refers to the fact that God's love is different from the natural inclinations of the sinful heart. Give a personalized example of how each of the following statements might appear in real life.

LOVE . . .
    does not envy
    does not boast
    is not proud
    is not rude
    is not self-seeking
    is not easily angered
    keeps no record of wrongs
    does not delight in evil

c. Which of the above qualities do you feel you lack most at the present time? Consider asking God to bless you with this particular quality of love.

d. Why do you suppose so many couples choose to have these qualities of love read at their wedding service? How necessary are these qualities in a Christian marriage?

e. What has Christ done for you to make these

qualities of love your very own? See **Romans 5:5–8.**

f. Notice how God's love bears up under all the pressures of life **(verse 7).** What do the words **"always trusts, always hopes, always perseveres"** mean to you?

LOVE NEVER FAILS

1. God's love will never end because love is the nature of God **(1 John 4:7–11).** This truth overcomes us: the love we experience now is the same love we will experience in even greater measure in the life to come. Read **verses 8–13.**

a. Our spiritual gifts will one day cease **(verses 8–10).** The gifts of prophecy, tongues, knowledge, and all other gifts will have completed their functions. Explain the reason for this.

b. Look at **verse 10.** To what does "perfection" refer? In what way might this describe our life in the resurrection to come? See **1 Corinthians 15:42–44.**

c. Spiritual gifts are important, but they are extremely insignificant when compared with the glory God has prepared for us in the life to come. How does **verse 11** express this truth?

d. We see God presently only as a poor reflection **(verse 12).** How shall we see God in the life to come? Share your thoughts about this. See **John 1:18** and **1 John 4:12.**

2. God's love is the greatest gift we will ever experience **(verse 13).** Faith and hope will remain in eternity, but love is even greater than these. Explain why this is so.

3. Consider what you have learned about God's love in this chapter. How would you apply His love in each of the following situations?

a. Your friend has gone through a frustrating experience in her home and is very much on edge. She suddenly lashes out at you and says some things that deeply hurt you.

b. You have a date to which you have been looking forward for some time. Your neighbor, however, asks you to babysit for her because of an emergency in the family.

c. Your greatest fear is to stand before a large group and speak. The pastor calls and asks you to say a few words about the youth group at the worship service on Sunday.

d. Your cousin is marrying a person of a non-Christian religion. Your family is so opposed to the marriage that they have decided to boycott the wedding. Your cousin, however, has asked you to be in the wedding party.

e. A group of your friends invites you to join them at a party where alcohol, marijuana, or other drugs will be used. They indicate that they will pay all your expenses for the evening and offer to buy your ticket for an upcoming concert if you will agree to serve as the designated driver—you will refrain from using the drugs, so that you can drive them home safely.

> Love in Christ is strong and living,
> Binding faithful hearts in one;
> Love in Christ is true and giving.
> May His will in us be done.
>
> Love is patient and forbearing,
> Clothed in Christ's humility,
> Gentle, selfless, kind, and caring,
> Reaching out in charity.
>
> Love in Christ abides forever,
> Fainting not when ills attend;
> Love, forgiving and forgiven,
> Shall endure until life's end.

Lutheran Worship, 376

And now I will show you the most excellent way. If I speak in the tongues of men and of angels, but have not love, I am only a resounding gong or a clanging cymbal. If I have the gift of prophecy and can fathom all mysteries and all knowledge, and if I have a faith that can move mountains, but have not love, I am nothing.

1 Corinthians 12:31b–13:2

SESSION 55

A God of Peace and Order

FIRST CORINTHIANS 14:1–40

DISORDER (A PARABLE)

In a certain church a guest preacher was invited to preach. He gave the church secretary the title of the opening hymn, "All Hail the Power of Jesus' Name." He did not know that the hymnal used in that church had three different tunes for the hymn.

The congregation was accustomed to singing the first tune. The choir director, however, liked the third tune and instructed the choir to sing it. The substitute organist, on the other hand, knew they were not using the regular tune, but at the moment the processional started couldn't remember whether to play the second or third tune. So she decided to play the second tune.

Consequently, when the service started, the congregation was singing the first tune, the organist was playing the second tune, and the choir was singing the third tune.

The choir detected the mistake first and started to sing the second tune. But the organist, seeing that the congregation wasn't singing well, decided she was in error and began playing the third tune. All the while the congregation was struggling bravely with the first tune.

The pastor tried to remedy the situation. He rose and announced loudly, "Let us all sing hymn number 164." This failed to end the confusion. As a matter of fact, people seemed more confused than ever, because all three tunes were numbered 164. After the announcement, the substitute organist was completely confused and stopped playing all together, while the choir director was shouting at her to play the first tune.

This parable of disorder in the church strikes us as humorous, but in real life such situations are closer to tragedy. God calls us to walk together in love, sharing our spiritual gifts for the edification of the common good. In this lesson we will be discussing how important it is to seek unity in our worship life and to follow God's design for peace and order.

SEEK TO EDIFY THE CHURCH NOT YOURSELVES

1. The Corinthian Christians were on a disaster course. Of all the spiritual gifts God freely gave them, they sought mainly the gift of tongues. Most of them spurned the more important gift of prophecy. Paul compares these gifts and their value in edifying God's church. Study **verses 1–17.**

a. Why is the gift of prophecy of much greater value to the church than the gift of tongues (**verses 1–4)?**

b. In what situations might the gift of tongues be of value to the church (**verses 5 and 13)?**

c. Summarize Paul's argument about the uselessness of tongues in building up the faith of the church (**verses 6–12).** What problems does tongue-speaking present to the person who hears them spoken?

d. In what way is praying in tongues different from praying with the mind (**verses 13–17)?** Which of the two is more edifying to the church?

2. When believers gathered for worship services, speaking in tongues created confusion and disorder in the assembly. Unbelievers who were present at the service were likely to snicker and mock the faith when they heard tongues spoken. Read **verses 18–25.**

a. Why does Paul say he would rather speak in a language people could understand rather than in tongues, a gift he himself enjoyed (**verses 18–19)?**

b. What words in **verse 23** hint at the fact that visitors at the worship service would interpret tongue-speaking as babble?

c. Contrariwise, what spiritual effect did the gift of prophecy have on the unbelievers at the worship service (**verses 24–25)?**

d. Does Paul forbid tongue-speaking? Has it any usefulness at all? Read **verses 39–40** and discuss these questions.

STRIVE FOR ORDERLY WORSHIP

The individualistic manner of the Corinthians created disorder in their worship services in ways other than tongue-speaking. Apparently everyone wanted to be on center stage! Paul admonishes them for such behavior in God's church. He reminds them that God is not a God of disorder but of peace (**verse 33).** Study **verses 26–33.**

1. How does **verse 26** suggest that there was confusion at the Corinthian worship services? What does

Paul tell them about how they should use their spiritual gifts in worship?

2. The use of prophets as speakers at worship was probably the early Christian manner of preaching. See **verse 29.** Why do you supppose Paul counsels the Corinthians to limit the number of speakers to two or three?

3. What instruction does Paul lay down regarding speakers at the worship service so that there would be order rather than confusion **(verses 30–33)?**

4. Someone has suggested that our modern liturgy is a more effective way for believers to contribute their spiritual gifts at worship services than the more open manner of the Corinthians. What is your opinion? Defend your answer.

THE ROLE OF WOMEN IN THE CHURCH

1. Another aspect of disorder in the life of the Corinthian church was the aggressive nature of women at the worship assembly. Contrary to the law of God and the accepted procedures of other Christian churches, the Corinthian women were usurping the roles reserved for men. Study **verses 34–36.**

a. Paul sets down the admonition that women should not be allowed to speak but must be in submission **(verses 34–35).** He states that this was a rule set down by God at the order of creation or through the Law. See **Genesis 3:16.** How does this passage establish the relationship between husbands and wives? See also **Ephesians 5:22–24** and **1 Peter 3:1–2.**

b. Study carefully Paul's discussion of the topic of womanly submission in **1 Timothy 2:11–15.** Notice how the major truth here revolves around the concept of authority. Women should not assume a function in the church beyond that which the Lord has assigned them. To speak out in the church would be to usurp the role of authority of men.

c. We must understand that the matter of womanly submission in no way suggests the superiority of the male. Both male and female are one in the Lord and are interdependent upon one another. See **Galatians 3:28** and **1 Corinthians 11:11–12.**

d. The basic issue Paul raises in this section deals with God's design for edification in the church. The roles of men and women differ only in respect to the concept of authority. Specifically, this means that women not hold positions involving the pastoral office or usurping authority over men.

e. Paul states that his understanding of this matter of male and female relationships in the church is founded on the Word of God **(verse 36).**

2. Women were very active in the early Christian church and assumed functions that contributed greatly to growth and edification in the body of Christ. A survey of some selected passages reveals the extensiveness of the activity of women in the New Testament church:

a. Priscilla possessed gifts of knowledge and teaching **(Acts 18:26).**

b. Phoebe may have been a deaconess **(Romans 16:1).** Note also the names of many other women in Paul's list of commendations.

c. Women have the major spiritual influence on children from birth through early childhood. This may be the gist of Paul's meaning in **1 Timothy 2:15.**

d. Women were active in prayer and prophecy **(1 Corinthians 11:3–10).**

3. Share your thoughts on this subject of the roles of men and women in the church. What are your feelings about the distinctions and the opportunities for members of both sexes to honor God through service?

4. We have no power of our own to bring about peace and order in God's church. Left to our own devices, we would contribute only confusion and disorder. We need the love of God in Christ to seek the way of peace.

a. God calls us to follow the way of love **(verse 1).** Review in your mind some of the truths you learned from **1 Corinthians 13.** How can we show love in the way we use our spiritual gifts in worship? How can God's love help us to understand the need for striving for the edification of the group, not just ourselves?

b. How has Christ shown you the full measure of His love so that you are compelled to live for Him and the unity of His church? See **2 Corinthians 5:14–15.**

The spirits of prophets are subject to the control of prophets. For God is not a God of disorder but of peace.

1 Corinthians 14:32–33

SESSION 56

We Shall Be Raised from the Dead

FIRST CORINTHIANS 15:1–34

Can you imagine the part of the Gospel message that seemed most radical to the pagans who heard it in ancient times? Do you know what caused an immediate reaction whenever this teaching was preached? *It was the message of the resurrection of the dead!*

The ancient world of Greece and Rome was a world of utter hopelessness. Archaeologists excavating Roman cemeteries discovered that nearly all the grave markers had seven letters carved on them—*NF F NS NC.* These were the first letters of four words, words so familiar to the Romans that the initials were sufficient for their identification.

The Words Were	The Words Mean
Non fui;	I was not;
Fui;	I was;
No sum;	I am not;
No curo.	I do not care.

The mood of these four words expressed a fatalistic surrender to the finality of physical death. The ancient world lived under the chill of that fatalism. Many modern people live under this same chill.

When Paul preached about Christ and the resurrection at Athens, many listeners reacted with snickering and mockery **(Acts 17:32).** Others, however, wanted to hear more. Deep within the human heart throbs the hope that death is not the final victor.

The preaching of the Gospel message (which included the resurrection) produced a people who were happy, vibrant, and filled with the hope of Christ. The power of the resurrection continues to change people today. Christ's victory over death guarantees that our future resurrection is certain and sure.

THE RESURRECTION GOSPEL

The Gospel of Christ stands or falls on the resurrection of Jesus Christ. The resurrection provides the certainty that our salvation is true. The certainty that Christ was raised from the dead has been attested by many eyewitnesses who saw Him alive. Read **verses 1–11.**

1. Notice how Paul sums up key elements of the Gospel in **verses 3–4.** This is, perhaps, the most compact statement of the Gospel in the New Testament. What are the key elements of the Gospel? Compare **Romans 4:25.**

2. What promise does God make to us through the Gospel **(verses 1–2)?** Why does Paul say that the Gospel is a matter of first importance **(verse 3)?**

3. Study carefully the list of eyewitnesses who saw Christ alive after His resurrection **(verses 5–8).** What important truths can we draw from this? How does this give us assurance that the resurrection is true?

4. Explain Paul's statement: **"and last of all He appeared to me also, as to one abnormally born"** **(verse 8).** Compare **Acts 9:1–9.**

5. An apostle is one who has personally seen the risen Christ and has been commissioned to preach the Gospel (see **Acts 1:21–22).** Why does Paul feel that he does not deserve to be an apostle **(verse 9)?** On the other hand, what has motivated him to diligently carry out his apostolic mission **(verse 10)?**

THE NECESSITY OF THE RESURRECTION

1. How essential is the resurrection of Jesus Christ to our faith? Without it, all is lost. We would have no forgiveness of sins, no hope, no future. Without it, our faith would be useless. Read **verses 12–19.**

a. Some of the Corinthians were denying that the dead could be raised **(verses 12–13).** According to Paul, what else were they guilty of denying?

b. Paul argues that the resurrection of Christ and the resurrection of the dead are linked together **(verses 13 and 16).** If one is true, the other must be true. If one is false, the other must be false. Explain this.

c. Explain how there could be no forgiveness of sins if Jesus Christ had only died on the cross but had not been raised from the dead **(verse 17).** How would faith in a "dead" Christ make our faith useless **(verses 14 and 17)?** Discuss this important point.

d. If the resurrection were a falsehood, of what could the world accuse Paul and the other apostles **(verse 15)?**

e. What prospect would exist for those who have died if there is no resurrection of the dead **(verse 18)?**

f. Look carefully at **verse 19.** What do you suppose Paul means when he says, **"If only for this life we have hope in Christ, we are to be pitied more than all men."?** Share your thoughts on this crucial truth.

2. How essential is the resurrection of Jesus Christ to our faith? Without it, our Christian witness would be futile. Our suffering for Christ would have no purpose. Life's noble meaning would be lost. Study **verses 29–34.**

Verse 29 is a difficult passage to interpret. Perhaps Paul is referring to a situation in which a dying friend or relative pleads with another person to be baptized in the hope of meeting the beloved person in the life of the world to come.

How does Paul describe the mission of his life because he *does* believe in the resurrection of the dead **(verses 30–32)?** If there is no resurrection, what does he suggest we do with our lives?

As we confess in the Third Article ("I believe in the resurrection of the body"), we will have our bodies in heaven. We know this from **Job 19:25–26,** it is exemplified by Moses and Elijah at Jesus' transfiguration **(Matthew 17:3),** and Jesus showed it in His resurrected body. With our minds and limited wisdom we cannot fully grasp what these bodies will be like, but we do accept the word of the Lord in faith.

THE HOPE OF THE RESURRECTION

1. The resurrection of Jesus Christ remains the central and all-controlling fact in human history. Our future hope is anchored to this vital truth. Because Christ has been made alive, we will be made alive. Read **verses 20–28.**

a. Take a look at the word *firstfruits* in **verses 20** and **23.** This word indicates that one day the rest of the harvest will follow. How is this a guarantee of your own resurrection from the dead? In what way does this bring hope to your life in the here and now?

b. If we were related only to Adam, we would have cause for despair. But because we are also related to Christ through faith, we have reason to rejoice. Examine **verses 21–22.** How would you use these passages to witness to an unbeliever about the hope of your future in the life to come?

c. Describe what will happen on the day of resurrection when Christ returns to this earth **(verses 23–26).** What thoughts come to your mind when you ponder the truth that death will forever be destroyed?

d. Some people consider death to be a friend. Paul

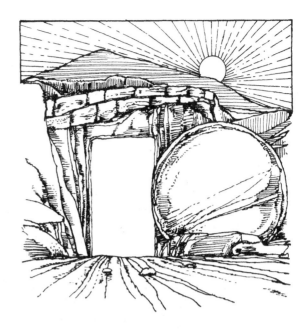

states that death is an enemy of God **(verse 26).** How do you resolve these two statements?

2. Does the hope of the resurrection make a difference in the way you live your life? in the way you react to the death of a Christian loved one? Write down at least three things the resurrection gives you that you would not have possessed otherwise. You may want to consult the opening section.

3. You may have heard the statement "Christians are not afraid to die because they have something to die for." What are your thoughts on this subject? Discuss this with your classmates.

4. Suppose you had a friend who was dying of a terminal disease. You feel led to share with her the hope of the resurrection promise. What would you say?

> The day of resurrection! Earth, tell it out abroad,
> The passover of gladness, the passover of God.
> From death to life eternal, From sin's dominion free,
> Our Christ has brought us over With hymns of victory.
>
> Now let the heav'ns be joyful, Let earth its song begin,
> Let all the world keep triumph And all that is therein.
> Let all things, seen and unseen, Their notes of gladness blend;
> For Christ the Lord has risen, Our joy that has no end!
>
> *Lutheran Worship,* 133:1, 3

Christ has indeed been raised from the dead, the firstfruits of those who have fallen asleep.

1 Corinthians 15:20

SESSION 57

We Shall Be Raised with Spiritual Bodies

FIRST CORINTHIANS 15:35—58

When Christopher Columbus was about to return to Spain after discovering a new land, he wondered how he could prove to skeptical Europeans that he had been to a strange and uncharted world. In order to dispel the skepticism of those he was to face, he took back with him several American Indians. These would provide the proof he needed. Now no one could doubt that he had discovered a world never seen before.

Many people express a skepticism about the type of body we shall possess in the resurrection. They wonder how human bodies that have died and decayed can be raised to life again. Some question the form and design of the resurrected body, especially the bodies of those who have died as small infants or as aged and infirm. Others wonder what life in the resurrection will be like. Will we know each other? How will we spend our time? What will be the nature of our life with God?

Scripture responds to such questions in a way that is marvelous to behold. In this lesson we will learn how all our questions concerning the body of the resurrection will find satisfaction in one divine answer: the glorious body of Jesus Christ! We will be clothed in a new garment of glory that will be fashioned like the glorious body of Christ. There is no greater proof of the riches and glory that await us in the resurrection to come.

THE RESURRECTION BODY

Paul answers many of the questions the Corinthians raised about the resurrected body. He states that the bodies we presently possess will be far different from the bodies we will possess in the resurrection. Study **verses 35—41.**

1. Why does Paul seem upset by the questions of the Corinthians **(verses 35—36)?** What attitude toward the resurrection of the dead do such questions reveal? What is your opinion?

2. What illustration does Paul use to contrast our present bodies with our bodies in the resurrection **(verses 36—38)?** Describe this contrast in your own words. In what way will our resurrected bodies be much different?

3. Why is it necessary for a seed to die before it can develop into a beautiful flower or another type of plant? Compare **John 12:24.** Tell how this illustration helps you better grasp the glory your body will possess in the resurrection.

4. All created life is different from other forms of life in its distinctive flesh, body, and splendor **(verses 39—41).** This is the Creator's work. Paul seems to be saying: cannot the Creator bring forth a new body that will far surpass our earthly body? Why is this a good argument against those who are skeptical of the resurrection?

5. After studying this section, tell why all our questions about the future ("What age will we be in heaven?" "What will we look like?" etc.) are insignificant and unfruitful. Explain how God has a marvelous plan in mind for our future. See **2:9.**

"IN THE LIKENESS OF THE MAN OF HEAVEN"

1. Our bodies in the resurrection will be spiritual bodies. They will be imperishable, and God will equip them with power and glory. Study **verses 42—44.**

a. Note how our future bodies are described as spiritual, as compared with our natural earthly bodies **(verse 44).** What does the term *spiritual* suggest to you? How might this term describe the principle by which our bodies receive life in the resurrection? See **6:19** and **2 Corinthians 5:4—5.**

b. Some people try to explain away the resurrection body by saying that we will be spirits in the world to come. How does **verse 44** completely disprove such a suggestion?

c. Our bodies in the resurrection are described as imperishable and made alive with power and glory **(verses 42—43).** What do these terms suggest to you? Compare **Revelation 7:16—17.**

d. What does Jesus say about the imperishability of our bodies in the resurrection? See **Luke 20:34—36.** What are Jesus' comments about marriage and family life in the resurrection? Why do you suppose there will be no marriage in the life to come?

2. God gives no greater promise about the state of our resurrected bodies than promising us that they

will be like Christ's glorious body. Read **verses 45–50.**

a. Notice the progression from our Adam-like existence to our Christ-like existence in the resurrection **(verses 45–47).** How do these passages clearly state that we will not at all resemble the likeness that we presently bear?

b. What does it mean to you that your body in the resurrection will be like the body of Christ **(verses 48–49)?** What light does **Philippians 3:21** shed on this important subject?

c. Explain why it is necessary that Christ give us new bodies that are not made of flesh and blood **(verse 50).**

d. Our earthly bodies are extremely frail, so easily diseased and hurt, and so given to the passions of sin. What does **Romans 8:23** say about our bodies' desire to be released from the power of sin into a new existence?

SHARING IN THE VICTORY TO COME

1. One of the great moments of Handel's *Messiah* is the aria that sings of the coming resurrection. At the sound of the trumpet, Christ will return and raise the dead incorruptible. Death will be defeated forever and all believers will share in Christ's eternal victory. Read **verses 51–57.**

a. At the resurrection Christ will change our natural bodies into spiritual bodies **(verses 51–52).** How long will this process take? What do you suppose Paul means by the phrase **"We will not all sleep"**? Compare **1 Thessalonians 4:15.**

b. What qualities will our new bodies possess that they did not possess previously **(verses 53–54)?**

c. Describe the victory God will give us at the resurrection **(verses 55–57).** Why does Paul say that the resurrection is a victory over sin and the Law as well as a victory over death?

d. How best can we thank God for this victory in the way we live today **(verse 57)?** Compare Paul's words in **Philippians 3:10–11.**

2. Some people say, "Christian funerals should not be tearful and sad occasions. They should be joyful celebrations because of the victory of the resurrection." Do you agree? Discuss your thoughts on this subject.

3. Because Christ will change our earthly bodies into spiritual bodies at the resurrection, some people believe that there should be no viewing of the body at the funeral service. They believe that memorial services at the church are more in tune with the Christian belief of the resurrection. What is your opinion?

4. Some Christians debate the rightness of cremations. Does this practice deny the resurrection of the dead, or does it uphold the resurrection? What do you think? Talk about it.

Jesus lives! The vict'ry's won!
Death no longer can appall me;
Jesus lives! Death's reign is done!
From the grave will Christ recall me.
Brighter scenes will then commence;
This shall be my confidence.

Jesus lives! And I am sure
Neither life nor death shall sever
Me from him. I shall endure
In his love, through death, forever.
God will be my sure defense;
This shall be my confidence.

Lutheran Worship, 139:1, 4

"Where, O death, is your victory? Where, O death, is your sting?" The sting of death is sin, and the power of sin is the law. But thanks be to God! He gives us the victory through our Lord Jesus Christ.
1 Corinthians 15:55–57

SESSION 58

Concluding Activities for Unit 6

Several activities are listed below to help you review the major truths of this unit. Following your teacher's directions, complete one or more of these activities.

REVIEW OF MAJOR THEMES

Select one of the major themes from this unit for further class discussion. Such themes may include the doctrine of spiritual gifts, the greatness of God's love, the role of women in the church, or the doctrine of the resurrection.

A BANNER: "LOVE IS . . . "

Create a banner to be placed in a worship sanctuary on the theme "LOVE IS . . . " The banner should contain all of the qualities of God's love listed in **1 Corinthians 13:4–13.**

Select a steering committee several days beforehand to make the design for the banner and to procure the materials.

A MINIWORKSHOP ON SPIRITUAL GIFTS

1. Conduct a miniature version of the workshop that many congregations are using in order to assist members in discovering their spiritual gifts. Remember that only an abbreviated list of spiritual gifts can be included in this survey. Begin this exercise with a prayer for God's blessing.

2. Read carefully the names and definitions of the spiritual gifts listed below. On a piece of paper make a note of those spiritual gifts that you consider to be your *dominant gifts*. Write down the name of each gift and write a *D* beside it. Also make a note of those gifts you consider to be your *subordinate gifts*. Write down the name of each gift and write an *S* beside it. If you have no feeling for a particular gift, do not include it in your list.

3. After you have completed your listing of dominant and subordinate gifts, give them a numerical ranking, with 1 as your highest ranked gift.

4. Divide the class into small groups in which each member will share his or her findings with the group. During this exercise the group should validate what each person feels are his or her dominant and subordinate gifts. If both the person and the group agree that a particular gift is dominant, this may be the gift that the Holy Spirit has appointed.

ADMINISTRATION

God empowers you to understand the particular needs of the church and to develop effective plans to meet these needs.

Evangelism

God empowers you to speak the Gospel with unbelievers. God uses your words to bring people to faith in Christ.

Wisdom

God empowers you to encourage and counsel members of the church so that they feel helped and uplifted. You have an insight into life's situations and know what to do and how to do it.

Giving

God empowers you to contribute your time and financial resources to the Lord with great joy, eagerness, and liberality.

Knowledge

God empowers you to understand and analyze the teachings of Scripture and to share this knowledge for the edification of other members of the church.

Leadership

God empowers you to set goals for the church which are in harmony with God's will and to organize and motivate members of the church to meet those goals.

Mercy

God empowers you to feel genuine concern for people and to help them find relief from their distressing problems.

Serving

God empowers you to use the talents He has given you, whether they be talents of music, craftsmanship, writing, or art, and to contribute them for God's work in the context of His church.

Teaching

God empowers you to communicate the truths of the Gospel and God's Word to others so that others are edified and strengthened as a result of your sharing with them.

Hospitality

God empowers you to provide food, lodging, or other needs and to care for strangers with joy and effectiveness.

UNIT 7

Faith Points Us to Service

SECOND CORINTHIANS

Somewhere in the western United States there is a Valley of Roses so extensive in size that the air is heavy for miles with the perfume of the flowers. Visitors who pass through the valley discovers that the scent hangs to their clothing. If they should walk into a room full of people at the end of their journey, the people would look at one another and smile, "We know where they have been!"

People notice also that we keep company with Jesus Christ. The aroma of Christ hangs heavy on our hearts and minds. The fragrance of the Gospel is obvious in the way we deal with our families and friends. People can sense a divine presence that directs and shapes our lives. They can say about us just as people said about Peter and John in Jerusalem, **"they took note that these men had been with Jesus" (Acts 4:13).**

In this unit we will be exploring our calling from God as ambassadors of Jesus Christ. Sharing the Good News ranks as the most privileged service we can render to God. But are we up to such a task? Won't people laugh at our clumsy efforts? Won't they snicker at our feeble words?

Do not worry! God Himself will provide the power and the glory. He will shine the light of Christ through us. And what is more, people will notice that we bear the **"aroma of Christ" (2 Corinthians 2:15).** *They will know where we have been!*

SESSION 59

The Glory of the New Covenant

SECOND CORINTHIANS 3:1—4:6

Have you ever thrown a tiny pebble into the smooth waters of a small pond? The impact of the pebble creates a small circle that immediately evolves into larger concentric circles. Soon the entire pond is filled with motion, the result of one tiny pebble.

Sharing the Good News of Jesus Christ often begins with a small, insignificant word. But the repercussions that follow produce results that challenge the imagination.

Years ago a Puritan doctor wrote a book called *The Bruised Reed.* He thought the book would never be of use to anyone. But Richard Baxter read his book and as a result penned *The Call to the Unconverted.* Later Phillip Doddridge read Baxter's book and was converted in the process. He wrote *The Rise and Fall of Religion in the Soul.* William Wilberforce read Doddridge's book and as a consequence was led to write *A Practical View of Christianity.* That book became so popular it finally reached Scotland, where Thomas Chalmers read it. Chalmers was so moved by Wilberforce's book that he began a crusade that set all of Scotland on fire for Jesus Christ.

We are moved to marvel at the power of God as we watch the glory of the Gospel shine brighter and brighter as it moves from one person to another. In our lesson today we will be discussing how God has called us to no less a privilege than to be ministers of His new covenant.

WE ARE MINISTERS OF THE NEW COVENANT

What a calling God presents to us! He has fashioned a new relationship (covenant) with the world through Jesus Christ. He offers to everyone the gift of a new life. And He calls us to help share that gift with others. Read **3:1–6.**

1. God gives us a title—ministers of a new covenant **(verse 6).** We usually think of a minister as a pastor. Does this passage mean that all members of the congregation are ministers? What's the difference between your ministry and your pastor's ministry? Talk about this.

2. How are we made competent to carry out the ministry of the new covenant **(verses 4–5)?** What special abilities do you have to witness about Jesus Christ? What are your thoughts on this important point?

3. God calls us to be ministers of a *new covenant* **(verse 6).** Compare the differences between the old covenant of Moses and the new covenant of Jesus Christ in the chart below:

Old Covenant	New Covenant
	a letter from Christ **(verse 3)**
	written with the Spirit **(verse 3)**
on tablets of stone **(verse 3)**	on tablets of human hearts **(verse 3)**
of the letter **(verse 6)**	of the Spirit **(verse 6)**
the letter kills **(verse 6)**	the Spirit gives life **(verse 6)**

4. Examine the features of the old covenant above. What did the old covenant give to everyone who failed to keep exactly the law of God **(verse 6)?**

5. By contrast what does God promise everyone in Jesus Christ through the new covenant **(verse 6)?** How does the Lord's Supper remind us that God has made us members of the new covenant? See **Luke 22:20.**

6. Look up **Jeremiah 31:31–33.** Notice the new covenant that God promised which would replace the old covenant. Where does Jeremiah say the new covenant would be written? How does **verse 3** relate to Jeremiah's prophecy?

7. Paul says that those people who came to faith in Christ through his ministry were "letters from Christ" **(verse 3).** What do you suppose he meant?

8. How would you feel if someone with whom you shared the Gospel one day became a "letter from Christ"? In what way does Christ use us in the "writing" process of these letters? Talk about this.

THE GLORY OF THE NEW COVENANT

How does it feel to be a privileged part of God's plan to share Christ with the world? Let's study how glorious God's new covenant really is. God has even planned to shine the glory of the new covenant through us. Study **3:7–18.**

1. Paul states that the old covenant was filled with the glory of God **(verses 7–8).** Read **Exodus 34:29–35.** Why did Moses have to wear a veil after receiving the Ten Commandments from God?

2. Paul claims that the glory of the new covenant far surpasses the glory of the old covenant **(verses 9–11).** What reasons does he give to substantiate this claim?

3. For those who still follow the old covenant a **"veil covers their hearts" (verses 13–15).** What does Paul mean by this statement? Explain how this "veil" is removed in the new covenant.

4. Explain how we reflect the Lord's glory inasmuch as we are led by the Spirit of God **(verses 17–18).** In what way do you suppose God's glory is translated into our lives?

5. In your own words describe the freedom you have to live completely for God in the new covenant. How does **John 10:10** state this truth?

WE WITNESS FOR CHRIST BOLDLY

1. In our witness to others we can talk about Christ honestly and plainly. We have nothing to hide. We are given power from God to speak our peace boldly. Read **4:1–2.**

a. What devious tactics are we to avoid when we witness to others of the Gospel **(verse 2)?** What might some of these tactics be?

b. Some preachers of the electronic church promise wealth and prosperity to all who accept Jesus Christ. What is your opinion of this type of evangelizing? Why?

c. Why is talking about Christ openly and honestly better than "beating around the bush"?

d. Why does Paul say that he can be bold in his witness of Christ **(3:12)?** How does the new covenant provide us with power and assurance to proclaim Christ as Lord?

2. We should not be so naive as to expect everyone to respond to our witness of the new covenant. The forces of evil oppose the Gospel of Christ. But we are confident that God will use our ministry in a marvelous way. Read **4:4–6.**

a. What keeps many people from accepting Jesus Christ as Lord and Savior **(verses 3–4)?** Who is this god of whom Paul speaks? See **11:14.**

b. What do you suppose blinds people to the abundant life that Christ promises **(verse 4)?** What other priorities stand in the way?

c. When we talk about Christ to others, what should be the substance of our witness **(verses 5–6)?** Translate this into your own words.

d. Leslie Weatherhead once said that the sight of his father praying on his knees by the bed was an image of Christ that he would never forget. How can our actions be a means by which God makes His light shine through us?

3. On the basis of this lesson, share with your classmates some of the ways you can be an effective minister of the new covenant.

> Come, Christians, follow where our captain trod,
> Our king victorious, Christ, the Son of God.
>
> *Chorus:* Lift high the cross, the love of Christ
>   proclaim
> Till all the world adore his sacred name.
>
> All newborn soldiers of the crucified
> Bear on their brows the seal of him who died.
> *Chorus*
>
> O Lord, once lifted on the glorious tree,
> Raise us, and let your cross our magnet be.
> *Chorus*
>
>   *Lutheran Worship*, 311:1, 3–4
>
> (Copyright © *Hymns Ancient and Modern*)

God, who said, "Let light shine out of darkness," made His light shine in our hearts to give us the light of the knowledge of the glory of God in the face of Christ.

2 Corinthians 4:6

SESSION 60

Don't Lose Heart

SECOND CORINTHIANS 4:7–5:10

Here is a strange paradox! When we think we are doing our best, the results are often ordinary. But when we feel we are doing our worst, we may produce our most significant work.

A woman who taught Sunday school in her younger years one day received a letter from a young man who had sat in her class as a boy. He was writing to thank her for changing his life. In his letter he reminded her of the time she challenged the class to follow Jesus Christ. He even mentioned the date when she had altered his entire outlook on life.

This woman had kept a diary, so she turned to the date the young man had mentioned. She discovered it was a time when she had come home quite disconsolate, almost determined to give up her Sunday school teaching. Her entry in the diary read:

"Had an awful time. The boys were restless. I am not cut out for this kind of thing. I had to take two classes together. No one listened except at the end. A boy from the other class called Tommy seemed to be taking it in. He grew very quiet and subdued. But I expect he was just tired."

How wrong she was! On that day that seemed so fruitless, her witness changed a young boy forever. It can be the same with us as well. In the midst of our gravest discouragements, God's grace will triumph. This is the message of faith we need to hear time and time again: *don't lose heart!*

TREASURES IN JARS OF CLAY

1. Life doesn't always treat ministers of the Gospel as kindly as we would like. We often suffer more abuse than others because of the message we preach. But God's Gospel shines through our human frailty. We rejoice that His power is at work in our weakness. Read **4:7–15.**

a. Notice the descriptive term Paul uses to characterize ministers of the Gospel—"**jars of clay**" **(verse 7).** Why is this such an appropriate term to describe our frailty as human beings? How do **verses 8–9** relate to this truth?

b. What is the treasure that God has placed in these jars of clay? Compare **verse 6.** What thoughts come to your mind when you realize that you bear the life-giving Gospel in your own body?

c. How does Paul explain that the power of the Gospel comes from God and not ourselves **(verse 7)?** In what way is our human frailty actually a testimony of God's power? Talk about this.

d. Ministers of the Gospel carry in their bodies the death of Jesus **(verses 10–12).** That is, they suffer mental anguish, persecution, and physical abuse for Jesus' sake. According to Paul, what good comes out of this?

e. No matter what abuse his body suffers, Paul says that he will not keep quiet about the Gospel **(verses 13–15).** What reason does he give? What motivates him to put his life on the line for Jesus Christ?

f. Have there been times in your life when you have felt put down by others because of your faith? How did you feel? What did you do about it? Share your thoughts with one another.

2. Here is encouragement for all ministers of the Gospel: don't lose heart! God renews us with His love. He fixes our faith on the kingdom of glory to come. Read **verses 16–18.**

a. When trouble comes, we have a ready resource who renews our faith and strengthens our determination **(verse 16).** What does **Philippians 4:6–7** counsel us to do in times of trial? See also **1 Peter 5:7.**

b. Note how Paul compares the present sufferings he endures with the glory God will give him in the life to come **(verse 17).** What does he say that puts all of

our discouragements in the proper perspective? See also **1 Peter 1:6–7.**

c. When we dwell on our present troubles, we have a tendency to become discouraged. Why is it a good practice to fix our faith on that which is unseen rather than on that which is seen **(verse 18)**? How does **Hebrews 11:1** relate to this truth?

d. Have you ever had an experience that shook your faith to its roots? Do you remember how you responded to this crisis? How did God's grace help you overcome? Talk about this with one another.

WE LIVE BY FAITH NOT BY SIGHT

1. We need not fear what the enemies of the Gospel can do to our bodies. God has designed new bodies for us in the resurrection to come. The indwelling presence of the Holy Spirit is the guarantee of a glorious future that awaits us. Study **5:1–5.**

a. Paul compares our present frail bodies with the new spiritual bodies of the resurrection. (You may want to review some of these truths discussed in **1 Corinthians 15:42–53.**) Examine the chart below:

Present Body	Resurrection Body
earthly tent **(verse 1)**	building from God **(verse 1)**
	an eternal house in heaven **(verse 1)**
	clothed with our heavenly dwelling **(verse 4)**
groan and are burdened **(verses 2 and 4)**	the Spirit as a deposit **(verse 5)**

b. What does the contrast between a tent and a building **(verse 1)** suggest to you? How does this contrast brighten your future hope?

c. What do you suppose is meant by the phrase **"we groan and are burdened" (verse 4)?** How does **Romans 8:23** help you understand this phrase?

d. The Scriptures are clear that we will be clothed with a body in the future **(verses 3–4).** How do these passages argue against the belief of many other religions that only the soul survives death? Talk about this.

e. Have you ever bought a gift on a layaway plan? You put down a deposit and promised to pay the balance at a later time. At the time of the final payment, you receive the gift. Paul argues: *the Holy Spirit within us is the deposit of the new body we will receive at the resurrection* (see **verse 5**). How does this truth give you confidence in your future with God? Share your thoughts on this.

2. God's promise of our future with Him makes us confident and fills us with faith. We are moved by His love to please Him with deeds that one day will be revealed at the judgment seat of Christ. Read **verses 6–10.**

a. We cannot see the reality of our future at the present time. Nevertheless, we live in the certainty that one day it shall be ours. How is this truth expressed in **verses 6–7?**

b. God empowers Christians who long to be with Christ and in the glory of His presence **(verse 8).** How does Paul state this longing for wholeness in **Philippians 1:21–24?**

c. At the coming judgment Christ will evaluate all of the deeds of our life and will reward the works of our faith **(verses 9–10).** This judgment will not determine our future salvation, which has already been determined by our faith in Jesus Christ (see **John 3:18**). The judgment for Christians on the Last Day will be for the purpose of rewarding the deeds we have done with gifts of glory. Study Paul's discussion of this topic in **1 Corinthians 3:10–15.**

d. How shall we live our life knowing that we will appear before the judgment seat of Christ **(verse 9)?** How does **2 Corinthians 5:15** point our lives in the right direction?

Come, my soul, with ev'ry care, Jesus loves to
    answer prayer;
He Himself bids you to pray, Therefore will not turn
    away.

Lord, your rest to me impart, Take possession of
    my heart;
There Your blood-bought right maintain And without a rival reign.

Show me what I am to do; Ev'ry hour my strength
    renew.
Let me live a life of faith; Let me die your people's
    death.

Lutheran Worship, 433: 1, 4, 6

We have this treasure in jars of clay to show that this all-surpassing power is from God and not from us. We are hard pressed on every side, but not crushed; perplexed, but not in despair; persecuted, but not abandoned; struck down, but not destroyed. We always carry around in our body the death of Jesus, so that the life of Jesus may also be revealed in our body.

2 Corinthians 4:7–10

SESSION 61

Ambassadors to the World

SECOND CORINTHIANS 5:11–6:2

Christianity's business is to wake people up! It is to rouse them from the sleep of spiritual death and to turn them to the waiting arms of God. It is to say, *"Now is the time of God's favor. Now is the day of God's salvation!"*

How urgently do we feel the need to share the Gospel? When opportunities come our way, do we take advantage of that solitary moment . . . or do the opportunities pass by, never to come again?

The ancient Greeks pictured *opportunity* in the form of a statue. The statue had the form of a human that stood on tiptoe, suggesting that it remained in any one spot for only a moment. On either side of its feet were wings, which represented the speed with which it passed by. The hair on the head was long at the front, which indicated that one must seize opportunity by the forelock whenever one met it. But the back of the head was completely bare, symbolizing that when opportunity passed, it could not be captured again.

Perhaps we would be more ready to seize opportunity by the hair if we better understood our high calling as Christians. It sounds overwhelming when we first hear it . . . but it's true. *Each of us is a personal ambassador of Jesus Christ*, a specially commissioned representative of the kingdom of God.

Let's explore this exciting truth today in one of the most quoted parts of the New Testament. You will be challenged by the King Himself!

CHRIST'S LOVE COMPELS US

1. What is the driving power behind our words and actions? What makes us tick? Christians respond with an answer clear as a bell. *"Christ's love compels us."* No greater influence shapes our lives. Read **5:11–15.**

a. Paul gives no apology for being a Christian, nor does he keep quiet about the mission of his life. How does he express this in **verse 11?**

b. Look at Paul's words in **verse 13.** Perhaps he refers here to his mystical experiences (**"we are out of our mind"**) as well as his more sober activities (**"we are in our right mind"**). Would you agree that Christ can be a part of the highs and lows of our emotional

life just as He is a part of our mental activities? Defend your answer.

c. The phrase **"Christ's love compels us" (verse 14)** means that His love holds us in its grip. His love pushes us to do works that benefit our neighbor. Mention some things you do that demonstrate the love of Christ in you. How might Christ's love develop in you even more? See **Colossians 3:16–17.**

d. Explain what Paul meant when he said that because **"[Christ] died for all, therefore all died" (verse 14).** Compare **Romans 6:3–4.**

e. Compare the difference between living for oneself and living for Christ **(verse 15).** Select an example from daily life and compare these two perspectives. Why are you able to live for Christ? Why were you not able to live for Him before you came to faith in Him?

2. Human standards don't apply to the goals and aspirations we seek after as Christians. The world does not write our agenda. Why? *We are a new creation! We are Christ's new people!* Read **verses 16–17.**

a. Paraphrase **verse 16.** Study **John 8:15–16.** How does Christ's love change the way you perceive other people? Share your thoughts on this.

b. Explain what you think it means that **"the old has gone, the new has come" (verse 17).** Compare **Isaiah 43:18–19.** Because we now belong to Christ, what old things have gone from our life? What new things have been added?

c. Apply the truth **"[you are] a new creation (verse 17)** to the following concerns of modern youth. How does the fact that Christ has brought a new order to your life affect your

    self-esteem;

    personal happiness;

    relationship with your family;

    relationship with your peers; and

    feelings about a worthwhile future?

d. With which of the concerns above do you feel most comfortable as a Christian? With which of the concerns do you feel your life in Christ needs to make more adjustments? (Answer privately. You need not share your answers.)

e. Look again at the above list of the concerns of modern youth. *As a class* identify the concerns that offer the most problems and challenges to a young person's life in Christ.

THE MINISTRY OF RECONCILIATION

When we share the Gospel with others, what are we to say? What message are we to communicate? Simply this one: *the message of reconciliation!* God seeks to be our Friend. He has made this friendship possible through Jesus Christ. Become God's friend! Study **5:18–21.**

1. Explain why it was necessary that God bring about the reconciliation between the world and Himself **(verses 18–19).** Why can't people reconcile themselves to God by saying on their own, "I want to be God's friend"? See **Romans 3:10–12** and **Ephesians 2:1.**

2. In order for friendship to be possible, God had to remove the problem that alienated the world from Himself. Describe what Christ had to do in order to remove the sin of all people **(verse 21).** What gift does God now offer to everyone in the world **(verse 21)?**

3. Suppose a person were to say to you, "But I still sin daily. How is it possible for God to accept me if I still am a sinner?" How does **verse 19** provide an answer to that question? See also **Romans 4:7–8.**

4. Christ offers each of us a marvelous privilege. He has called us to be His personal ambassadors to share the message of reconciliation **(verses 19–20).** Why is the title *ambassador* an appropriate term for the task He has given us?

5. Has God ever made an appeal through you **(verse 20)?** Share your experiences with one another. Is it possible for God to even speak through small children? In what way? See **Matthew 21:16.**

THE URGENCY OF OUR TASK

1. How urgent is our calling as Christ's ambassadors? It's as urgent as the need for those who hear the Gospel to accept it! The time of God's favor will not always be with us. *Today is the day to be reconciled to God!* Read **6:1–2.**

a. If you were sharing the Gospel with someone, how would you present the matter of the urgency of receiving Jesus Christ today **(verse 2)?**

b. Why do you suppose so many people delay their response to God's appeal through the Gospel? What was Felix's response to Paul's witness of the Gospel **(Acts 24:24–25)?** What was Herod Agrippa's response **(Acts 26:28–29)?**

c. Why must members of a Christian congregation be challenged each Sunday to God's message of reconciliation **(verse 1)?**

d. Pastors sometimes talk about deathbed conversions to Christ that they have witnessed. Explain the danger for those who wait until the last moment of their life to respond to God's appeal.

2. Suppose a young couple married with one disagreement between them as they started their life together. She was fervent in her love for Christ. He, however, did not take spiritual things seriously. What would you suggest the young wife do to make their marriage as happy as possible while at the same time showing concern for her husband's spiritual welfare? Should she insist that he attend worship services with her? Should she say nothing about her faith in Christ? See **1 Peter 3:1.**

3. Do you have friends who have still not responded to God's appeal in Christ? Some Christians have an active prayer list from which they pray daily or weekly for all such people to have open hearts to God's pleading.

4. After completing this lesson, what thoughts come to your mind about taking advantage of every opportunity to share Christ with others?

Spread the reign of God the Lord,
Spoken, written, mighty Word;
Ev'rywhere his creatures call
To his heav'nly banquet hall.

Tell of our Redeemer's grace,
Who, to save our human race
And to pay rebellion's price,
Gave himself as sacrifice.

Tell of God the Spirit giv'n
Now to guide us on to heav'n,
Strong and holy, just and true,
Working both to will and do.

Lord of harvest, great and kind,
Rouse to action heart and mind;
Let the gath'ring nations all
See your light and heed your call.

Lutheran Worship, 321:1, 3, 4, 6

(Stanzas 3, 4, and 6 from *Lutheran Book of Worship,* copyright © 1978. Concordia Publishing House representing the publishers and copyright holders. Used by permission. Stanza 1 copyright 1982 by Concordia Publishing House.)

Christ's love compels us, because we are convinced that One died for all, and therefore all died. And He died for all, that those who live should no longer live for themselves but for Him who died for them and was raised again.

2 Corinthians 5:14–15

SESSION 62

God Loves a Cheerful Giver

SECOND CORINTHIANS 9:1–15

Wherever Christians have advanced the Gospel, they have left behind a tell-tale sign. *Believers in Christ are generous people!*

Christians are almost always the first to respond to victims of hurricanes, famines, floods, and other such disasters. They willingly accept refugee families into their churches and homes, providing them with hope and encouragement to begin a new life. Those who are homeless and hungry know that followers of Christ are prepared to share what they have even when everyone else has said no. Because of the Christian Gospel, they have become aware that true compassion for another person means to minister to that person's total needs.

A missionary in Burma relates the story about a Buddhist man dying of throat cancer. At a Christian hospital in a highland village he was given food and medical assistance. The dying man was so touched by the kindness of the Christian staff that he asked about their God. Never in his life had he been treated so kindly and with such cheerful compassion. A few days later he died in the saving faith of Jesus Christ.

In this lesson we will be applying this theme of generous giving to our own lives of faith. We will examine questions that challenge us, questions like: How cheerful a giver am I? How willing am I to respond to the needs of those who look for the face of Jesus Christ in me?

THE COLLECTION FOR THE SAINTS

Because of unfortunate circumstances, the Christian saints in Jerusalem were in dire straits and were suffering. A collection for their welfare was being gathered in all the churches of Greece and Asia. Delegates were chosen to gather the funds and were even now ready to come to the church at Corinth, which had promised a generous offering. Read **verses 1–5.**

1. How does Paul describe the Corinthians' interest in the collection for the saints in Jerusalem **(verse 2)?** See also **8:10–11.**

2. The apostle had boasted to the Macedonians about the Corinthians' eagerness in this project of as-

sistance **(verse 2).** Look at **8:1–5.** How did the Macedonian Christians respond to this same appeal?

3. Because the delegation was ready to come to Corinth, what concern did Paul have about the Corinthians' offering **(9:3–4)?**

4. Being generous differs from giving a large offering grudgingly **(9:5).** What do you suppose that difference is? See also **8:12.**

SOW GENEROUSLY AND REAP GENEROUSLY

The more we spread, the more we receive (smiles, kindness, etc.). The more we share our possessions with those in need, the more our lives will be enriched by God's blessings. Study **9:6; 9–11.**

1. Notice how generosity begets generosity **(verse 6).** How do **Proverbs 11:24–25; 19:17;** and **Luke 6:38** express the same truth?

2. God especially commends being generous to the poor **(verse 9).** How does **James 2:14–17** remind us that we who have in abundance should share with the poor?

3. What does God promise to give to those who are generous with others **(verse 10)?** What does he mean by **"harvest of your righteousness"?**

4. In what way does God provide the resources that allow us to be generous to those in need **(verse 11)?** How does this passage assure us that when God touches our hearts, we will find the wherewithal to give?

5. Study **Mark 12:43–44.** Explain why the widow at the temple can truly be called a generous giver. Why did Jesus commend her gift so highly?

GIVE CHEERFULLY AS GOD GIVES

Generous givers give cheerfully after the manner of Christ Himself. They think not of themselves, but of the need of others. Study **verses 7–8.**

1. What do you suppose Paul means by the statement, **"Each man should give what he has decided in his heart to give" (verse 7)?** Why is Christian giving a matter of the heart's inner desire? How does this

relate to cheerful giving? How did Paul express this thought in **8:5?**

2. Our love for Christ motivates us to be cheerful givers. What blessing does God freely give us so that we will want to give **(verse 8)?** How does **8:9** speak of the generosity of God toward us?

3. What are some reasons why a person might give reluctantly or under compulsion **(verse 7)?** Is giving reluctantly better than not giving at all? Compare **8:12.** Talk about this.

4. God does not expect us to become poor so that others become rich. How does **2 Corinthians 8:13–15** speak about the problem?

5. What is sacrificial giving? What do you read about this topic in **8:3** and **Luke 21:1–4?**

THANKS BE TO GOD FOR HIS GIFT

1. Generous giving produces consequences that go far beyond meeting the needs of those in want. Our gifts of love encourage others to praise God for the grace of God that motivates us to help them. Read **9:12–14.**

a. When other people take note of our generosity, do they evaluate our spirituality as well? How do **verses 12–13** help answer that question?

b. Discuss this statement: *Generous giving is an expression of how seriously we are confessing our commitment to the Gospel of Christ.* What is your opinion? Give a reason for your answer.

c. Notice how generosity encourages others to become spiritually closer to us **(verse 14).** Explain why this is true. If possible, give an example.

2. Christian giving lies at the heart of the Gospel of Jesus Christ. *We are generous givers because God in every way gives generously to us.* What is the indescribable gift we have received from God that compels our hearts to rejoice with thanksgiving **(verse 15)?**

3. Examine the scene of the Last Judgment in **Matthew 25:34–40.** The topic of Christian giving will be an important aspect of the judgment.

a. Describe the gifts Christ considers to be an essential part of our faith in our life on earth.

b. In what way is Christ in all of the needs of oppressed and impoverished peoples of this earth?

c. What is your opinion of the necessity of our gifts to the needy after studying this Scripture?

4. Sometimes we just don't feel like contributing generously to the needs of others. Paul says, however, that God loves a cheerful giver **(9:7).** Does that mean

God doesn't love you? If not, describe the problem that does exist. Also describe the solution to that problem.

5. Talk about how you and your classmates can show your thanksgiving to God by participating in a class project. Here are some suggestions:

a. Take an offering for a needy family in your area and have representatives of the class deliver the gift in person.

b. Take a special mission offering to send to a missionary overseas with a thank-you letter from the class. Express your thanksgiving that the missionary and his or her family are representing you in the mission field.

c. Write some prayers of thanksgiving to the Lord that can be read at worship services in local churches.

> Lord of glory, you have bought us
> With your lifeblood as the price,
> Never grudging for the lost ones
> That tremendous sacrifice;
> And with that have freely given
> Blessings countless as the sand
> To the unthankful and the evil
> With your own unsparing hand.
>
> Grant us hearts, dear Lord, to give you
> Gladly, freely of your own.
> With the sunshine of your goodness
> Melt our thankless hearts of stone
> Till our cold and selfish natures,
> Warmed by you, at length believe
> That more happy and more blessed
> 'Tis to give than to receive.
>
> *Lutheran Worship, 402:1–2*

Each man should give what he has decided in his heart to give, not reluctantly or under compulsion, for God loves a cheerful giver. And God is able to make all grace abound to you, so that in all things at all times, having all that you need, you will abound in every good work.

2 Corinthians 9:7–8

SESSION 63

When I Am Weak, Then I Am Strong

SECOND CORINTHIANS 12:1–10

The young man in the hospital bed awoke to consciousness with a look of horror on his face. His hands were gone! He looked at the end of his arms and everything inside of him went cold and numb. There were only stumps where his hands had been.

"What good am I now?" he thought bitterly. "What can a man do without hands? My life is over."

But he was wrong. His life was not over. The most radiant and successful years of his life were ahead of him. The loss of his hands was to be the turning point in his life.

The young man without hands was Harold Russell. He had lost his hands in an accident as a paratrooper in World War II. While in the hospital he had met another man without hands who said to him: "Russell, you are not crippled. You merely have a handicap."

Harold Russell could not forget the words of his friend. Having a handicap meant that his life would be tougher, but he could still win. That was the important thing.

With this new mental attitude, Harold Russell fought his way back from bleak despair to victory. He became a motion picture star and the winner of Hollywood's Academy Award. He married his childhood sweetheart and later he became a successful author and lecturer.

"My weakness," said Harold Russell, "turned out to be my greatest strength. It is not what you have lost but what you have left that counts."

Talk about the story you read. Explain how Harold Russell used his weakness as a strength. In what way are possibilities for success always available in "impossible" situations? Have you ever experienced this in your own life?

Our lesson will focus on the theme of strength through weakness. No matter how weak we may become, God's grace is near at hand. His power can turn weaknesses into strengths.

WHEN "THORNS IN THE FLESH" COME INTO OUR LIVES

1. God had abundantly blessed the apostle Paul with wisdom from above. He showered Paul with revelations and divine mysteries to equip him for his work as an apostle. Few people have seen the mind of God as had Paul. All of these blessings and gifts prepare the stage for Paul's "thorn in the flesh." Read **verses 1–4.**

a. The Lord spoke to Paul in visions and revelations **(verse 1).** God frequently communicated His divine truths in such a manner. Read **Galatians 1:11–12.** What does Paul say about the Gospel he preached? In what manner did he receive this divine message?

b. Notice that Paul was caught up **"to the third heaven" (verse 2)** and **"to paradise" (verse 4).** These terms may be synonymous and may refer to the highest realm of heaven. What meaning does it have for you that the apostle heard utterances that came from heaven itself?

c. Study these Biblical references of people who received visions from God: Jacob **(Genesis 28:10–17)** and Peter **(Acts 10:9–16).** In what way do these visions remind you of Paul's experience **(verses 2** and **4)?**

d. Paul wrote 13 books of the New Testament canon, more than any other author. How does **verse 4** add to your confidence that Paul's writings have been inspired by God Himself? How do **2 Timothy 3:16** and **2 Peter 1:20** substantiate this truth?

2. A terrible and painful affliction assaulted Paul despite his dedication to God as an apostle. Satan wounded him with a thorn in the flesh, a malady that

Paul begged the Lord in prayer to remove. Study **verses 7–8.**

a. Explain why God permitted Satan to torment Paul with a painful bodily affliction **(verse 7).** In what way can affliction be the means by which God draws us closer to Himself?

b. Have you ever experienced a severe setback in your life in which you felt God was sending you a message? Do you believe God works through such afflictions as sickness, family disunity, or broken relationships? Share your thoughts on this with one another.

c. God *did not* send Paul his thorn in the flesh. The imposer of all such afflictions that torment God's people is Satan **(verse 7).** How did Jesus describe Satan's activity in the sicknesses and diseases that people bear **(Luke 13:16)?**

d. Look up **Job 2:6–7.** How does this passage show us that God allows Satan freedom to send trials to believers but within certain boundaries and limitations?

e. Do you sometimes feel that God has it in for you? Why are such feelings really a form of self-pity? How does **Romans 8:28** reveal that God always has your best welfare in mind through all the trials of life?

f. We do not know the exact nature of Paul's thorn in the flesh **(verse 7).** It must have hurt him severely because he prayed continuously ("three times") for the Lord to remove it **(verse 8).** Some people believe that Paul suffered a painful eye disease. See **Galatians 4:15** and **6:11.** Why could Paul be happy with God's answer to his prayer?

g. Describe a situation in your life, for example, a sickness in your family or a problem at school, in which you prayed desperately for God to intervene. What answer did God give you? How did you feel about His answer?

STRENGTH THROUGH WEAKNESS

1. God answered Paul's prayer in a way that made the apostle stronger in his faith and a more effective minister of the Gospel. Study the Lord's loving way of helping him turn his affliction into a strength. Read **verses 9–10.**

a. The Lord did not remove Paul's affliction but gave him the grace to live with it **(verse 9).** Explain how affliction leads us to depend on God's grace. Why is God's grace the most valuable gift we can receive? See **Romans 8:31–32.**

b. In what way does God's power show itself in our weaknesses **(verses 9–10)?** How is God able to accomplish so much when we are weak? See **Galatians 4:13–15.**

c. The lesson Paul learned through this personal experience (**"when I am weak, then I am strong"**) prepared him for a lifetime of suffering in his ministry for Christ. Read **2 Corinthians 11:23–30.** Explain how Paul's ministry for Christ became stronger when he became weaker.

d. How does **Galatians 2:20** explain Paul's dedication to use his weakness to honor Christ?

2. Examine the Biblical personalities below. How did each through God's power turn weaknesses into strengths?

a. Moses and his speech defect **(Exodus 4:10–17)**

b. Gideon and his tiny army of 300 men **(Judges 6:14–16; 7:19–23)**

c. David, when facing Goliath **(1 Samuel 17:41–47)**

3. Apply the truths you have learned in this lesson to the following situations from modern life. In each situation show how the weakness the person is suffering can, by God's grace, be turned into a strength:

a. After reaching the height of 5′3″, Tom stopped growing. He finds it difficult accepting his short stature because of the remarks of others, who often ridicule him.

b. Diana's parents rarely criticize her older brother, but they seem to constantly criticize her clothing, her music, her friends, and her behavior. In their eyes she can do nothing right. Her self-esteem is at a low ebb.

c. Paula dreamed of going to college to study art. Because of a need to support her widowed mother and two small sisters, she had to forego her college education and go to work. It seems now that she will never be able to fulfill her art career.

> If you but trust in God to guide you
> And place your confidence in Him,
> You'll find Him always there beside you
> To give you hope and strength within.
> For those who trust God's changeless love
> Build on the rock that will not move.
> *Lutheran Worship,* 420:1

[God] said to me, "My grace is sufficient for you, for My power is made perfect in weakness."
2 Corinthians 12:9

SESSION 64

Concluding Activities for Unit 7

Several activities are listed below to help you review the major truths of this unit. Following your teacher's direction, complete one or more of these activities.

WRITE A LETTER TO A PASTOR OR A MISSIONARY

Write a personal letter of encouragement to a pastor or a missionary. In your letter mention your gratitude to God for calling that person into the special ministry of the Lord's work. Talk about your own ministry in the Gospel. Include something about yourself, your family, and your school.

Ask your teacher or pastor to supply you with a list of names and addresses of pastors and missionaries in your church body.

MAKE A CROSS-CULTURAL COLLAGE

Create an awareness of being ambassadors to the world by constructing a collage of the many diverse cultures that make up the world.

On sheets of large posterboard (as many as will be needed) place interesting pictures of people from various cultures. Divide the assignment. Perhaps each member of your class can secure a picture of one cultural group. Stretch your creativity to make the collage appealing and to communicate a message.

Place appropriate Scriptural verses (such as those studied in this unit) on the collage and display it in a prominent area.

UNIT 8

The Joy That Proceeds from Faith

STUDIES IN PHILIPPIANS

What do these three persons have in common?

1. *A soldier has been stationed at a lonely overseas outpost for 18 months. He has not had one opportunity to see his wife or young son. One day when he returns from duty he is told by his commanding officer to pack his bags. He is being sent home immediately.*

2. *A young woman has experienced a difficult pregnancy, and the delivery has been filled with complications and pain. But when she opens her eyes, she sees the doctor holding a crying but very healthy baby girl.*

3. *An elderly man has been waiting outside the operating room for more than three hours. He agonizes that his wife, whose life is in the balance, may not survive this critical operation. Suddenly the door of the operating room opens and the doctor appears with a smile on his face: "She's going to be fine. The danger is past."*

All of these people are experiencing the most profoundly happy feeling humans are capable of—JOY! It is impossible to adequately define or describe the meaning of joy. But those who have experienced it know that there is no feeling to be compared to it.

Did you know that one of the greatest gifts God gives us is the gift of joy? Joy proceeds from our faith in Jesus Christ. It is God's way of assuring us that we are His and He is ours—forever!

In this unit you will study the Bible's book of joy, the letter to the Philippians. Joy characterized the apostle Paul's life. We will discover how it can be a dominant theme in our lives as well.

SESSION 65

Joy in Advancing the Gospel

PHILIPPIANS 1:3–29

Can anything good come out of a prison? How can God have anything to do with a person who has been labeled a criminal?

Don't draw any conclusions too swiftly. Some of the world's greatest deeds were done in a prison and by people the world labeled as dangerous criminals.

Martin Luther began his translation of the Bible into German while kept (by his friends) in Wartburg Castle for an entire year. This was the first modern translation of the Bible into a native tongue, and people have been blessed ever since by having the Bible in their own language.

John Bunyan wrote *Pilgrim's Progress,* one of the most popular Christian books in modern history, while incarcerated in Bedford jail.

St. John wrote the **Book of Revelation** while in exile on the island of Patmos.

Some of St. Paul's epistles, including his letter to the Philippians, were written while the apostle was a prisoner of the emperor.

Jesus Christ Himself was made a prisoner of Pontius Pilate and was labeled a vile criminal, condemned to die the shameful death of crucifixion on a cross.

We can only marvel at how God can work blessings out of what seem to be hopeless situations. The Gospel is too powerful to be kept in check by the whims of people. *Even a prison can be the pulpit from which God shares His mighty love with a world that needs Jesus Christ!*

CHRISTIAN JOY AS A "PRISONER FOR CHRIST"

1. The apostle Paul was most likely a prisoner of the emperor at Rome. He had been accused of disturbing the Roman peace and was awaiting trial for his life. Notice Paul's attitude as he writes to the Philippians about witnessing for the Gospel. Read **verses 3–11.**

a. What did Paul mean when he spoke of the Philippians as being his "partners"? Why do you suppose this gave him a feeling of joy **(verses 4–5)?**

b. Describe the affection Paul felt toward the Philippians **(verses 7–8).** Have you ever felt this way about other Christian brothers and sisters? What situation prompted this affection?

c. If Paul were alive today, would he also consider you a "partner" in the Gospel? How do you feel about using your life as a witness to the love Christ has for you? Talk about this with one another.

d. Look at Paul's beautiful prayer in **verses 9–11.** Why is this a good prayer for the purpose of "bringing Christ to the nations"? Do you believe that prayer can advance the cause of the Gospel? Explain.

2. No wonder Paul sounds *joyful.* His imprisonment has actually advanced the preaching of the Gospel! Other people have been converted to Christ through his "chains." Look at **verses 12–19.**

a. What does Paul say has happened throughout the palace as a result of his "chains" **(verse 13)?** Whom do you suppose were the recipients of his Christian witness?

b. What effect did Paul's imprisonment have upon other Christian preachers **(verse 14)?** Give a reason for your answer.

c. Not every Christian liked Paul personally. Some were jealous of him and preached the Gospel to advance themselves rather than Christ **(verses 15–18).** Explain how preaching the Gospel for *wrong* motives can still effectively be a way of proclaiming salvation in Jesus Christ.

d. Look especially at **verses 18–19.** Identify the two kinds of assistance Paul received which gave him confidence during his imprisonment. Relate the assistance he received to the Christian joy he felt. Explain how these go together.

CHRISTIAN JOY WHETHER DYING FOR CHRIST OR LIVING FOR CHRIST

1. What if you were in Paul's situation in a Roman prison? How would you face the prospect that your faith in Christ might mean being *put to death?* What are your thoughts about martyrdom for Christ? Let's examine Paul's response to that possibility. Read **verses 20–26.**

a. Notice how the apostle keenly looks to his future

(verse 20). What is he so confident about?

b. What does the phrase, "**to die is gain**" (**verse 21**), mean? Why does Paul look forward to his own death?

c. Are you looking forward to your death as did Paul? Talk about this as honestly and openly as you can. What aspects of dying make you joyful? What aspects make you troubled? Compare **John 14:1–3.**

d. Describe the dilemma that Paul refers to in **verses 22–26.** What reason does he give for his statement that "**it is more necessary for you that I remain in the body**"?

e. Discuss Paul's reason for wanting to remain alive **(verse 22).** Then apply Paul's thinking here to your own life. Do you believe that every Christian who is alive has a "purpose" on this earth? Share your opinions about this question.

CHRISTIAN JOY: FACING TROUBLES IN MY OWN FUTURE

1. God does not give us a crystal ball to discover when we might be called to suffer for our faith in Christ. The Philippians themselves had seen Paul suffer (compare **Acts 16:22–34**). Now suddenly they were facing the same kind of persecution. Read **verses 27–30.**

a. What advice does the apostle give the Philippians as they endured trials and tribulation? What will happen to those who oppose the Gospel and persecute Christians?

b. What important truth does God reveal to you in **verse 29?** How does **1 Peter 3:14–17** state the same truth?

2. *A discovery exercise.* Look at the following areas of the world and rank them in the order of where Christians might expect the most severe persecution. Share your findings with other members of the class and discuss your answers.
Latin America

Soviet Russia
Saudi Arabia
Your own city
Central Africa
China
Israel

3. Suffering for the sake of the Gospel may not be physical in nature. Sometimes suffering takes the form of verbal abuse or shunning. Identify some situations in which people might shun you or label you as "strange" if you spoke openly about Jesus Christ.

4. Suppose you are going through a trying circumstance in your life because of your Christian faith. Explain how you can still experience Christian joy despite the suffering and abuse you feel.

5. Write a letter to a friend who is facing a severe trial in his or her faith. What would you say to bolster his or her confidence and joy?

What a Friend we have in Jesus
All our sins and griefs to bear.
What a privilege to carry
Everything to God in prayer
Oh, what peace we often forfeit,
Oh, what needless pain we bear
All because we do not carry
Everything to God in prayer.

Have we trials and temptations?
Is there trouble anywhere?
We should never be discouraged
Take it to the Lord in prayer.
Can we find a Friend so faithful
Who will all our sorrows share?
Jesus knows our every weakness,
Take it to the Lord in prayer.

Lutheran Worship, 516:1–2

He who began a good work in you will carry it on to completion until the day of Jesus Christ.

Philippans 1:6

SESSION 66

The Ultimate Role Model

PHILIPPIANS 2:1–16

Who is the one person you admire more than anyone else in the whole world?

Think about this person for a few moments and get a clear picture of this person in your mind. Then ask yourself whether this person possesses the following qualities:

- has an attractive personality
- is intelligent
- has been gifted with certain skills
- possesses a good moral character
- is humble and self-giving

How did the person you selected match up to the qualities listed above? In which qualities did your selection score high? In which qualities did your selection seem deficient? Talk about this for a few minutes.

Now let's take this test one more step. Apply these same qualities to Jesus Christ and ask yourself this question: *Which quality in the list above best describes Jesus Christ in His mission of salvation on earth?*

After you have made your selection, share your opinion with others in the class.

It is perfectly normal to admire another person and use that person as a role model. According to psychologists, much of our learning development in life comes from emulating role models. The same process happens spiritually. Christians follow the Ultimate Role Model, Jesus Christ, whose life is a shining example for our own Christian behavior.

Let's turn now to our lesson and discover how Christ models Himself to us. By God's grace and power we can begin to walk in His footsteps.

AM I A HUMBLE PERSON?

1. Benjamin Franklin—so the story goes—fashioned a long list of virtues he was determined to keep. A friend noticed his list did not include the virtue of "humility" and asked Franklin why he left that virtue out. Reportedly, Franklin made this reply: "That is one virtue I cannot keep."

Let's study **verses 1–4** and discover why humility is such a difficult quality for humans to practice.

a. What attitudes toward other people are we urged to possess **(verses 1–2)?** What reasons does Paul give for possessing these attitudes?

b. Study **verse 3** carefully. Is it possible to do anything without selfish ambition (for example, take a test, compete in an athletic contest)? Why or why not?

c. What does Paul mean by **"consider others better than yourselves" (verse 3)?** How is this type of behavior to be done? What does **verse 4** say about this issue?

2. What does the word *humility* suggest to you as a behavioral style? Is it a virtue that American society ranks highly? Defend your answer. What kind of treatment would a "humble person" receive in our world?

3. Where would you rank yourself on the following scale of humility?

THE ULTIMATE MODEL OF HUMILITY

1. We do not learn humility by studying a word. We learn humility by imitating the Person who practiced it supremely in His own life. **Verses 5–11** are probably an ancient Christian hymn, sung by Christians in adoration of Jesus Christ, God's Humble Servant. Look at **verses 5–8.**

a. Explain how **verse 6** demonstrates that Jesus is GOD in His very nature. Discuss Jesus in His preexistence as God. (Compare **John 1:1.**) Which words in the Nicene Creed refer to Jesus as God?

b. How does **verse 7** demonstrate that Jesus is HUMAN in His very nature? (Compare **John 1:14.**) What word describes the "role" that Jesus took on earth by becoming a human being?

c. Examine **verse 8** carefully. Describe the many ways that Jesus humbled Himself in His earthly ministry. Describe how dying on the cross was also an important aspect of His humility. Whom did He "obey" by dying for our sins on the cross?

d. Living as a humble servant demands ultimate commitment. What must Jesus have felt in His heart toward the world to adopt the role of a servant? See **Romans 5:6–8.**

2. Isaiah had prophesied the role of Jesus as God's humble servant. That portion of Scripture relates to the section we are studying in Philippians. Look carefully at some of the key verses of **Isaiah 53.**

a. How does **Isaiah 53:2–4** describe Jesus in His servant ministry on this earth? Discuss what these verses mean to you.

b. The shameful death of Jesus is described in **Isaiah 53:5–12.** How do these verses say to you that it was God's will that His Son bear our sins on the cross? What words suggest that Jesus died voluntarily because of his self-giving love?

c. On the basis of **Isaiah 53,** tell why it was necessary that Jesus become a Servant for the world to receive salvation.

3. God sent His Son to this earth in humility, but received Him back in glory. Here is an important truth: *Humility is followed by exaltation.* Study **Philippians 2:9–11.**

a. What does it mean that Jesus is now exalted "to the highest place"? To which words of the Apostles' Creed might this phrase relate?

b. Notice the emphasis on the *name* of Jesus. Describe how His name compares with all other names. Why is His name so important? (Compare **Acts 4:12.**)

c. Describe the *title* God gives to the exalted Christ **(verse 11).** Why is this title an important part of the Christian confession of faith? (See **Romans 10:9.**)

4. Reflect for a few minutes on the *attitude of humility.* To reach out to others in self-giving love is God's way. To be a servant is to help and build up other people. God so honors this attitude that He honors it by exalting the person who practices it. Read **Luke 14:7–11.**

a. According to this story, what happens to the person who has an attitude of selfish ambition and conceit?

b. What happens to the person who purposely and humbly takes the lower seat?

c. What are the key words of this story?

SHINING AS STARS

1. God supplies us with the power and grace to live humbly—as Jesus did. His hand is in our lives to produce some marvelous spiritual victories. Because of God's power, we can "shine as stars" in a world that is dark. Look at **verse 12–16.**

a. How does living out our salvation "in fear and trembling" relate to the fact that God Himself is working His purpose in our lives **(verses 12–13)?**

b. Explain how living a humble and self-giving life is possible without complaining and arguing **(verse 14).** Where do you get the power to live such a life?

c. What activity do Christians practice so that they appear as "stars" shining in a crooked and depraved world **(verses 15–16)?**

2. *An activity summing up this lesson.* Write down your three strongest qualities as a person. Next to each of these qualities mention how each can be used in a humble, self-giving way for the benefit of others.

"Come, follow Me," said Christ, the Lord,
"All in My way abiding;
Your selfishness throw overboard,
Obey My call and guiding.
Oh, bear your crosses, and confide
In My example as your Guide.

"I am the Light; I light the way,
A godly life displaying;
I help you walk as in the day;
I keep your feet from straying.
I am the Way, and well I show
How you should journey here below."
Lutheran Worship, 379:1–2

Do everything without complaining or arguing, so that you may become blameless and pure, children of God without fault in a crooked and depraved generation, in which you shine like stars in the universe as you hold out the Word of life.
Philippians 2:14–16

SESSION 67

Strive for the Goal and the Prize

PHILIPPIANS 3:7–21

It took place at the 1984 Summer Olympics in Los Angeles. A woman long-distance runner from Switzerland circled the Coliseum track as the final lap of the women's marathon. The crowd was hushed. The runner, barely able to walk, weaved back and forth, her face revealing an excruciating torment. It was obvious that she was in extreme distress from heat exhaustion and dehydration.

Race officials offered her first aid, even though this would have meant disqualification. But she spurned their assistance and doggedly continued the lap, now hunched over and dragging one foot behind her. She inched closer to the goal. Members of the crowd were crying . . . cheering . . . sitting in stark amazement with eyes riveted on this solitary runner who would not quit. When at last she struggled over the finish line, collapsing in the arms of anxious officials, the Coliseum shook with an emotional roar seldom experienced in human events.

She had done it! Fighting against every bodily desire, she put it all aside to attain the one important goal pulsating within her—to finish the marathon she had started.

WHAT IS LIFE'S SUPREME GOAL?

1. Spend a few moments reflecting on the story you just read. Share your opinions as you think about the following questions:

Why do you suppose the crowd so identified with the runner?

In your opinion, was finishing the race worth the pain and agony the runner suffered? Why or why not?

What values about life does this story suggest to you?

2. The Christian life presents a goal worth enduring for as well. Let's see what Paul desired to have from God that he would give up everything to possess. Read **verses 7–9.**

a. What is the "surpassing greatness" Paul speaks of in **verse 8?** How is this stated in **verse 9?**

b. Why do you suppose Paul refers to all the earthly advantages he possessed as "rubbish" **(verse 9)?** (These "advantages" are summarized in **verses 4–6.**)

c. In your opinion, is it wrong to have earthly ambitions and desires? In what ways can earthly ambitions distract from a Christian's relationship with Jesus Christ?

d. How does the Christian balance the desire for earthly things and the desire for a personal relationship with Christ? See **Matthew 6:31–34.**

e. Explain how a person enters into a "personal relationship" with Jesus Christ **(verses 8–9).** What does it mean to "gain" Christ?

f. If you were to tell a friend about the way of salvation in Jesus Christ, how would you say it?

3. Our salvation includes more than knowing Jesus Christ personally. We look forward to the day of resurrection when Christ will raise our bodies from the dead. At this time God will complete the work of salvation He has already begun. Look at **verses 10–11.**

a. Why is the resurrection the supreme prize of the Christian life? Why is it *essential* that our resurrection be included as part of God's plan for our total salvation? See **1 Corinthians 15:16–19.**

b. By whose power will your body be raised from the dead **(verse 10).** See also **John 6:40.**

c. Look at **verses 20–21.** What do these verses say about the resurrection of our bodies?

PRESSING ON TOWARD THE GOAL

1. Think again of that runner in our opening story. She struggled in pain to finish the race, and she finished it. Paul compares the Christian life to a race. We Christians run as hard as we can with our eyes on the finish line. See **verses 12–16.**

a. How does **verse 12** explain that no one finishes the race of faith in this life on earth? What would you say to a person who insisted that he or she was "spiritually perfect"?

b. What is the Christian to keep his or her eyes on while running the race of faith **(verse 14)?** Say this in your own words. What is the "prize" to which Paul refers?

2. *A Self-inventory:* "HOW HARD AM I RUNNING THE RACE OF FAITH?" Choose one of the following as an indication of how you rate your spiritual life at this time. (A self-inventory is simply a checkup.)

a. **Not a winning performance.** I seem to pay more attention to worldly goals than to my life with Christ. I'm not running as hard as I can.

b. **A struggle, but I'm doing better.** I have good days and bad days. Sometimes Christ means everything to me, and sometimes I forget Him completely.

c. **I'm starting to enjoy the race.** I feel like my life is finally faced in the right direction. Christ means more to me year after year.

Whatever rating you gave yourself, remember that God's grace makes it possible for you to run the race of faith. Spend a moment in prayer thanking God for your new life in Christ. Pray also for the strength to improve your performance.

3. Athletes train rigorously for important races. The greater the discipline in training, the better the prospects for a superior performance. Notice how Paul applies discipline to our lives of faith in **1 Corinthians 9:24–27.**

a. Describe how Paul trains himself for running a good race of faith.

b. Mention a few things you might do in your own life to add some discipline to your life of faith. Share your answers with others.

THE POWER BEHIND OUR PERFORMANCE

1. Let's not imagine that we are running the race of faith on our own feeble power. Instead, God freely supplies us with His strength because He desires that we reach the goal and receive the prize. Look at **verses 17–21.**

a. What must we keep looking at in order to be open to God's power and strength **(verse 20)?** What phrase in **verse 21** suggests to you that God is both our trainer and our coach?

b. **Verses 18–19** describe those who are "enemies of the cross of Christ." What false goal of life are these people following?

c. Does God's promise in **verse 21** make a difference to you in how you run the race of faith today? Explain.

2. Some runners drop out of the race and give up long before they reach the finish line. On the basis of what you have learned in this lesson, explain why you are certain that you will finish the race of faith.

3. Suppose you were discussing your faith with a girl who is unsure she will be with Christ in heaven. She mentions that she doesn't believe she is "good enough" to deserve God's eternal life. How would you answer her?

Run the straight race through God's good grace;
Lift up your eyes and seek his face.
Life with its way before us lies;
Christ is the path and Christ the prize.

Cast care aside, lean on your guide;
His boundless mercy will provide.
Trust, and enduring faith shall prove
Christ is your life and Christ your love.

Faint not nor fear, his arms are near;
He changes not who holds you dear.
Only believe, and you will see
That Christ is all eternally.

Lutheran Worship, 299:2–4

Whatever was to my profit I now consider loss for the sake of Christ.

Philippians 3:7

SESSION 68

Rejoice in the Lord

PHILIPPIANS 4:4—13

Here's an experiment for you. Imagine yourself in a church during worship. Look around at the people, notice the decorations in the chancel, observe the appointments within the nave, listen to the organ music and to the people singing. Visualize the pastor preaching or reading the lessons. Try not to miss a thing.

Now do this: *Write down all the symbols or indications of Christian joy that come to your mind. Include everything that strikes you as being cheerful and happy.*

What did you include in your list? Share your findings with others in the class.

How much joy do Christian believers share with each other? How much joy do Christian believers show the world outside the church? What are your thoughts on this subject?

We do know that Christian joy *should* be a dominant part of our faith in Jesus Christ. Jesus Himself was the most radiant man in all history. People loved being around Jesus. The crowds hovered near Him to hear the good news He preached. Children sat on His lap as He spoke to them of God's love. Wherever the Gospel has been preached, joy has been born in the hearts of people. This is because joy is a fruit of faith.

Let's explore this topic and discover the reasons why Christians deserve to be called the most cheerful people on earth.

THE SECRET OF CHRISTIAN JOY

1. Paul gives the Philippians a watchword to advertise their faith to the world. He tells them to "rejoice in the Lord always." **Read verses 4–5:**

a. In your own words, what does it mean to "rejoice in the Lord?" Think of another word or phrase that might mean the same thing as "joy."

b. Where does Christian joy come from? See **Galatians 5:22; Romans 15:13; 1 John 1:3–4.** Why is joy a distinctive mark of being a Christian?

c. Why do you suppose people were "glad" when they were around Jesus? Study **Mark 12:35–37; John 20:19–20.** What has Jesus done to make your life happier? See **Matthew 9:2; John 15:9–11; Luke 2:10–11.**

d. What joyful behavior **(verse 5)** are Christians to practice before Christ returns to earth? Why is it important how we appear to people in the world?

2. Martin Luther was deeply impressed by the joy of the Christian faith. He wrote many words about it, including the following paragraph:

God can make Himself known only through those works which He manifests in us, and which we feel and experience within ourselves. But where there is this experience, there a hearty love for God is born, the heart overflows with gladness, and goes leaping and dancing for the great pleasure it has found in God.

(From *Luther,* by Robert F. Fischer, Philadelphia: Lutheran Church Press, 1966.)

a. Explain how Christian joy comes from personally experiencing God's works of love and salvation.

b. Have you ever had these feelings Luther talks about? Discuss this subject.

WHAT IS JOY LIKE?

Paul lists several reasons why Christians should always rejoice. All of these reasons have to do with God's constant care of His people. Let's discover what joy is like by examining three situations in which God is there with us to give us His power and peace.

1. **Joy is like a playful child.** Christians have anxieties and worries like everyone else. But they can re-

solve these worries through prayer. Just like a contented and carefree child who plays near her mother or father, so Christians can live joyfully because God's peace has replaced their cares and concerns. Read **verses 6–7.**

a. What does Paul prescribe to the Christian who is anxious and worrisome **(verse 6)?** Be sure to list every part of his prescription.

b. What does it mean to "petition" God in your prayer? Why does Paul add the word *thanksgiving* when praying in an anxious situation?

c. What is God's promise to you if you take your cares and worries to Him in prayer **(verse 7)?** How can God's "peace" guard you against further anxiety?

d. Suppose one of your friends professes to be a worry wart. She says she can't help worrying because that is her nature. On the basis of what you have learned, how would you counsel her?

e. In your own words, tell how you can be joyful like "a playful child" even when the worries and anxieties of life get you down.

2. **Joy is like a beautiful song.** Sin causes a lot of squalor and ugliness in the world. But Christians can focus their thoughts on a higher plane of life where beauty and purity reside. Even though we live in a sinful world, God brings joy to our lives as He leads us to think good thoughts that are as lovely as a beautiful song. Read **verses 8–9.**

a. Identify the seven types of godly thoughts that bring pleasure and joy to the mind. Give an example of each.

b. When we think healthily as these verses prescribe, what promise of God will take place in our lives **(verse 9)?**

c. What might be a Christian response to a person who tells dirty jokes or off-color stories again and again?

d. In your own words, tell how the types of thoughts that occupy your mind are related to being joyful in the Lord.

3. **Joy is like a tranquil sea.** Certainly there are times when Christians are "broke," with not even "two pennies to rub together." At other times it seems as if we have more than enough to spare. Despite the ups and downs of our lives, we can maintain a spirit of Christian cheerfulness throughout. God gives us joy to live tranquil lives no matter what the environment we are in. Read **verses 10–13.**

a. Paul apparently had been living in poverty. How-

ever, he says that this fact did not upset him. How was he able to face it so cheerfully **(verses 10–12)?**

b. What was Paul's great secret to live life so tranquilly **(verse 13)?**

c. Explain in your own words how God's strength can blunt the pain of being in need. (Compare **Matthew 6:25–34.**)

d. Do you consider it a sin to worry about the material things of life? Give a reason for your answer.

e. In your own words, describe how you can "rejoice in the Lord" if you are (1) rich; (2) poor.

CELEBRATE THE JOY OF FAITH

Do the following activity with your class. It emphasizes the joy of the Lord in praise and thanksgiving.

Divide the class into two sections. While the first section reads the following paraphrase of **Psalm 108,** the other section rhythmically claps its hands in unison. Then reverse the sections and repeat:

PSALM 108

My heart is glad today, O God
      and I am determined to serve You!
I celebrate your presence.
I glory in Your love for me.
I sing Your praises
      and yearn to proclaim Your loving concern to all. . . .

I know to whom I belong,
      and I know where I am going.
I know that You are my Lord
      and that You will accompany me
            as I walk the streets of the city and
                  mingle with the groping
                  inhabitants.

I pray, O Lord, that You will use me,
      that through my fumbling efforts
            You will touch some soul with healing
            and love.

My heart is glad today, O God.
Grant that I may communicate to others
      some measure of this eternal joy.

(From *Psalms Now* by Leslie Brandt. Copyright © 1973 by Concordia Publishing House.)

Rejoice in the Lord always. I will say it again: Rejoice!

Philippians 4:4

SESSION 69

Concluding Activities for Unit 8

Several activities are listed below to help you review the major truths of this unit. Following your teacher's directions, complete one or more of these activities.

GROUP DIALOG

1. In a group of about four students, with an equal distribution of boys and girls in each group (if possible), take turns selecting your favorite role models in each of the following categories. State the reason for your choices.

    a. my personality role model

    b. my intellectual role model

    c. my athletic role model

    d. my artistic role model

    e. my spiritual role model

2. Staying in your same groups, point out how the person you selected also possesses other godly and moral qualities to be a worthy model to follow.

3. If time permits, volunteers may share their selections with the entire class.

"I WAS THERE . . . "

Write a short story about being captured by terrorists on a flight to the Middle East. Describe the tension and anxiety in this situation in which death looms as a distinct reality. At the same time, describe how your joy in Christ would sustain you in this crisis. In a sense, imagine that you were St. Paul captured by terrorists.

Make your story as vivid as possible, but reasonably short. Be ready to read your story to the class.

A BANNER OF JOY

Make a class banner celebrating the themes of this unit, all of which feature some dimension of Christian joy. Your class should be divided into groups, each with a different assignment in the task of constructing the banner.

When completed, your class may want to hang the banner in your home room or in your worship facility.

UNIT 9

Faith Expressed by Hope

STUDIES IN FIRST AND SECOND THESSALONIANS

Have you ever wondered about the end of the world? What will the last day on earth be like? When will it take place? What will happen?

Occasionally a person will appear and announce that the end of the world is near. Such a person claims that God has revealed to him or to her the exact date of Christ's return. We often see a flurry of excitement. Some people, in fact, take the announcement so seriously that they make actual preparations for the announced day. But when Christ does not come as predicted, the enthusiasm of the people wanes, and life returns to normal.

Many people today believe that the possibility of the end of the world seems more real now than in former times. A nuclear war could destroy most of the inhabitants of this earth. Those that did survive may not live long, because some scientists predict that a "nuclear winter" would envelop the earth soon afterward. (Even non-Christian scientists see that the end of human history is a possibility).

In this unit we will examine some of the Bible's teachings about the "end times" (sometimes called *eschatology*). The Thessalonian Christians were concerned about the Day of the Lord (the day of Christ's return to the earth). They wondered about the same questions you and I might ask: "What will that day be like?" "When will that day appear?" "How are we to prepare in anticipation of that day?"

Scripture gives us some clear answers to these questions. We will discover that God in His love has prepared a marvelous future for us. Even now He fills our hearts with the assurance of faith that Christ is surely coming. We pray the prayer of Christian Hope—"AMEN. COME, LORD JESUS."

SESSION 70

Living to Please God

FIRST THESSALONIANS 4:1–12

Have you heard about the pastor whose "congregation" was made up entirely of prostitutes?

A Christian minister in New Orleans believed that the hardened "girls of the street" needed to hear the Gospel of Jesus Christ. He was called the "chaplain of Bourbon Street." Going from bar to bar, he gained the trust of these women by his friendly manner and by his concern for their spiritual destiny.

Many of his fellow pastors felt that "streetwalkers" would scorn and mock the "chaplain of Bourbon Street." But he discovered that these prostitutes hated what they were doing. Trapped in a hopeless way of living with no future, they welcomed the liberating message of the Good News of Christ. Many were converted to Christ and began new lives filled with meaning and joy.

You may see here a curious relationship between how people see their "future" and how they behave in the "present." If people's attitudes about their future are changed, their present behavior may change as well.

The situation at the church in Thessalonica resembled the situation faced by the chaplain of Bourbon Street. The problem of sexual immorality was getting out of hand. These Christians had to be challenged to the truth of their high calling in Jesus Christ and the promise of a better life to come.

THE CALL TO HOLY LIVING

1. Sexual immorality was rampant in the pagan world of Paul's day. Prostitution, adultery, and homosexuality were common practices and were accepted as part of the framework of normal living. The Christians at Thessalonica struggled with this "old way of life" and their "new calling in Jesus Christ." Paul reminds them that God has called them to holy lives patterned after His will. Read **4:1–7** and discuss the following questions.

a. In what ways is sexual immorality against the will of God **(verses 1–3)?** Why do you suppose our sexual behavior is so important in our Christian walk of faith? (Compare **3:13.**)

b. **"Passionate lust" (verse 5)** is considered normal by many people today, just as it was in ancient times. How do such people view the purpose of their bodies? How does God want us to view the purpose of our bodies **(verse 4)?**

c. Someone once said, "God created us to *love* people and to *use* things. But sinful people have changed that instead to *use* people and to *love* things." How does sexual immorality "use" people as "things"?

d. God will punish those who engage in sexual immorality **(verse 6).** To what kind of punishment do you suppose this refers?

2. Developers of modern media know that "sex" both attracts viewers and sells magazines and books. Rate the following types of media in their presentation of sexual behavior. Use a scale of 1 to 5 with the extreme of "passionate lust" as 1 and the extreme of "holy use of the body" as 5. Give reasons for your answers and talk about this powerful influence of our culture.

a. TV sitcoms

b. TV soap operas

c. Romance magazines

d. Paperback novels

e. Movies (parental gudiance)

f. Movies (restricted)

3. Do the sexually explicit signals of our culture cause stress to Christian teenagers, or are these cultural influences overrated? Defend your opinion.

4. How would you respond to a Christian friend who said that she really "loves" her boyfriend and sees nothing wrong in having sexual relations with him?

THE POWER AT WORK WITHIN US

God gives us the strength to abstain from "passionate lust" and to walk the high road of holiness. Each of us is a "temple" in which the Holy Spirit lives. Read **verses 8–10.**

1. How does the Holy Spirit lead us to a proper use of our bodies **(verse 8)?** (Refer also to **1 Corinthians 6:18–20.**)

2. Some people say they are addicted to sex just as other people are addicted to alcohol and other drugs.

They claim they cannot help themselves. What answer to this problem do you find in **verse 9?**

3. Many girls resent being thought of as "sex objects." How can a healthy Christian love turn a person's thoughts from "lust" to a higher view of the other person's humanity?

4. Some Christians preserve themselves from immorality until a strong temptation enters their lives. Why is Paul's advice in **verse 10** so important for young Christians who believe they will never succumb to immorality?

INFLUENCING THE WORLD AROUND US

1. The Gospel has a marvelous answer to the so-called "attractions" of sexual immorality. It suggests that we present to the world an even more "attractive Christian lifestyle" and thus win the respect and admiration of unbelievers. Study **verses 11–12.**

a. How can the advice in **verse 11** bring admiration from unbelievers and cause them to seek after the true God?

b. Someone has said that our influence on others is the "shadow that trails behind us." In what ways might you influence the following to Jesus Christ?

- your brother or sister
- your close friends
- your classmates
- a stranger on the street

c. Why do you suppose Paul considered it important that Christians **"not be dependent on anybody" (verse 12)?**

2. Far too often Christian guys and girls are tempted to compromise their morality in order to be "popular." How can being "wholesome-minded" be an even more popular and envied life-style in today's world?

3. Look again at **1 Thessalonians 3:13.** Explain how our *future* with Christ affects our behavior in the present world.

The man is ever blessed
Who shuns the sinners' ways,
Among their counsels never stands,
Nor takes the scorner's place.

He like the tree shall thrive,
With waters near the root;
Fresh as the leaf his name shall live,
His works are heavenly fruit.

Not so the wicked race,
They no such blessings find;
Their hopes shall flee like empty chaff
Before the driving wind.

How shall they bear to stand
Before the judgement seat
Where all the saints at Christ's right hand
In full assembly meet?

Lutheran Worship, 388:1, 3, 4–5

Make it your ambition to lead a quiet life, to mind your own business and to work with your hands, just as we told you, so that your daily life may win the respect of outsiders and so that you will not be dependent on anybody.

1 Thessalonians 4:11–12

SESSION 71

The Coming Day of the Lord

FIRST THESSALONIANS 4:13–18

The early Christians lived with the fervent hope that the second coming of Jesus Christ would occur soon. Many expected to see Jesus return in triumph in their own lifetime.

An air of excitement about the imminent coming of Christ filled the Christian community. One of the earliest prayers in Christendom was, **"Amen. Come, Lord Jesus" (Revelation 22:20).**

Sometimes waiting for something exciting causes people to become impatient. We all know how small children tend to become nervous and temperamental the week before Christmas. Christians at times have also demonstrated anxiety about the time or the date of Christ's second coming rather than simply trusting the promise.

The Thessalonian Christians were especially troubled about certain aspects of the Day of the Lord. As a result of this anxiety, their joy was beginning to erode. In this session we will discover how Paul gives these Christians an assuring answer to an important topic.

LIVING WITH A SURE HOPE

The Thessalonian Christians were struggling with an issue concerning those Christians who had already died. When Christ returns, won't those Christians who have died be at a disadvantage? How could they share in Christ's victory if they are dead? Let's examine Paul's response to this question in **verses 13–15.**

1. Notice how Paul refers to the dead as **"those who fall asleep" (verse 13).** Why do you suppose this term is so frequently used in the New Testament to desribe death? (Compare **Luke 8:52–54; John 11:11–13; 1 Corinthians 15:6.**)

2. In what way does the term "fallen asleep" assume that there is a resurrection to come?

3. Describe what will happen to the Christian dead on the day that Christ returns to earth **(verse 14).**

4. Will there be an advantage to those who are alive when Christ returns **(verse 15)?** How does this truth give assurance to the troubled Thessalonians?

5. Many in the ancient world considered death as utter hopelessness. One Greek poet said that it would be better never to have been born at all, since death was the killer of human hope. How does **verse 14** reflect this pessimistic attitude? What kinds of statements have you heard that reflect the same attitude?

6. Because of Jesus Christ we Christians live with a sure hope about our future. How does **verse 14** explain the reason why we are assured a future life with God? Also note **1 Corinthians 15:20–23.** What do these words say about the resurrection and our future hope?

THE DAY CHRIST RETURNS

It is important to our faith to be clear about the events surrounding the return of Jesus Christ to this earth. Let's examine **verses 16–17** and understand the Scripture's teaching about the Last Day.

1. Look again at the phrase, *the coming of the Lord,* in **verse 15.** What promise did Jesus make about His coming again in **John 14:3** and **Mark 13:26–27?** How does **Hebrews 9:28** refer to Christ's coming at the Last Day?

2. Describe the scene of Christ's return as if you were an eyewitness **(verses 16–17).** What will happen on that day?

3. Look carefully at **Matthew 24:30–31.** Who will accompany Christ at His return in glory? What will be their mission?

4. Why do you suppose Christ's return will be announced by the **"call of the trumpet" (verse 16)?** Compare **Exodus 19:13, 16, 19; Zephaniah 1:14–16.**

5. Notice how the dead in Christ will be raised *first* and then will join the other believers who are alive **(verses 16–17).** Will those who are alive at Christ's coming go through a physical change? See **1 Corinthians 15:51–53.** Describe what you think will happen.

6. What marvelous promise about our future with Christ is mentioned in **verse 17?** Share with one another what this means to you.

TELL THE WORLD ABOUT IT

1. The teaching of Christ's return not only comforts Christians with its message of hope. It also encourages

us to give hope to those who grieve or who live without hope in this world. See **verse 18.**

a. Think of a loved one from your family who has died and was a consecrated Christian. Will you see that person again on the day Christ returns in glory? Give a reason for your answer.

b. What would you say to a good friend whose father suddenly died of a heart attack? What words of encouragement would bring comfort to your friend?

2. Teenage suicide is now the third leading cause of death among young people in our nation. Why do you supppose so many teens kill themselves? Do they have hopeless thoughts about their future? What would you say to a friend who contemplated suicide?

3. Suppose you were to give a talk on "The Second Coming of Christ and Its Meaning for Me." What major themes would you include in your talk?

Jerusalem the golden,
With milk and honey blest,
Beneath your contemplation
Sink heart and voice oppressed.

I know not, oh, I know not
What joys await us there,
What radiancy of glory,
What bliss beyond compare.

Oh, sweet and blessed country,
The home of God's elect!
Oh, sweet and blessed country
That eager hearts expect!
In mercy, Jesus, bring us
To that dear land of rest!
You are, with God the Father
And Spirit, ever blest.

Lutheran Worship, 309:1, 4

The Lord Himself will come down from heaven with a loud command, with the voice of the archangel and with the trumpet call of God, and the dead in Christ will rise first. After that, we who are still alive and are left will be caught up together with them in the clouds to meet the Lord in the air. And so we will be with the Lord forever. Therefore encourage each other with these words.

1 Thessalonians 5:16–18

SESSION 72

The Suddenness of That Day

FIRST THESSALONIANS 5:1–18

What would you do if you knew that Jesus Christ was coming back to earth tomorrow?

Would you make a special attempt to make this last day "more Christian" than any day you have ever lived? Would you try to mend all the "broken fences" in your life and to heal all the hurts you have caused? Do you think you might spend the day in prayer or Bible reading? Perhaps you would want to just spend more time with your family and discuss your thoughts, hopes, and ideals with them. *Share your thoughts on this question with your classmates.*

Someone once asked Martin Luther this same question. He reportedly answered, "If I knew that Jesus Christ was coming tomorrow, I would plant an apple tree today."

Think about Luther's answer for a moment. Luther said, in effect, that he would spend his last day no differently than he would spend any other day. *He was ready for Jesus Christ to come at any time!* In other words, "live each day as if it might be the day that Jesus Christ comes again in glory."

Our lesson today focuses on this theme of being prepared for the second coming of Christ. How prepared are we? Let's find out.

DON'T BE UNPREPARED

The Thessalonian Christians didn't like being "kept in the dark" about the coming of the Lord. Many of them desired special information about the possible date Jesus might appear. Just like some Christians today, they believed that knowing the date in advance would give them an advantage in being prepared for the Second Coming.

Notice how Paul responds to this improper attitude. Read **verses 1–3.**

1. What phrase in **verse 1** reflects the interest of the Thessalonians in trying to figure out the date of the Second Coming? If possible, tell about any Christian groups that seek to do the same thing today.

2. How does Paul admonish the Thessalonians for their misguided interest in times and dates **(verse 2)?**

How instead does he describe the day of Christ's coming? (Compare **Matthew 24:36–44.**)

3. Look closely at **verse 3.** In what way do these words characterize the coming of Christ as a sudden event?

4. If someone should try to prove to you that Christ was returning to this earth at a specific date, how would you respond?

5. Why do you suppose God "keeps us in the dark" about the exact date Christ will return? What spiritual benefit do we derive by *not* knowing the time of His coming?

LIVE IN THE LIGHT NOT IN THE DARK

When Christ returns, He will find two groups of people on earth: the children of light and the children of darkness. Those who are waiting for Christ's coming behave in a vastly different way from those who are not. Study **verses 4–11.**

1. To what people is Paul referring when he uses the term darkness **(verses 4–5)?** Contrariwise, who are the "sons of light"? How do the terms "darkness" and "light" help us understand the conflict between God and evil? Explain how Christ has made you a child of the light. (See **verse 9.**)

2. How will the coming of Christ emotionally affect those who live in darkness **(verse 4)?** How will it affect those who belong to the light? How about you? Would you be surprised if Christ were to come tomorrow? Should you be?

3. Describe the behavior of those who are not waiting for Christ's return **(verses 6–8).** What difference do you see in those who *are* waiting with anticipation for the Savior's return?

4. Read the parable of the 10 virgins in **Matthew 25:1–13.** What truth does Christ teach in this parable? Why is it so necessary that we be prepared for the day of His coming?

5. Explain what Christ will give to the children of light at His coming **(1 Thessalonians 5:9–10).** What will happen to the children of darkness?

6. What great action by Christ motivates us to live

in anticipation of His coming (verse 11)?

7. Does it seem to you that more people today are living in darkness than in the light? Discuss this question with your classmates. (You may want to look at Matthew 7:13–14.)

FAITH PREPARES US FOR CHRIST'S COMING

What is the best way for you to live today if you knew that Jesus Christ was coming tomorrow? Remember Luther's advice. Keep yourself busy in a life of faith and you will always be prepared! Read 1 Thessalonians 5:12–18 for some practical advice on living productive and joyful lives for Christ.

1. To whom do you suppose Paul is referring when he names "those . . . who are over you in the Lord" (verses 12–13)? Why should they be treated with respect and regarded highly in love? How does Hebrews 13:7 suggest the same attitude?

2. Each of the phrases in verses 13–14 are Christian duties to our brothers and sisters in the Lord. In your own words, what do these phrases mean to you?

3. Which of the Christian duties above have you actively incorporated into your life? Which of them do you find difficult to do? Why?

4. Why is getting even with someone (verse 15) so opposed to the life to which God has called you? How did Jesus deal with those who treated Him wrongfully?

5. Is it possible to be joyful always, to pray continually, and to give thanks in all circumstances (verses 16–18)? What do you suppose these verses mean?

6. How would you organize your day on the basis of verses 16–18? Would you feel better prepared for Christ's coming if your daily schedule focused on these activities? Why or why not?

> The clouds of judgment gather,
> The time is growing late;
> Be sober and be watchful,
> Our judge is at the gate:
> The judge who comes in mercy,
> The judge who comes in might
> To put an end to evil
> And diadem the right.
>
> Arise, O true disciples;
> Let wrong give way to right,
> And penitential shadow
> To Jesus' blessed light;
> The light that has no evening,
> That knows no moon or sun,
> The light so new and golden,
> The Light that is but one.
>
> *Lutheran Worship, 463:1–2*

Since we belong to the day, let us be self-controlled, putting on faith and love as a breastplate, and the hope of salvation as a helmet. For God did not appoint us us to suffer wrath but to receive salvation through our Lord Jesus Christ. He died for us so that, whether we are awake or asleep, we may live together with Him. Therefore encourage one another and build each other up, just as in fact you are doing.

1 Thessalonians 5:8–11

SESSION 73

The Appearance of the Antichrist

SECOND THESSALONIANS 2:1–17

Does it sometimes appear to you as if a great war is being waged on our earth between the forces of good and the forces of evil?

The theme of a conflict between goodness and evil has driven the imagination of writers for years. Our literature and drama are filled with it. Even Hollywood has found this to be a compelling theme. Successful science fiction films portray the dark forces of the universe fighting to the death against the forces of good. Perhaps people never tire of this topic because they see this conflict as a stark reality.

The Scriptures portray this warfare, however, to be far more serious than any science fiction film could picture it. The Word of God reveals that the battle between the army of Satan and God's army (the church) continues relentlessly. Even now the war wages about us; we are involved as participants. At no time is the conflict more deadly than when we battle the Antichrist, the enemy of God, who appears in various forms even now, and will be very extreme in the so-called last days.

This lesson focuses on the teaching of the Antichrist and the assurance we have from God that He will strengthen us to stand firm in faith against this messenger of Satan. We live with a lively hope that God will win this final victory over the forces of evil. When Christ returns, He will bring judgment to the earth. He will share with us forever the glory of His triumph and His kingdom of love.

THE APPEARANCE OF THE ANTICHRIST

1. A rumor about the Coming of Christ was circulating among the Thessalonian Christians and was causing a grave disruption in the congregation. Some of the members were under the impression that the Day of the Lord had already come. Paul replies that such a rumor could not possibly be true. Read his response in **verses 1–3.**

a. Why do you suppose the Thessalonians were so quick to believe that the Day of the Lord might actually have already come (**verses 1–2**)?

b. Why is it important not to be gullible when people try to persuade you to believe an interpretation of the Scripture that is different from what you have been taught? Compare **1 John 4:1.**

c. What reason does Paul give the Thessalonians that the Day of the Lord had not yet come (**verse 3**)?

2. The teaching of the Antichrist (the man of lawlessness, **verse 3**) is recorded in many parts of the Scripture. This teaching helps us understand the events that will transpire before the Day of the Lord. Carefully examine the following Biblical truths, which lay out clearly the doctrine of the Antichrist. Read **verses 3–12.**

a. The Antichrist is the archenemy of God, the representative of Satan, who will seek to destroy God's church. He is called the man of lawlessness (**verse 3**), the abomination of desolation (**Matthew 24:15**), the beast (**Daniel 7:19; Revelation 13:1**), and the Antichrist (**1 John 2:18**). He will make his appearance shortly before the Day of the Lord.

b. When the Antichrist appears, he will lead a rebellion against the church and will make war on the saints (**verse 3**). See also **Daniel 7:19–23.**

c. The Antichrist will attempt to make the entire earth worship him instead of the true God (**verse 4**). So radically will he oppose God that he will set up his rule in the church itself. See **Revelation 13:1–8.**

d. The days of the Antichrist will be so oppressive for believers in Jesus Christ that God will shorten the days of his rule on earth. See **Matthew 24:15–22.**

e. The coming of the Antichrist is being held in check until the proper time (**verse 6**). However, certain aspects of his oppressive rule have already begun (**verse 7**). See also **1 John 2:18.**

f. On the Day of the Lord, when Christ returns to earth, He will destroy the Antichrist and the power of evil (**verse 8**). See also **Daniel 7:21–22** and **Matthew 24:29–31.**

3. The Antichrist will use a deadly weapon to attract worshipers in his war against God's church. He will employ the Satanic lie (**John 8:44**) in a massive effort to deceive the peoples of the earth. Read **verses 8–12.**

a. Examine the activities of the Antichrist in his

campaign to delude the world **(verse 9).** Why are these effective ways to attract followers? Give examples from history in which such activities deluded the masses

b. How successful will the Antichrist be in his great campaign of turning the world against God and to himself **(verse 10)?** Do you suppose some who had been believers will deny Christ and follow the Antichrist? Explain your answer.

c. How do we know that the work of the Antichrist is really the work of Satan **(verse 9)?** See also **Revelation 13:1–8.**

d. Why do you suppose God will allow the Antichrist to delude so many people **(verses 10–12)?** If people are deluded, what gift of God are they rejecting in favor of a lie?

e. How does **John 16:7–11** make clear the truth that God must bring judgment to the world of sin and to all who reject Jesus Christ?

f. How will the reign of the Antichrist come to an end? When will God destroy his evil kingdom **(verse 8)?**

STAND FIRM IN CHRIST

As believers in Christ we live not in fear of the Antichrist but in the joyful assurance that we belong to God. Through the power of the Gosepl, God gives us strength to stand firm in our faith against all evil. Read **verses 13–17.**

1. What words in **verse 13** give you the assurance that you belong to God and that you will be with Him forever?

2. Do you thank God daily that you are loved by God and are one of His chosen people? Discuss the benefits of beginning and ending each day with such a prayer of thanksgiving **(verse 13).**

3. Describe how God has called you and other believers into His kingdom **(verse 14).** Why is it important for you to do everything you can to let others have the same opportunity to know Christ?

4. How does God enable us to stand firm in our faith against every evil foe **(verses 15–17)?** Describe the resources God gives us so that our faith remains strong.

5. Think for a moment of all the martyrs and saints who died in Christ's name, resisting the forces of evil. How does **Revelation 2:10** relate to them? How would it relate to you if a similar situation should arise in your life? Talk about the topic of standing firm with your classmates.

For all the saints who from their labors rest,
All who by faith before the world confessed,
Your name, O Jesus, be forever blest.
Alleluia! Alleluia!

You were their rock, their fortress, and their might;
You, Lord, their captain in the well-fought fight;
You, in the darkness drear, their one true light.
Alleluia! Alleluia!

But then there breaks a yet more glorious day;
The saints triumphant rise in bright array;
The King of Glory passes on his way.
Alleluia! Alleluia!

Lutheran Worship, 191:1, 2, 7

Concerning the coming of our Lord Jesus Christ and our being gathered to Him, we ask you, brothers, not to become easily unsettled or alarmed by some prophecy, report or letter supposed to have come from us, saying that the day of the Lord has already come. Don't let anyone deceive you in any way, for that day will not come until the rebellion occures and the man of the lawlessness is revealed, the man doomed to destruction.

2 Thessalonians 2:1–3

SESSION 74

In the Meantime, Live by Faith

SECOND THESSALONIANS 3:1–16

One of the most exciting things about being a teenager is getting your first job. Being hired by an employer means that someone else considers you a responsible person. It also means earning money and making your own decisions about how you will spend it.

Working hard can be one of life's most enjoyable experiences. Unfortunately, it can also become tedious, boring, and oppressive. So much depends upon one's attitude toward work and the type of work one is doing.

1. Do you like to work? What are some of the positive benefits you feel a person derives from working? What experiences, if any, have you found distasteful?

2. Think about two common but extreme approaches to work in our own society—the workaholic and the idler. How would you differentiate between these two approaches? What do these approaches say about the people who practice them? Why do both of these approaches fall short of a God-pleasing attitude toward work?

In this lesson we will exlore the connection between our Christian faith and our attitudes toward work. The love of Christ makes a big difference in the way we approach our work. Because of what Christ has done for us, our work can be a joyful expression of the high calling we have received from God.

DON'T BE AFRAID OF EVIL

Before Paul talked to the Thessalonians about proper Christian attitudes toward work, he gave them encouragement in the persecution of their faith. The Thessalonians were going through a rough time. Evil people were opposing their faith and the preaching of the Gospel. What were they to do? Read **verses 1–5.**

1. Paul believed strongly in the power of prayer in mission work **(verse 1).** He was persuaded that prayer made possible the rapid spread of the Gospel. What force in the world was trying to hinder the work of the Gospel **(verse 2)?**

2. Are you an active "prayer-er"? Do you have a prayer list of people you pray for daily? Why is it necessary to pray for people to hear the Gospel of Christ and receive salvation **(verse 2)?**

3. What promise of God do you find in **verse 3** that assures you God will never forsake you to the power of evil? In what ways does God come to your aid so that Satan does not harm your faith?

4. Notice how perservering ("hanging in there") with Christ is associated with having one's heart filled with Christ's love **(verses 4–5).** Do you think this means that the more we have God's love, the less we will be afraid of evil? Defend your opinion.

5. What is the greatest fear you have about your faith? (You don't have to tell anyone about it). On the basis of these promises of God, isn't God's love for you greater than your fear or the power of evil? *Talk about this.*

MAKE EACH DAY PRODUCTIVE

A problem had arisen at Thessalonica involving the idleness of several of the congregation's members. Apparently these members believed that since Christ's coming might be very soon, they no longer needed to work and be productive. Paul responds to this problem by pointing them to a proper model of a true Christian worker—his own ministry. Read **verses 6–15.**

1. What does Paul mean in **verse 6** when he says to keep away from every brother who is idle? Does he mean that we are to shun fellow Christians who do not support themselves by working? What do you think might be the purpose of Paul's remarks? (Compare **verses 14–15.**)

2. What problems do idle people cause to those who work hard to earn their food **(verse 8)?** What attitudes of many idle people disrupt the harmony of the Christian congregation **(verse 11)?**

3. The words in **verse 10—"If a man will not work, he shall not eat"**—have often been misinterpreted by Christians. Does this mean that absolutely no one should be helped through Christian charity or government welfare? What about those who are sick, mentally ill, desperately poor, or have handicaps? What does God tell us in this verse?

4. Notice how Paul offers his own ministry as a model of working hard for the Gospel until the day that Christ returns **(verses 7–9).** Describe how Paul worked among the Thessalonians even when he was their pastor. How was he supported?

5. Do you think pastors should conduct their ministry free of charge, that they should earn a living by taking another job on the side? Do pastors have the right to be paid for the preaching of the Gospel? (Study Paul's comments on this subject in **1 Corinthians 9:3–18, Galatians 6:6,** and **1 Timothy 5:17–18.**)

6. Do you agree or disagree with this statement: "Every member of the congregation should assume his or her 'fair share' of the congregation's financial burden"? Give a reason for your answer.

BE BUSY AT YOUR WORK AND SERVE THE LORD

God calls us to work for Him in those vocations in which He has given us the particular aptitudes and skills to be successful. Work is a gift from God which we offer back to Him through faith. Look again at **verses 6–15.**

1. What words in **verses 11–15** describe how we are to serve God in the best possible way as employees? Explain in your own words what this might mean in the job in which you are currently employed.

2. What has Christ done for you to motivate you

to work hard at your job and to be worthy of the salary you earn **(verse 12)?**

3. How would you react to a situation at your job in which other employees complain that you are working too hard and making them look bad?

4. Jot down three or four vocations in which you believe you have the necessary aptitudes and skills to be successful. Then answer these two questions for each of the vocations you have chosen:

a. How do you plan to prepare yourself for this vocation?

b. How could you best serve Christ in this vocation?

5. Through faith in Christ we are motivated to work in the name of the Lord Jesus Christ **(verse 6).** Explain how working in Christ's name can keep us from the two extremes of idleness and being a workaholic?

6. Think of a person who is a model worker. What qualities does this person bring to his or her work that impresses you so much? Share your opinions with your classmates.

Earth and all stars, Loud rushing planets!
Sing to the Lord a new song!
Oh, victory! Loud shouting army!
Sing to the Lord a new sing!
He has done marvelous things.
I too will praise him with a new song!

Engines and steel! Loud pounding hammers!
Sing to the Lord a new song!
Limestone and beams! Loud building workers!
Sing to the Lord a new song!
He has done marvelous things.
I too will praise him with a new song!

Classrooms and labs! Loud boiling test tubes!
Sing to the Lord a new song!
Athlete and band! Loud cheering people!
Sing to the Lord a new song!
He has done marvelous things.
I too will praise him with a new song!

Lutheran Worship, 438:1–2, 5

(Copyright © Augsburg Publishing House. Used by permission.)

We hear that some among you are idle. They are not busy; they are busybodies.... Yet do not regard him as an enemy, but warn him as a brother. Now may the Lord of peace Himself give you peace at all times and in every way. The Lord be with you.

2 Thessalonians 3:11, 15–16

SESSION 75

Concluding Activities for Unit 9

Several activities are listed below to help you review the major truths of this unit. Following your teacher's directions, complete one or more of these activities.

"GOOD THINGS TO WHICH I LOOK FORWARD . . . "

Take a sheet of paper and write the above title at the top center of the page. Just below the title create two headings, one on each side of the page. At the left write, "While I Wait for Christ's Return." On the right side of the page write, "When Christ Returns in Glory."

Under each heading list those things to which you look forward. You may refer back to the lessons in this unit for some ideas for your lists.

When you finish, share your list with your classmates.

Rejoice! You have just sketched out a marvelous future which has been shaped and molded by God's power in Christ.

A CLASS DEBATE

Christian believers agree that the sexual immorality of our age dishonors God's will. Such activities as prostitution, pornography, and homosexuality and such consequences as herpes, syphilis, and AIDS have created a severe social problem. Although we agree on the problem, not all Christians agree on the solution to the problem.

Prepare a class debate on this topic, "Resolved that Christians should respond to the sexual immorality of our society by leading a life of purity that will influence people in our society to live the high calling of Jesus Christ. They should not respond by passing laws restricting immoral sexual behavior."

Choose one or two members of the class to take a position favoring the resolution and one or two members to take a position opposing it. Use a standard debate format. Each presentation should have a time limit.

Let other members of the class share their opinions after the presentations. How much does your class agree on this complex social problem? Do you favor the resolution or oppose it? Or do you take a position somewhere in between?

UNIT 10

Knowing What We Believe: Studies in Luther's Large Catechism

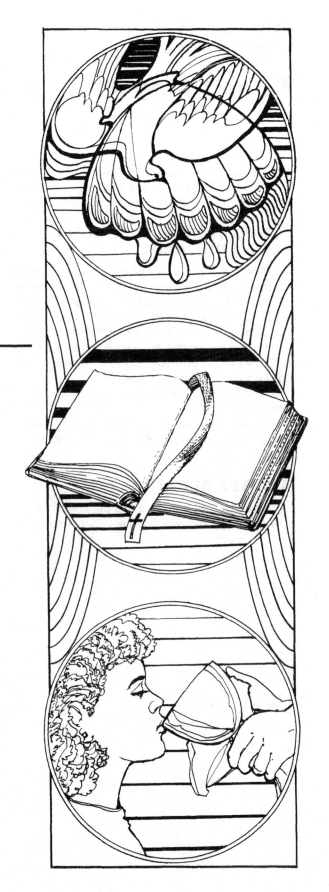

"I believe the St. Louis Cardinals are the best team in the National League this year," a friend tells you.

"Oh, really," you respond. "Why do you believe that?"

"Based on the facts." your friend replies. "They have the best all-around defense, they're hitting well, and their pitching is pretty good."

Those facts presented by your friend could prove to be wrong, but the point is that your friend bases her faith in the St. Louis Cardinals as the best team in the National League on the facts *as she perceives them.*

Our Christian faith is based on facts—*not facts as we perceive them, but facts as they have been given to us by God.* As God works in us to keep our faith strong, He wants us to know what those facts are.

The facts of our faith are summarized in the principle teachings of Christianity. These are the Ten Commandments, the Apostles' Creed, the Lord's Prayer, Baptism, and the Sacrament of the Altar. The Spirit helps us keep our faith strong as we review these teachings regularly.

In this unit we will study the Large Catechism of Dr. Martin Luther. The purpose of this study will be to review the main teachings of our Christian faith so that we may better understand and more deeply appreciate what we believe. Ultimately, we study the Large Catechism so we can apply these teachings to our daily lives.

SESSION 76

Basic Christian Teachings Revisited

LARGE CATECHISM: PREFACE

If you attended a Lutheran elementary school or a Lutheran Sunday school, you probably are familiar with Luther's Small Catechism. Your teachers used the Bible and that little book of questions and answers to present the main teachings of Christianity.

If you are a confirmed member of a Lutheran church, you no doubt have spent a great deal of time studying—and perhaps memorizing—Luther's Small Catechism. And you may have thought that when you were confirmed, your days of studying the catechism were over. So you may have been surprised and somewhat puzzled when you discovered that this unit is based on the catechism.

The catechism on which this unit is based, however, is less well-known and little used in most Lutheran churches. It is Luther's *Large Catechism*. In it Luther presents the same teachings as in his Small Catechism, but in greater detail.

"Why should we study this?" you may ask. "We've spent lots of time in Sunday school, in confirmation class, and even here in high school studying the main doctrines of the Christian faith."

In this session we will turn to the Bible and to Luther himself to answer that question. In his two prefaces to the Large Catechism Luther tells us why we need to be engaged daily in studying the main teachings of our Christian faith.

A MODEL FOR STUDYING BASIC CHRISTIAN TEACHINGS

In the Old Testament God gave the Israelites specific instructions about how to study His commandments and how to keep those commandments constantly before them. These instructions can be of help to us as we consider how we can best study the main teachings of our Christian faith.

1. Read **Deuteronomy 6:4–9.** Think about what these words suggest to you about how Christians are to study the Scriptures.

a. What were the Israelites to do with the commandments they had been given by God?

b. Why do you suppose God told the Israelites to tie these commandments on their hands and foreheads, and to write them on their doorframes and gates?

c. What does this passage suggest to us about how we ought to study the main teachings of our Christian faith?

2. In his 1528 preface to the Large Catechism, Luther also suggests how basic Christian teachings are to be studied. Read that preface on pages 10–13 in Luther's Large Catechism (LC).

a. What instructions does Luther give about how the basic Christian teachings are to be studied? Why did Luther consider this so important?

b. Luther says his catechism "contains the minimum of knowledge a Christian should have," and that "whoever lacks this knowledge cannot be counted among Christians." Do you agree? Why or why not?

3. Two years later, Luther wrote a different preface to his Large Catechism. Read this preface on pages 5–9 of the Large Catechism.

a. To whom was this preface addressed? Why do you suppose Luther wrote it?

b. If Luther were writing his Large Catechism today, to whom do you think he would have addressed the preface? What do you suppose he would emphasize?

c. Luther suggests specific opportunities pastors of his time would have for daily catechism study. When would be your best time for such study?

REASONS FOR STUDYING BASIC CHRISTIAN TEACHINGS

1. In his preface of 1530 Luther suggests that one reason for studying basic Christian teachings is that "to occupy oneself with God's Word, talking about it and thinking about it is . . . a most tremendous help against the devil, the world, the flesh, and all evil thoughts." Read the paragraph that begins with these words and also the next paragraph on page 7 of the Large Catechism.

a. How does studying basic Christian teachings help you resist the devil?

b. How does studying basic Christian teachings help you resist evil thoughts?

c. What does Luther say we should do with the catechism besides studying it?

2. 1 Peter 5:8–9a also speaks about driving out the devil. How is this to be accomplished according to this passage?

PUTTING BASIC CHRISTIAN TEACHINGS INTO PRACTICE

We study Christian teachings, of course, so we can apply them to our lives. Look at the summary of basic Christian teachings on pages 11–13 of the Large Catechism. List at least five ways these teachings will have an influence on how you live your daily life. What role does the Holy Spirit have in the way you live out those teachings?

PRAYER

Lord, as we study about the main teachings of our Christian faith, help us to put into practice what we learn in our daily lives. We ask it in Jesus' name. Amen.

LOOKING AHEAD

Read The First Commandment and Luther's Explanation of the First Commandment on pages 13–20 of the Large Catechism.

Be self-controlled and alert. Your enemy the devil prowls around like a roaring lion looking for someone to devour. Resist him, standing firm in the faith.

1 Peter 5:8–9a

SESSION 77

What Makes God God?

FIRST COMMANDMENT

Look at the checklist below. On a sheet of paper, rank in order from 1 to 10 the 10 most important things in your life right now.

my car	my record collection
my girlfriend/boyfriend	drugs
sports	my friends
my parents	church
getting good grades	preparing for college
having a good time	God

Did you rank God number 1? If you did, why did you do so? Is He really number 1, or did you just write that because you thought it was what you were expected to write? What makes God number 1 in a person's life?

WHAT MAKES GOD NUMBER 1?

1. In the Large Catechism Luther says, "To whatever we look for any good thing and for refuge in every need, that is what is meant by 'god.' "

a. Name some things to which people look "for any good thing." When would you consider these things to be "gods"?

b. Look at the list of the most important things in your life. When and how might one or more of these things become "gods"?

c. How can you keep these things from becoming your "god"?

d. Where do people today turn for help in time of need? How may this become idolatry?

2. Luther says that "to *have* a god is nothing else than to trust and believe in Him from the heart. . . . True worship and service of God takes place when your heart directs all its trust and confidence only toward God and does not let itself be torn away from Him; it consists in risking everything on earth for Him and abandoning all for His sake."

a. What are some false gods that people throughout history have worshiped and served?

b. Of what does idolatry really consist?

c. How can there be idolatry even in worshiping the true God?

d. How can we guard against such idolatry?

OUR GOOD GOD

Luther says "we are to trust in God alone, look to Him, and expect to receive nothing but good things from Him."

1. Look at **Exodus 20:1–2.** What good things that the Israelites had received were to motivate them to call the true God their God? What similar good things have we received to move us to call the true God our God?

2. What are some of the ways good things come to us?

3. If good gifts come to us in natural ways, how can we say that they come to us from God?

4. How can we keep the good things God gives us from becoming our idols?

A THREAT AND A PROMISE

In the "Appendix to the First Commandment" God threatens to punish those who disobey His commandments and promises to bless those who keep His commandments.

1. Why are these words attached to the First Commandment? What does it mean that God is a Jealous God?

2. If God threatens to punish all those who do not acknowledge Him as God, why do godless people often prosper?

3. If God promises to bless those who obey His commandments, why do good people sometimes suffer much more than their godless neighbors? What is the greatest blessing you have received from from God?

4. With so much evil in the world today, how can you talk about God as the source of all good?

5. What are some of the implications of the First Commandment for your personal life?

PRAYER

Lord, help me to fear, love and trust in You above all things. Amen.

LOOKING AHEAD

Read the Second and Third Commandments on pages 20–29 of the Large Catechism.

The devil took Him to a very high mountain and showed Him all the kingdoms of the world and their splendor. "All this I will give You," he said, "If You will bow down and worship me."

Jesus said to him, "Away from Me, Satan, for it is written:

'Worship the Lord your God, and serve Him only.' "
Matthew 4:8–10

SESSION 78

How to Serve God

SECOND AND THIRD COMMANDMENTS

Eric had not been to church for several weeks. Oh, he had every intention of going each Sunday. but every week he would stay up too late on Saturday night—sometimes partying with his friends, sometimes just reading or watching TV.

Eric's mother lived in a different city. About once a week she would call Eric on the phone. She would ask Eric. "Are you still going to to church regularly?" And Eric would reply, "Yes. I am. Mother, I swear to God I am!"

It is obvious that Eric was violating both the Second and Third Commandments. But before you point the accusing finger at Eric too quickly, let's look to see how each of us may violate these commandments and how we might keep them better, remembering always that we seek to live according to God's will because our Savior, Jesus, loved us and gave Himself for us.

IT'S ONLY A LITTLE LIE FOR GOD'S SAKE!

You might look at Eric in the above story and think, "I don't see what's so terrible about what Eric told his mother. It was only a little lie, and it really didn't hurt anyone." But little lies do hurt people . . . including those who tell them. And they are especially damnable when God's name is used to support them. That's why God adds a warning to this commandment. Read that warning in **Deuteronomy 5:11.**

1. Look at **Matthew 26:69–75.** How did Peter violate the Second Commandment? Whom did this hurt? How?

2. What are some ways in which people today use God's name to lie and deceive?

3. What are the results of using God's name in this way?

USING GOD'S NAME FOR TRUTH'S SAKE

Some of the Old Testament Jews who interpreted God's law very strictly and lived in great fear of dis-obeying it decided that in order to avoid using God's name in vain, they would never use it at all. Luther says, however, that this commandment ought to remind us not only how we are not to use God's name but also of how we ought to use His name properly.

1. Identify as many ways as you can think of in which God's name can be used properly.

2. Choose two of the ways of using God's name properly. Tell how you might use God's name in these ways in specific situations.

3. What is the most important way for us to use God's name?

KEEPING GOD'S DAY HOLY FOR HIS SAKE

1. Luther says there are two reasons for observing a "holy day" each week: first, for the sake of the body and its needs; and second, to have time and opportunity for divine worship.

a. Which of these two reasons for observing a "holy day" do you consider more important? Explain your answer.

b. Why should people go to church on Sunday? Is it a sin not to go to church?

2. Luther says that there are two categories of people who violate this commandment: "Those . . . who neglect God's Word because of greed or frivolity or [drunkenness, and those] who listen to God's Word as to some entertainment and come merely by the force of habit and leave again with as little understanding . . . as at the beginning."

a. What is the difference between these two types of violators of God's Word?

b. Do you think a church service should be entertaining?

c. Listed below are some things people do on Sunday. Which of these can a person do and still sanctify the holy day?

Play golf	Mow the lawn	Sleep late
Go to church	Have a picnic	Go jogging
Visit with family	Work	Read the Bible
Go to a movie	Play tennis	Attend a sports event

Luther says that the main point of the Third Commandment is that we should use Sunday as a time to hear the Word of God. "And even if no other benefit or need drove us into the Word, everyone should be impelled by the fact that our using the Word shows the devil the door and drives him away."

LOOKING AHEAD

Read the Fourth Commandment on pages 29–40 of the Large Catechism.

Call upon Me in the day of trouble; I will deliver you, and you shall glorify Me.

Psalm 50:15

SESSION 79

Honoring Parents and Other Authorities

FOURTH COMMANDMENT

People at a church planning conference several years ago were asked to identify the problems the church needs most to address today. On the list were such expected subjects as alcoholism and drug abuse, the problems of aging, and sexual promiscuity. But at the top of the list was concern about the breakdown of the family.

The Fourth Commandment specifically addresses issues of family living. It speaks primarily about how children are to relate to their parents, but as it does this, it also gives an indication of how parents are to relate to their children. We will be studying both of these relationships in today's class session. We will also be looking at what our relationship to others in authority should be, since their authority is derived from the authority given parents by God.

THE SPECIAL PLACE OF PARENTS

1. The Second Table of the Law says that we are to "love our neighbor as ourselves." The Fourth Commandment does not, however, command us to love our parents or even, for that matter, to obey them. Rather it tells us to *honor* them.

a. What is the difference between "honoring" someone and "loving" someone?

b. Why does God tell us to honor our parents?

c. How do we show that we honor them?

d. What about children whose parents are not worthy of honor? Does this commandment apply in such a situation?

2. Honoring parents may seem to be an area of service to God that is easily defined. Sometimes, however, circumstances may make honoring parents very difficult.

a. What are some circumstances that might make it difficult to honor parents?

b. An aging parent who is experiencing physical infirmities that are causing great pain asks a son or daughter to provide a means for ending her own life. In this situation, what should the son or daughter do to honor that parent?

THE SPECIAL GIFTS OF PARENTS

1. Parents are special gifts of God to us, Martin Luther says in his Large Catechism. We are to prize and value them as earth's greatest treasure.

a. How can we show that we prize and value our parents?

b. In what ways can parents help us to do good works?

2. Not only are parents special gifts of God, parents also give special gifts of God to us.

a. What are some of the special gifts your parents have given you?

b. What are some other special gifts that parents sometimes give to their children?

c. What is the greatest gift parents can give to their children?

ON BEING PARENTS

Luther also speaks to parents in his explanation to this commandment. He says that "parents should recognize their responsibility to obey God and, above all, to be genuinely and faithfully concerned to fulfill all duties of their office."

1. What are the two main responsibilities of parents?

2. How do they fulfill these responsibilities?

3. What will happen if parents take these responsibilities seriously?

4. What effect do you suppose this would have on society?

OTHER AUTHORITIES

Luther says that others in authority over us derive their authority from this commandment. We are to honor them just as we are to honor our parents.

1. List as many people as you can think of who have authority over you.

2. From a human point of view, from what do they derive that authority?

3. Where does their authority really come from?

THE PROMISE

As Luther points out, this is the only commandment in the Second Table of the Law to which God attaches a promise. Read God's commandment and the promise attached to it in **Deuteronomy 5:16 and Ephesians 6:2–3.**

1. Why does this commandment have a special promise attached to it?

2. What specifically is God's promise?

3. If a child dies early in life, does that mean that child has not honored his parents? Defend your answer.

4. What happens to those who do not keep this commandment?

LOOKING AHEAD

Read the Fifth, Sixth, and Seventh Commandments on pages 40–53 of the Large Catechism.

Children, obey your parents in the Lord, for this is right.

Philippians 6:1

SESSION 80

Out among Our Neighbors

FIFTH, SIXTH, AND SEVENTH COMMANDMENTS

"You do that again and I swear, I'll kill you!"

"Boy! That's one sexy lady. I'd sure like to get into her pants!"

"This must be my lucky day! The lady at the store gave me a dollar too much in change!"

You've probably heard those words before. In fact, you've probably said them . . . or at least some of them.

It doesn't take much imagination to realize that those statements represent a violation of the Fifth, Sixth, and Seventh Commandments.

Most of us are not guilty of murdering another person, of committing adultery, or even of deliberately stealing another person's property. Yet we live out of relationship with others in so many ways that in one way or another we are all guilty of violating these commandments.

That is why Christ came into our world and went to the cross: So that when we fail in our attempts at relationships with God and with others, He might restore us to right relationships once again.

CHARTING YOUR REQUIRED RELATIONSHIPS

1. In this session we will proceed somewhat differently than in other sessions in this course. Below you will find a model by which to chart the relationships with your neighbor required by the Fifth Commandment. On three separate sheets of paper, complete a similar model for the other two commandments being studied in this class session.

Thou Shalt Not Kill

	Forbidden	Encouraged
Thoughts, emotions	Anger, hatred, hostility	Forgiving, love
Words	Angry words, curses	Words that protect the other person from harm
	Offering counsel to a killer	
	Encouraging someone else to	
Actions	hate or kill Murder, physical violence of any kind	Defense of neighbor Taking advantage of the opportunity to do good to him/her.

2. Look at the Scripture passages that follow and tell how they are to be applied in relationship to one or more of the commandments being studied in this session:

   a. **Matthew 25:42–43**
   b. **Matthew 5:27–28**
   c. **James 5:1–5**

SOME PRACTICAL MATTERS

Below are several statements related to the three commandments being studied in this session. Tell whether you agree or disagree with the statement. Defend your answer.

1. You should avoid extramarital sex because you might get AIDS or another venereal disease.

2. It is all right to keep extra change received from an unattended vending machine.

3. If someone hits you in anger, never hit that person back.

4. More important for a husband and wife than not committing adultery is their mutual love and respect for one another.

5. The Sixth Commandment only applies to married people.

6. Since it is natural for teenagers to have sexual fantasies about members of the opposite sex, there is really nothing wrong with such fantasies.

7. Killing the enemy in wartime is not a violation of the Fifth Commandment.

8. People who spend time talking socially instead of working during the time when they are being paid to work are in reality stealing from their employer.

9. In general, men and women should get married.

10. God does not really expect anyone to keep these commandments.

PRAYER

Father, we want to do Your will. We ask You to give us the will and the strength to live in right relationships with others. When we fail, Father, because of our human weakness, forgive us, as You have promised, for the sake of Jesus Christ Your Son, our Lord and Savior. Amen.

LOOKING AHEAD

Read the Eighth, Ninth, and Tenth Commandments, and the Close of the Commandments on pages 53–67 of the Large Catechism.

So I say, live by the Spirit. and you will not gratify the desires of the sinful nature.

Galatians 5:16

SESSION 81

Don't Even Think It!

EIGHTH, NINTH, AND TENTH COMMANDMENTS AND CLOSE OF THE COMMANDMENTS

"Have you heard about Sue?"

Those words are intended to get your attention—and they probably will.

How often have you heard words like that? How often have you spoken them yourself? When you heard or said them, it was pretty obvious that it wasn't something good about Sue that would follow. Whether what you then said about Sue was true or not, in that situation you were probably guilty of violating the Eighth Commandment—bearing false witness against your neighbor.

Or perhaps you carry around another kind of guilt. Maybe you just can't stand it that Bob has that lovely red convertible and you don't even have a car. It's not just the convertible that makes you jealous of Bob, however. It's also the fact that Jane is Bob's steady girlfriend, and you've had your eye on Jane for a long time . . . or, if you're a girl, maybe it's Jane who has the car and Bob that you would like to have as your steady date. Either way, you have problems with what is forbidden in the Ninth and Tenth Commandments.

So let's take a look at commandments 8, 9, and 10. Let's see what they say to us about how we ought to live and what they show us about what our righteousness really amounts to in the sight of God.

WHEN NOT TO SPEAK

1. As Luther points out, the Eighth Commandment has to do with our neighbor's reputation. In it we are forbidden to say anything about our neighbor that would damage his or her reputation.

a. What three specific situations does Luther say are expressly forbidden by this commandment? What is the most prevalent form of "bearing false witness?"

b. Luther says that in this commandment we are forbidden to say anything at all bad about our neighbor. There are, however, he said, some exceptions . . . some people who are allowed to say bad things about others. Who are they? Why are they allowed to say bad

things about others, according to Luther? Do you agree? Why or why not?

2. If someone sins against you, you are not to say bad things about that person. There is a proper way to deal with such a sinner, however. It is found in **Matthew 18:15–17.**

a. What are the steps in dealing with someone who sins against you according to **Matthew 18:15–17?**

b. What does it mean that the one who refuses to repent is to be treated like "a pagan or a tax collector"?

3. When you look at what the Eighth Commandment forbids, it would almost seem best not to say anything about your neighbor at all.

a. Is it ever proper to speak openly about a neighbor's sin?

b. What should you do when someone else says bad things about another person?

FORBIDDEN DESIRE

When we think of forbidden desire, we usually think of sexual lust. There is, however, another kind of lust that is just as damning. That is the lust for another's material goods. Let's look at an example of both of these kinds of forbidden desire—and of one that falls somewhere in between.

1. A man who has no living spouse or children dies. He leaves his money to a favorite nephew. That nephew's brother brings a lawsuit against his brother, claiming that he has an equal right to his uncle's inheritance. Is this an example of coveting? Why do you think God forbids such covetousness?

2. You are a division manager in your company. One day the president calls you into his office. He tells you that Mrs. Smith would be a great asset to your company. He says you should offer her whatever it takes to get her to take a job in your division, and that if you do, there's a salary increase for you. The only problem is that Mrs. Smith works for a rival firm. What should you do?

3. Remember Bob in that lovely red convertible? You've just learned that Bob really can't afford that car. In fact, he has defaulted on his last loan payment. Jane tells you that the loan company that financed the car

in the convertible than she is in Bob. What do you do now?

THE BOTTOM LINE

In his comments on the Close of the Commandments, Luther says that "The First Commandment is to run through all the commandments like the wire frame or hoop that runs through a wreath joining the end to the beginning and holding everything together."

1. What does Luther mean by this statement?
2. What purpose do the commandments serve?

LOOKING AHEAD

Read the introductory section of the Creed and the First Article on pages 67–70 of Luther's Large Catechism.

So in everything, do to others what you would have them do to you, for this sums up the Law and the Prophets.

Matthew 7:12

is about to repossess it, but that they will turn it over to anyone who will agree to make the rest of the payments. Jane intimates that she's much more interested

SESSION 82

The Father of Us All

FIRST ARTICLE

Albert Einstein once said, "The presence of a superior reasoning Power . . . revealed in the incomprehensible universe forms my idea of God."

What forms your idea of God? How much are you influenced by the universe? What else shapes your idea about God?

Surely we cannot ignore facts like the following:

- We live in a massive universe, composed of millions of stars and galaxies in an orderly array.
- Through the process of photosynthesis green plants combine energy from light with water and carbon dioxide to make food and produce oxygen.
- Every 15 to 30 days the human body replaces the outer layer of skin.
- Nearly all the cells in the body are too tiny to see without a microscope. Yet packed within each cell is the machinery that the cell needs to carry out its many activities.
- The human body maintains a constant temperature. When it needs to retain heat, the blood vessels in the dermis narrow (maybe we get goosebumps) and so limit heat loss. When the body needs to give off heat, these vessels expand and so increase heat loss.
- As soon as a sperm fertilizes an egg, the egg has a complete blueprint of a new human being. (A new life exists!)
- When a severe bacterial infection is present in the body, the bone marrow produces far more neutrophils (a kind of white blood cell) than usual. The neutrophils move to the area of infection, swallow up the bacteria, and destroy them with enzymes. After the bacteria have been destroyed, the neutrophils break apart.

Imagine the massiveness of God's creation! Imagine the miracles that occur in your body every moment of every day—that are also occurring at the same time in every other human being, in every animal, in every plant, and in all other parts of God's creation! What a miraculous God and Father we have!

Our God has created and rules over a great universe. Yet He cares about you—about every part of your body, about everything that happens to you, and, above all, about where you will spend eternity! God cares. He has power beyond our imagination. And He uses that power in love that defies our comprehension.

INTRODUCING THE APOSTLES' CREED

1. We have completed our study of the Ten Commandments and are now moving into our study of the Apostles' Creed.

a. What is the purpose of the Apostles' Creed?

b. What is the relationship between the Creed and the Ten Commandments?

2. Luther says that the Creed was originally divided into 12 articles. It is not important to know what those 12 articles were, but it is important to realize and identify the many statements of faith contained in the Creed.

a. Summarize in one sentence each of the three articles of the Creed.

b. Identify the basic teachings of Christian faith contained in the Creed. How many "articles" do you have?

c. Discuss the importance of the Creed in relation to your everyday life.

THE ALMIGHTY MAKER

1. Luther says that the First Article of the Creed gives us the nature, will, activity, and work of God the Father.

a. What does the First Article say about the Father's nature? Why is this important for us?

b. What do we learn in the First Article about the Father's will? What is the significance of this for our lives?

c. Describe the activity and work of God the Father. How does this help us in our lives?

2. God describes the creation of the world in **Genesis 1–2.** He accomplished this marvelous feat in six days.

a. The writer of **Psalm 104** was impressed with God's creation, so he wrote this psalm of praise to God. In verse after verse he listed things that impressed him. Suppose you are going to write a similar psalm of

a. How does God show that He cares for each and every one or us?

b. Read **Psalm 139:13–16.** What insights about your life, your body, and your Creator do you receive here? How do these insights affect your attitude toward abortion? toward the way you treat your body? toward the way you treat other people?

c. Read **Psalm 8.** What does this psalm tell you about our Creator God? What does it tell you about yourself?

REPLY TO MY FATHER

In response to all that God the Father has done and is still doing for you, Luther says you are to "love, praise, thank and serve Him." Identify some ways you can do that *today*.

LOOKING AHEAD

Read the Second Article on pages 70–72 of the Large Catechism.

Praise the Lord, O my soul. O Lord my God, You are very great; you are clothed with splendor and majesty. . . . How many are Your works, O Lord! In wisdom You made them all. . . . I will sing to the Lord all my life; I will sing praise to my God as long as I live. May my meditation be pleasing to Him, as I rejoice in the Lord. But may sinners vanish from the earth and the wicked be no more. Praise the Lord, O my soul. Praise the Lord.

Psalm 104:1, 24, 33–35

praise. What impresses you—what are some things in God's creation that you will include in *your* psalm?

b. Discuss reasons why you must reject theories of evolution recorded in many science textbooks.

c. What significance do you find in the fact that God created people as male and female?

d. What message do you find for yourself in the fact that God told His created people to subdue and rule the earth?

3. Not only did God create everything else in the world, He also created *me*. God has a personal investment in me, therefore He cares about me.

SESSION 83

Jesus Is Lord

SECOND ARTICLE

Some religions stress the sovereignty of God. Their teachings center around the lordship of Jesus. Because He is Lord of the universe and Lord of our lives, they say, we are to worship and serve Him.

Jesus is indeed the Lord of our lives. But His lordship does not consist in Him having simply declared Himself our ruler. Jesus is Lord because He is our Redeemer. With His own life's blood shed on Calvary's cross He bought us back from the rule that sin, death, and the devil had over us. Jesus is Lord because He paid the supreme price—His very life—to reestablish His lordship. This is Luther's emphasis in his explanation to the Second Article of the Apostles' Creed.

JESUS THE REDEEMER

Romans 5:6–11 provides a succinct summary of how Jesus reestablished His lordship over us.

1. Explain in your own words what St. Paul is saying here about how Jesus reestablished His lordship over us.

2. Look at the statements below, which seek to explain each portion of the Second Article. Mark each statement true or false. Tell why you did so.

a. Jesus is partly God and partly a human being.

b. Jesus was conceived without His mother ever having had sexual intercourse.

c. Jesus really died, was buried, and rose bodily from the dead.

d. Jesus sits on the right hand of the Father as a place of special privilege.

e. Jesus is now in heaven forever.

3. Tell how much it cost Jesus, what He underwent, and what He risked in order to bring us back under His rulership.

THE HEART OF THE MATTER

Note what Luther says in his concluding remarks about this article: "The entire Gospel that we preach depends on our thorough grasp of this article. Upon it rests our entire salvation and joy, and it is so rich and inclusive that it will keep challenging our efforts to learn it."

1. Choose one act that Jesus went through to regain His lordship over us. Write a brief essay on why this was necessary for our redemption.

2. Why would Jesus come into the world, endure suffering and shame, and die for us? Obviously, He loves us with a love so great that we can't comprehend it. And He didn't stop loving us after He rose from the dead and ascended into heaven.

Probably, you have gone through times in your life when you had thoughts such as, "I'm so awful! Jesus can't be loving me now!" But He did. And He does. Think of the time when you felt least lovable. Then meditate for 30 seconds about the fact that Jesus still loved you—even then.

3. The love of Jesus motivates His children to act in marvelous ways. One doctor turned down a lucrative practice in a large city to treat poor people, many of whom could pay him only by trading some product or service for his service, such as a bag of potatoes from a garden or plowing his garden. A housewife spent her spare time making quilts, which she sold; she gave all the money from those sales to the church.

Who is the person you know who best reflects the love of Jesus? (If you wish, give the person a fictitious name.) Write down some of the "unreasonable" things this person does because he or she is a child of God. Why does such behavior make the verbal witness about Jesus "believable" when it come from him or her?

4. Do two things for each of the following:

- *Describe a loving act you can do.*
- *Mention about a message from God that you can share.*

a. A friend is extremely depressed. You think he or she might be thinking about committing suicide.

b. A friend has a dependency on alcohol or another drug.

c. A friend's parents are getting a divorce.

d. A friend's father or mother is dying of cancer.

e. A friend discovered she is pregnant.

f. A football player dropped a pass in the end zone that would have won the game, which your team lost.

PRAYER

Almighty God, our Heavenly Father, You sent Your Son to be our Savior. By His life, death, and resurrection, He has redeemed us from the power of sin, death, and the devil and brought us back to life with You under His royal reign. Thank You, Father, for sending Your Son into our world, to the cross, and through the grave, that through Him we might have eternal life. We thank You for Your goodness and praise You for Your mercy in Jesus Christ, our Lord. Amen.

LOOKING AHEAD

Read the Third Article in Luther's Large Catechism, pages 72–78.

For God so loved the world that He gave His one and only Son, that whoever believes in Him shall not perish but have eternal life.

John 3:16

SESSION 84

The Holy-Maker

THIRD ARTICLE

Look at the statements below. Choose the one you think is most correct.

1. I am holy.
2. I am holier than most people.
3. I am holy sometimes.
4. I am not holy at all.

The third person of the Trinity is the Holy Spirit. He has a special assignment from God the Father. He is the "Holy-Maker," as Luther puts it. His work is to make us holy. In this session we will attempt to better understand how He accomplishes that task.

HOW THE HOLY SPIRIT WORKS

1. Luther points out that the Holy Spirit works through the community of saints.

a. What precisely is the community of saints?

b. How does the Holy Spirit come to us through the community of saints?

c. Why is the Christian community such an important place?

2. Look up **1 Corinthians 12:3.**

a. What does this passage tell us about the importance of the Holy Spirit's work?

b. How does this passage connect the Third Article's teaching to the teachings of the Second Article of the Creed?

3. Look up **Galatians 5:16–18.** What does this passage say about the Holy Spirit's task of making us holy?

4. Now check **Ephesians 4:3–5.** What do you think is meant here by the "unity of the Spirit"? How does this relate to the idea of the Holy Spirit as our "holy-maker"?

THE HOLY SPIRIT AMONG US

1. Think about the blessings you have received from the Holy Spirit through the communion of saints. Write a paragraph or two about one of the following: A time when

- I received comfort from the communion of saints.
- I felt "down," and another Christian "lifted me up."

- being in the communion of saints made me feel close to God.
- someone in the communion of saints helped me remember that I'm a child of God.
- someone in the communion of saints brought me (back) to God.

2. Together identify someone with a spiritual need. Discuss ways you can serve as instruments of the Holy Spirit to build up that person.

3. Write an ending to this sentence: What I think we could do to build up our school is . . .

4. As part of the communion of saints we share our faith with others, both inside and outside the communion.

a. Write an ending to this sentence: One big problem I have sharing the faith is . . .

b. Discuss ways to address the problems you identified in *a*.

BEYOND THE CHRISTIAN COMMUNITY

Our relationship to the Christian community—at least our physical relationship with that community—ends when life ends. Luther suggests, however, that that is not an end. It is rather the beginning of a better relationship with God and the culmination of the Holy Spirit's work. That is why we confess that we believe in "the resurrection of the body, and the life everlasting." In our life beyond the grave, God's holiness will be perfected in us, and we will be holy even as He is holy.

Turn to **1 Thessalonians 4:13–18.** What do these verses tell you about what your coming life of holiness will be like?

PRAYER

Come to us, Holy Spirit. Through the Word of God, keep pointing us to Jesus, our Savior, that we may have the forgiveness of our sins and look forward to life everlasting with Him. In His name we pray. Amen.

LOOKING AHEAD

Read the introduction to the Lord's Prayer on pages 78–84 of Luther's Large Catechism.

No one can say "Jesus is Lord," except by the Holy Spirit.

1 Corinthians 12:3b

SESSION 85

Prayer Talk

INTRODUCTION TO THE LORD'S PRAYER

During a time of extreme drought, a preacher gathered his congregation to pray for rain. Before he began his prayers, the preacher looked around at the assembled congregation.

"We came here to pray for rain, did we not?" he asked.

Heads nodded, and there were murmurs of assent from those present. "Then I'm sure surprised," the preacher said, "that as far as I can see, not one of you brought your umbrella!"

That's how it often is with prayer. We pay lip service to its effectiveness, but we don't really believe it works. We agree we ought to pray, but seldom take the time to do it. Today we want to reflect on why we ought to pray, how we ought to pray, and for what we ought to pray.

EXCUSES, EXCUSES

1. People who do not pray regularly can find all kinds of excuses for not doing so. Look at the list below. Tell how you would counteract each of these excuses.

a. "There's not enough time."

b. "I don't know how to pray."

c. "God already knows what I need."

d. "I'm not good enough to pray."

e. "There's nothing for which I need to pray right now."

2. Use the checklist below to help you take a personal prayer inventory. What does this inventory tell you about your prayer life? (Answer this question privately. Do not share your answers unless you want to.)

a. I prayed privately today.

b. I pray at least once a day.

c. I pray when I'm in trouble.

d. I pray when I need something from God.

e. I never pray.

f. I pay attention to the prayers in church.

g. I pray the Lord's Prayer daily.

h. I think prayer is a waste of time.

WHY PRAY?

1. Luther wrote in the Large Catechism that we ought to pray because God has commanded us to pray and has promised to hear our prayers.

a. On page 78 Luther says that prayer is commanded by God in the Second Commandment. However, the Commandment does not specifically mention prayer. It tells us that we should not misuse the name of the Lord our God (or, "take the name of the Lord, thy God, in vain"). How is that command related to prayer?

b. Look at **Psalm 50:15.** Identify the command and the promise in this verse.

c. Turn to **Matthew 7:7–11.** Explain what these verses say about God's command to pray and His promise to hear our prayers.

2. Think of your own prayer experiences and the experiences of people you know. If you are willing, tell about a time when your or someone else felt very close to God during prayer. What led you (or the other person) to feel that way? How did God answer the prayer?

HOW TO PRAY

1. You can come to God in prayer in a variety of ways. You can use a formal, written prayer. You can pray *ex corde*—just use whatever words come to mind. You can pray silently or out loud. You can pray in public or in private. All of these prayers are acceptable to God. However, God does reject some prayers. We need to be aware what these prayers are so that we avoid praying them.

a. Turn to **Matthew 6:5–8.** What kind of prayers does God reject?

b. What kind of prayers are pleasing to God?

2. Jesus Himself gave us the model for our prayers in the prayer He taught us to pray, the Lord's Prayer. Luther says that in this prayer "all the needs that constantly beset us are gathered up, each one of which is so great that it ought to drive us to pray about it as long as we live."

a. List in a word or phrase each of our needs that is presented in the Lord's Prayer.

b. Write a prayer of your own, asking God to meet one of these needs.

3. Some people find it easy to pray at any time in any place. Others prefer to pray in an environment that helps them pray. For example, they go to their room, turn off their stereo, and read from the Bible or a devotional book before they pray. What kind of environment works for you? Talk about it.

4. What kinds of prayers do you pray? Do you often forget to pray for things for which you had intended to pray? What practices might help you remember? Talk about it.

LOOKING AHEAD

Read the First, Second, and Third Petitions on pages 84–89 of the Large Catechism.

Ask and it will be given to you: seek and you will find; knock and the door will be opened to you. For everyone who asks receives; he who seeks finds; and to him who knocks, the door will be opened.
Matthew 7:7–8

SESSION 86

Prayers of God's Family

FIRST, SECOND, AND THIRD PETITIONS

Most of us turn to prayer at our times of special need. We ask God to help us when we are frightened, when we are in trouble, when we are sick, when we have specific problems, and when we have special needs. We should certainly pray at all those times. God invites us to bring all our needs and wants to Him, and He promises to hear and answer our prayers.

In the Large Catechism, however, Martin Luther says that the Lord's Prayer shows us that our physical needs and wants should not be our first priority. Rather, we should pray first of all for God to satisfy our spiritual needs. That is what our Lord teaches us to do in the Lord's Prayer as we pray first of all to our Father: "Hallowed be Thy name. Thy kingdom come. Thy will be done on earth as it is in heaven."

When we have prayed for spiritual treasures, we can be confident that God will also satisfy our physical needs, for He has promised: **"Seek first His kingdom and His righteousness, and all these things will be given to you as well" (Matthew 6:33).**

HONORING THE FAMILY NAME

"He comes from such a good family. Their name is a well-respected one in our community. It's certainly a shame he turned out so badly. He's a disgrace to his family's name."

1. You've probably heard someone says words like those above. What brings disgrace and dishonor to a family name? Think of an instance where a famous person has brought dishonor to his or her family name. What caused the dishonor?

2. Look up **Matthew 7:15–20.** What are some ways a member of God's family might dishonor the name of the Father? What happens when the Father's name is dishonored?

3. What does all of this tell us about what we are praying for in the Lord's Prayer when we pray "Hallowed be Thy name"?

4. Describe a person or situation in which you see a demonstration that God has answered someone's "Hallowed be Thy name" prayer.

5. Probably, you can think of times when you failed to keep God's name holy. Maybe you feel more like a poor, miserable sinner than like a child of God. However, what blessings do you enjoy through your faith in God? What difference do those blessings make in your life?

INHERITING THE FAMILY FORTUNE

When parents die, they usually leave most of the material wealth they have accumulated to their children. They may, however, choose not to leave that inheritance to children who have been unfaithful to them or who have displeased them in some way.

Some parents choose to share some of their material goods with their children before they die. They want the joy of seeing for themselves the happiness this brings to their children.

1. The Second Petition of the Lord's Prayer is "Thy kingdom come." What does this petition tell us about the inheritance we have from our heavenly Father? When can we expect to receive that inheritance?

2. Look at **Matthew 7:20–21.** What must God's children do to receive their inheritance from their heavenly Father?

3. Describe things or people in your school which demonstrate that God's kingdom has come among the people in this special place.

4. Write a brief prayer based on the words "Thy kingdom come."

DOING THE FAMILY'S WILL

Probably your parents expect certain things of you—things that contribute to your family. Maybe they expect you to be home at certain times for meals and at other specified times on Friday and Saturday nights. Maybe they expect you to take out the trash, help with the dishes, care for a younger sister or brother, and clean your room. Maybe they expect you to use the money from your job to buy some of your clothes.

In the Third Petition Jesus instructs us to pray that

our heavenly Father's will be done among us in our spiritual family.

1. Notice what Luther says about the devil on pages 88–89 of the Large Catechism. Luther recognized that when God grants the requests we make in the first two petitions of the Lord's Prayer, the devil will become very concerned. Therefore we need God's help in a special way—in a way that will keep us faithful to Him.

Luther paraphrased the Third Petition on page 89 ("Dear Father, . . . weakness or apathy"). Make the language even more simple and contemporary. Paraphrase Luther's paraphrase!

2. What is God's will for us?

3. Why should we pray that His will would be done?

Isn't God's will always done in the world?

4. We pray, "Thy will be done on earth *as it is in heaven.*" Describe how God's will is done in heaven.

5. Describe what happens on earth when people do God's will in the same way that it is done in heaven.

6. Write a short prayer based on the petition "Thy will be done on earth as it is in heaven."

LOOKING AHEAD

Read the Fourth, Fifth, Sixth, and Last Petitions on pages 89–97 of the Large Catechism.

Seek first His kingdom and His righteousness, and all these things will given to you as well.
Matthew 6:33

SESSION 87

Prayers for Deliverance

FOURTH, FIFTH, SIXTH, AND LAST PETITIONS

From ghosties and ghoulies, from beasties and things that go bump in the night, good Lord deliver us.

That ancient prayer of the church asked God for deliverance from unexplainable terrors. That prayer may seem silly to us today, but those who prayed it many years ago were serious in their plea for God's deliverance.

Unexplainable terrors still exist today, even in our scientific, technological age. They take many different forms: alcoholism, drug abuse, divorce, AIDS, guilt over sexual misbehavior, unwanted teen-age pregnancy, unemployment. These are just a few of the multitude of terrors that may surround us today. Certainly from all of these terrors and many more, we need to pray "Good Lord, deliver us."

GIVE US THE THINGS WE NEED HERE ON EARTH

In the Fourth Petition our Lord tells us to pray, "Give us this day our daily bread." Speak this prayer silently. Then pause to think about it. For what are you praying as you speak these words?

1. Look at **Matthew 6:25–34.** Why does our Lord tell us to pray for daily bread?

2. Luther says this prayer is not just a prayer that our bread box would be filled, but a prayer that God would prevent all the evil things that might interfere with the meeting of our physical and material needs.

a. List as many of those needs as possible.

b. Now list all those things that might interfere with meeting those needs.

3. Tell how God uses other people to provide the things you need.

4. Tell how God can use you to provide things that others need.

5. Write a short prayer, asking God to deliver you from all the evil that might interfere with receiving your daily bread.

DELIVER US FROM GUILT

In the Fifth Petition we pray "Forgive us our trespasses, as we forgive those who trespass against us." Jesus further explained this petition in **Matthew 6:14–15.** Read these verses and think about what they mean.

1. God forgives our sins by His grace. His forgiveness comes to us even before we ask for it. Why, then, should we bother to pray for His forgiveness?

2. Our Lord says we should pray, "Forgive us our trespasses, *as we forgive those who trespass against us.*" Does this mean that God's forgiveness of our sins is dependent on our forgiving others? Explain your answer. For help, read Luther's words on pages 93–94 of the Large Catechism.

3. Why is it so very important that our sins be forgiven?

DELIVER US FROM TEMPTATION

In the Sixth Petition our Lord teaches us to pray "Lead us not into temptation." As Luther rightly points out, this is not a prayer that God would not tempt us. It is a prayer that God would give us the strength to resist the temptations of the devil, the world, and our flesh, that is, our own sinful being.

1. Identify the specific temptations that, according to Luther, come to us

   a. from our flesh;

   b. from the world; and

   c. from the devil.

2. Choose one temptation in each category. Tell how that temptation might come to you today or tomorrow.

3. What can you do to ward off these temptations?

4. Is it sinful to feel temptation? Explain your answer.

As Luther points out, the Fourth, Fifth, and Sixth Petitions are summarized in the Seventh Petition. There we pray for deliverance from the Evil One, from the devil himself.

We pray in these petitions that God would deliver us from all those things that would interfere with our relationship with Him. We pray these prayers confidently, because our Lord has commanded us to pray and has promised to hear our prayers. We pray in faith, believing that "**He who did not spare His own Son, but gave Him up for us all—how will He not also, along with Him, graciously give us all things?**" (Romans 8:32).

LOOKING AHEAD

Read the section on Baptism on pages 97–109 of Luther's Large Catechism.

The Lord will rescue me from every evil attack and will bring me safely to His heavenly kingdom.
2 Timothy 4:18

SESSION 88

Living In/Out Your Baptism

SACRAMENT OF HOLY BAPTISM

Luther says that we should remember our Baptism daily. Think about that. What does he really mean? Am I to stop every day to remember that many years ago some pastor poured or sprinkled water over me and said some words? What good can come from remembering that?

When Luther says, "Remember your Baptism," he means something quite different. He is saying, "Remember what God did for you through your Baptism. He came to you with the forgiveness of sins, applied to you through the water and Word of Holy Baptism, and made you His own child!"

That's Baptism. It's something to live *in,* and it's something to live *out.* It's something to live in every day, because it daily assures you of God's forgiveness of your sins. It's something to live out, because as you are reminded of that forgiveness through which you became a child of God, you are challenged to live out your life as God's child.

In this session we want to look at Baptism. We want to look at it not as something that happened once in your life, but as something that gives you the power to live by faith in Christ day after day.

BAPTISM IS

Below are some multiple choice questions about Baptism. Choose the best answer. Be ready to explain why you chose the answer you did.

1. The words on which Baptism is founded are found in
   a. **Matthew 28:19.**
   b. **Mark 16:16.**
   c. **Romans 6:4.**
   d. *a* and *b.*
2. Baptism is
   a. a human invention.
   b. commanded by God.
   c. not specifically commanded in Scripture.
   d. *a* and *b.*
3. Baptism is
   a. optional.
   b. not necessary.
   c. necessary for salvation.
   d. a good idea.
4. To be baptized in God's name means
   a. that we must be sure to speak God's name when we baptize someone.
   b. that Baptism is not human action, but the action of God.
   c. that Baptism is invalid if the one doing the baptizing does not believe in God.
   d. none of the above.
5. Baptism gets its power from
   a. the water.
   b. God's Word.
   c. the water and the Word.
   d. the pastor.

6. The benefits of Baptism are received
   a. automatically.
   b. if the person administering the Baptism has faith.
   c. later in life.
   d. by faith of the one being baptized.
7. Baptism offers
   a. membership in the church.
   b. victory over death, the forgiveness of sins, and the power of the Holy Spirit.
   c. eternal salvation.
   d. the promise of a happy life.
8. Infants should be baptized, because
   a. Baptism is effective automatically.
   b. God has commanded it.
   c. children need to be baptized, because they also sin.
   d. little children can have faith.

THE INS AND OUTS OF BAPTISM

Luther uses the same imagery that St. Paul used in **Romans 6:4.** Thereby he showed

a. what Baptism signifies; and

b. why God ordained this outward sign and external observance for this sacrament by which we are first received into the Christian church.

1. You studied **Romans 6:4** in session 15. Briefly review what you learned there. What is St. Paul saying?

2. How does Luther apply what St. Paul says in **Romans 6:4** to the daily life of a Christian?

3. Skim the verses that follow **Romans 6:4.** Summarize how Baptism changes you.

4. Look at **Romans 6:14.** Think of these words as a promise from God rather than a command. What is God's promise here? What does it mean for your life?

5. In **Colossians 2:9–12** Paul compares Baptism to circumcision. Circumcision marked the covenant God made with Abraham **(Genesis 17).** Describe the covenant relationship we enjoy through Baptism.

6. Circumcision placed a visible mark upon the one who was circumcised. In Baptism God also marks us, but in a way not visible to the human eye. However, that mark is visible to God, to the angels, and even to Satan. You are a new creation.

a. According to **Colossians 2:13–15,** how have you been changed?

b. Skim **Colossians 3:1–17.** What are some ways God has moved us to respond to the grace He showed in our Baptism?

c. Paul describes our lives as a new creation in **2 Corinthians 5:15–21.** Identify three aspects of this life that stand out in your mind as you read this text.

7. Recall the last time you witnessed a Baptism. What went through your mind? You didn't see Jesus healing a blind man or taking a young girl by the hand and restoring her physical life. But you did witness a miracle. What was it?

8. Briefly state what it means to daily remember your Baptism. What are some things you can do to help you remember?

9. At least once or twice while you identified the way Baptism changes people, you probably wondered, "Does all this refer to me? I'm not sure I'm really a new creation. After all, I still like to do sinful things at times. Maybe I'm not really a child of God, after all."

What's a good thing to do when such thoughts enter your mind? How can you be sure you are still a child of God?

10. Summarize the reasons for practicing infant Baptism.

PRAYER

Lord, help me to remember my Baptism daily. Help me to see it as my everyday clothes, to be worn constantly that the devil may not lead me into any kind of temptation, and that I may live in the assurance of the forgiveness of my sins, through Christ Jesus, my Savior, in whose name I pray. Amen.

LOOKING AHEAD

Read the Sacrament of the Altar on pages 111–121 of Luther's Large Catechism.

He who believes and is baptized will be saved; but he who does not believe will be condemned.

Mark 16:16

SESSION 89

Bread and Wine, Body and Blood

SACRAMENT OF THE ALTAR

Have you ever sung the song, "Sons of God, Hear His Holy Word"? If so, you may remember the refrain, "Gather 'round the table of the Lord, eat His body, drink His blood." The result of such eating and drinking? We will live forever.

Recall what you know about the Lord's Supper.
- What is it?
- Who should receive it?
- What benefits does God give us when we receive it?

Think about the importance of the Lord's Supper in your life. Continue thinking about this by considering the words our Lord used when He instituted the Lord's Supper (called "The Sacrament of the Altar" in the Large Catechism).

THIS IS . . .

1. In **Luke 22:20** Jesus takes the cup containing the wine and says, "This cup is the new covenant in My blood." We learn what that new covenant is from **Jeremiah 31:31–34.**

a. What is the content of God's new covenant with His people?

b. What is the sign of God's new covenant with His people?

2. In **1 Corinthians 11:23–26** St. Paul repeats the words with which Jesus instituted the Lord's Supper.

a. What do these words tell you about the bread and wine in the Lord's Supper?

b. When do the bread and wine become the body and blood of Christ?

c. What are the benefits you receive from partaking of the Lord's Supper?

FOR *YOU* . . .

You've probably heard commercials that try to impress you with how important you are in order that you will be moved to purchase the product. These commercials use words like "It's not for everyone."

1. These words could be applied to the Sacrament of the Altar. In a very real sense, it's not for everyone.

Who is it for? Think about that as you read **1 Corinthians 11:23–28.** Then make two lists:
- In one list identify who the Lord's Supper is for.
- In the other list identifying those who should not partake of the Lord's Supper.

2. What is the basic difference between these two lists?

DO THIS

The Lord's Supper is not a spectator sport. It is something in which God's children are to be involved regularly and often. That's what our Lord meant when He said, "Do this in remembrance of Me."

1. How should you prepare yourself to go to the Lord's Supper?

2. How often should a person go to the Lord's Supper?

3. Why should a person go to the Lord's Supper?

4. What should a person do if he or she feels no need to go to the Lord's Supper?

CONSIDER THIS

A high school student partied late on Saturday night. He had a few beers with his buddies—in fact, he had a few too many. When he came home late that night (well, actually early Sunday morning), his mother met him at the door. She let him know that his behavior had offended her. She also told him that she expected him to go to church with the family that morning.

The student made it up for church, but he could hardly stay awake during the service. In fact, at one point his sister gave him an elbow jab and whispered that he had been snoring loudly.

A little later, he looked up and saw that the Lord's Supper was being served and that an usher was standing at the end of his pew.

What should he do now? Should he go to the Lord's Supper? What would you do?

As you think about these questions, read the following:

On feeling worthy

I know how difficult it was for you

to celebrate Communion today.
I know how you have been struggling
    with the meaning of your life.
I know of your doubts and weaknesses.
I know about your unkept promises
    and your failings.
I know of your struggles
    and your victories.

I want you to know I am happy
    that you came to My Supper today.
    You have opened yourself to My forgiveness.
    You have availed yourself of My strength.
    You have remembered Me and My work for
      you.
    You have tasted My love.

You are not a hypocrite for coming.
    The sick man is not a hypocrite
      for coming to the doctor.
    The hungry man is not a hypocrite
      in showing up for breakfast.
    You came because
      you know you are sick.
    You came because
      you know you are hungry.

I am happy that you came to My Supper today.
    I am going to heal your illness of spirit.
    I am going to feed your soul.
      I do not reject the sick.
      I do not turn the hungry away.

I know how difficult it was for you
      to celebrate Communion today.
    In your eyes it was not an easy decision.

You wondered whether you were sincere.
You wondered whether you really wanted
My help.
      But you came.
    And I'm glad.
In your eyes it was not an easy decision.

I want you to know that I am happy that you came
    to My Supper today.
    In My eyes you were an important guest.
    I was waiting for you.
    I was waiting to feed you.
      You came.
      And I'm glad.
    In My eyes you were an important guest.

I want to be a part of your struggles.
I want to give you My strength for your life.
I want to forgive all your sins.
    Please keep coming to My Meal.
    It is a happy occasion when you're there.

I know how difficult it was for you to celebrate Com-
    munion today.
    But please know I'm happy you came.

(Adapted from "Listening Excursion No. 3," in the *Perforated Mood-Swing Book* by Ronald M. Redder. Copyright © 1972 by Concordia Publishing House.)

LOOKING AHEAD

Read the Brief Admonition to Go to Confession on pages 122–127 of Luther's Large Catechism.

Whenever you eat this bread and drink this cup, you proclaim the Lord's death until He comes.
                    1 Corinthians 11:26

SESSION 90

"I'm Guilty, But . . ."

CONFESSION

As a monk Martin Luther searched for peace but could not find it. No matter how he tried to atone for his sins, he never felt that he had done enough to satisfy a just God who requires perfect obedience of His children.

Then one day God gave Luther new insights into **Romans 1:16–17: I am not ashamed of the Gospel, because it is the power of God for the salvation of everyone who believes: first for the Jew, then for the Gentile. For in the Gospel a righteousness from God is revealed, a righteousness that is by faith from first to last, just as it is written: "The righteous will live by faith."**

Until that day Luther thought that *righteousness of God* meant His judgment. Because God is perfect, Luther imagined that we can satisfy Him only by following His rules perfectly. But now Luther realized that righteousness refers to something God gives us through faith; we receive a righteousness from God because of His mercy, not because of our ability to earn it.

This insight from God changed Martin Luther's life. Now he realized that his relationship with God did not depend on what he did but on what God had done. He could have peace with God because Jesus had died for him and his sins were forgiven.

That realization also changed Luther's attitude toward private confession. He no longer saw private confession as an act in which one enumerated his or her sins to a priest so that the priest might assign duties to the penitent person to help that person atone for his or her sins. Now confession—public or private—became an act by which a person confessed conscience-troubling sins before God so that he (or she) might be assured of the forgiveness of his sins; a person receives forgiveness solely by the grace of God and not because of anything he or she has done.

Today we want to consider what place confession should play in the life of God's people today.

THE THREE CONFESSIONS

Luther suggests that there are three ways by which we confess our sins.

1. Identify these three kinds of confession.
2. Explain why we should confess our sins before God.
3. Tell why we should confess our sins before another person.
4. What is the purpose of private confession?

THE TWO PARTS OF CONFESSION

Indicate whether you agree or disagree with the statements below. Be prepared to defend your answers.

1. Confession is my own work and action.
2. The most important thing about confession is enumerating my sins.
3. I should only go to private confession if I really want to do so.
4. If you are a poor, miserable sinner, you should confess your sins so that others realize how bad you really are.
5. To desire confession is to desire to be a Christian.

PRACTICALLY SPEAKING

Confession assumes repentance. When you confess sins to God, you approach Him with an attitude of faith and repentance. God forgives freely ; as a matter of fact, He forgives you even before you speak your words of repentance. Confession reestablishes a good relationship between you and God.

When you confess sins to other people, you also make your approach with an attitude of repentance. In a sense you show faith in them, too—faith that they will deal gently with you instead of laughing at you or making a big scene in connection with the wrong you committed. You hope that a better relationship will exist between them and you as a result of the this encounter.

Thus confession becomes a part of a process that leads to better relationships.

1. Privately (not in a form to be shared with your teacher or classmates) write a paragraph in which you describe how an act of confession by you can restore

or enhance your relationships with one of the following:

    a. God

    b. A parent

    c. A friend

    d. A teacher

    e. A brother or sister

    f. Your pastor

Also describe the way you will approach the person. Include the very words you will use for confession.

2. Look at confession as suggested in a hymnal. Choose one form that is especially meaningful to you. What makes it meaningful?

    a. *Lutheran Worship,* pages 136–37, 158, 178, 308–09, or 310–11.

    b. *The Lutheran Hymnal,* pages 6, 16, or 46–49.

Therefore confess your sins to each other.

James 5:16a

CPSIA information can be obtained
at www.ICGtesting.com
Printed in the USA
FSOW03n2343070916
24713FS

9 780758 650498